The Ranch

CHRIS PECK

Forward

Welcome to the world of free form writing. The book you are about to read is the first attempt by a newcomer to the literary trade. By profession I'm a telephone man and I don't yet consider myself a wordsmith. I do consider myself trainable. I have worked very hard to become one of the best, or at least one of the most interesting damn phone men the world has ever known. I've been perfecting my vocation for more than forty years. If this book goes well my next attempt will tell the "telephone man story." This book, however, is about my personal military experience during the Viet Nam War. There has been a deep seated need to do this in my heart for a very long time and after some soul searching, confidence building, and a sizable but well regulated quantity of alcohol and some very well cared for flowers from an also well regulated plant that grows wild all over the earth, I figured "what the hell I'm going to be dead sooner than later and this story must be told."

    I grew up without a father at a time and place where almost everyone else had at least one. I can remember being asked by the kids in grade school what happened to my father. Because my mother would wait until I was twenty-one to tell me the story of the handsome, Irish, heavy equipment operator who got her pregnant and left her to raise me, I was forced to make up a story. My story revolved around a war hero who was killed in the heat of battle when a German soldier shot him with a bazooka. I was born in December of 1948. The Germans had stopped shooting anyone with anything in May 1945. When I was seven I hadn't learned much about the second World War. If my school mates were a little smarter they would have done the math and realized that my mother would have had to been pregnant for at least three and a half years. It's true, my sad story didn't have a wooden leg to stand on.

Being the son of a war hero was sort of cool and I even started to convince myself that my story was true. To this day I can see my dad standing on top of a burning tank, smoking the stub of a nasty cigar, blazing away with Thompson submachine guns in each hand. He shrugs off the bullets that are tearing away at his uniform and his body when suddenly he is turned into a crimson cloud of smoke and flying body parts by a shoulder mounted rocket fired by a German soldier wearing a Nazi helmet. My story got better the more times I told it and before long my fantasy father had killed enough Germans to fill up a Volkswagen factory before they blew him to red white and blue smithereens. I sold myself this story to such an extent that I felt I had something to live up to. I wasn't exactly born to be in the service but I somehow convinced myself that someday I would become the best damn soldier since Conan the Barbarian.

I've been employed in and around the Veterans Medical Center here In Albuquerque, New Mexico since 1978. During that time I've met and gotten to know veterans from all of our wars going back to World War II until this current batch returning from Iraq and Afghanistan. Every one of these Veterans is different but they are also very much the same. Those of us who joined up or were drafted, all have the basic military experience in common. It doesn't matter if you wound up storming the beach at Normandy or driving the Admiral to the golf course in a very clean Jeep, there is a commonality involved with anyone who has been indoctrinated into military life.

This isn't a war novel, so if you are expecting descriptions of huge fiery explosions with bloody assholes and elbows flying in all directions from cover to cover you need help, you also need to find yourself a different author. There is one chapter that involves a terrible deadly aircraft accident and another where torture, rape and murder are important elements, and of course some typical, nearly deadly, Navy horse ranch adventures, but this book is mostly a study in the fact of war and how I personally dealt with the one that was thrown directly in my path. I've included a number of rants directed at the rich and powerful who put monetary gain ahead of the lives of the young men and woman who are sacrificed every day in the name of wealth and misplaced glory.

I must now warn you that I have dropped a few carefully targeted "F" bombs here and there to remind you, the reader, that people in the service curse. I'm from New Jersey where the word fuck can be used five or six times in a sentence without being repetitious or redundant. As in "If you fuck with my sister I'm going to fuck you up so bad your dog will walk with a fucking limp you stupid fucked up mother fucking fuck." People in the military swear like sailors and when they return home they have to readjust to the world they came from. If you come from New York or Boston for instance that adjustment is minimal but a farm boy from Kansas could raise a few eyebrows when he slips and asks his mother to "Please pass the fucking okra." Just guessing but his next sentence could very well be "Daddy could you please put down that fucking axe handle?"

This book is a mostly nonfictional, autobiographical account of a few very important years of my life, and I feel that I was brutally honest as I tried to describe the good the bad, the humorous and the stunningly sad. The legal and the not so much. I don't make myself a role model in this story but I've tried to rationalize all the crazy shit we did and the madness that surrounded those of us who were trying to serve our country during that incredibly interesting time in our nations history. In the process we didn't hurt anyone. (well there was a guy in judo class) I like to think I helped turn a few heads around. I hope you can forgive me for some things you will read about me here. If you can't......you might want to take a deep breath and try relaxing, just a little bit.

The men and women who have served overseas in the line of fire while "defending our country" deserve our undying thanks and respect. They also deserve an education, a job, free health care and a VA loan when they get home from their tour of duty. Not two years after they get back, I mean the day they get back. They earned these things and many of them have paid a very high price. High school kids who join the service are thinking many things when they sign the paperwork at the recruiters office. Today some are hoping to get an education, some are planning how to spend the sign-up bonus, some are trying to find a way to make a difference, and some just want to cash in on all the "tail" they think they will get when they put on the uniform. None of these young wide eyed kids pictures themselves in a wheel chair or a plastic bag with their arms and legs strewn around someone else's neighborhood, ten thousand miles from the town they grew up in. This book is for those young men and women who are considering a lifetime, or at least what will seem like a lifetime in the military. My greatest wish is that this book will make you laugh, perhaps shed a tear, and what is more important, I hope that it makes you think.

The United States armed forces has nearly as many job descriptions as it has people wearing odd looking hats. There are practical reasons for the shape of those hats of course but you wouldn't see someone on Wall Street for instance wearing a "Jump Cap," a "Dixie Cup," or a "Cunt cap." Sorry about that last one. I didn't make up the name. It's called a garrison cap in mixed company.

The US military employs cooks and mail delivery personnel, there are drivers of trucks and drivers of flight line maintenance equipment. There are those who paint ships, those who navigate ships. There are people who drag deadly weapons to the flight deck and attach them to the wings of the scariest airplanes in the world, and then, of course, the pilots of those sexy aircraft who fly those armed weapons over to somebody's house or place of employment and push a button that, after a few seconds, removes that building from a map along with the people who were living or working there. This list of military jobs is almost endless. Each military branch is a well run self contained unit. Everything that is done in civilian life is duplicated within the confines of the military structure, whether it is writing paychecks, repairing plumbing, providing communications services, distributing prescription medications, or perhaps feeding and caring for a herd of large four legged creatures on a "Navy horse ranch." This is a story about the experiences revolving around the very odd and "Twilight Zone" like jobs that I performed in my nearly four year career as a member of the most expensive and dangerous navy that a giant shit load of money can buy. Mostly however, this story is about how I wound up doing those jobs and the carnival of changes that took over my life along the way.

CHAPTER 1

In the beginning there was chalk

Let us begin this story in the prehistoric year of 1966. That's a long, long, very long time ago to those of you who "twitter." This means I am older than sunlight, and I don't generally regard the opinion of people who were born after the end of the Viet Nam war. This is just a guideline not a hard as nails rule. There are plenty of damn smart kids out there with their hearts in the right place who I respect and I pray they get a chance to lead our brave new world in the right direction......someday.

One particularly overcast October afternoon I was seated at my at my desk in our high school science class. The desk was big and made from solid wood with a thick black fireproof coating that had two gas outlets protruding from the surface, one for each student. The fireproof feature came in handy when kids would try to use the burners to light cigarettes the instant the teacher left the room. The science room had eight of these lab desk work stations. I think. You couldn't take pictures with your phone back then and cameras required giant evil smelling flash bulbs. My memory of those days is a little blurry so if there were nine desks you can sue me. There was a slight aroma of formaldehyde from the biology class that shared the same class room and we were surrounded by the ghostly spirits of the countless frogs and piglets that had given their lives for science.

This was my senior year in the slightly above middle class town of Cedar Grove, New Jersey, and I was about halfway through the process of determining my destiny. At the time I probably should have been listening to my science teacher, who was doing his very best to explain how television worked. Fortunately I knew he would be totally stumped by my question when I asked it. I had read the whole science book early on in the school year and if something wasn't in the lesson plan, Mr. "looks up girls dresses all day" wouldn't have a clue and would ramble on hopelessly for the rest of the period. It was a little game I played with him and my classmates loved me for it, especially the beautiful young girl who sat next to me in the front row with the short skirt and the most wonderful tanned legs in the whole school. Her name was Rhea, and she had recently moved to New Jersey from southern California.

Rhea knew that when I asked Mr. "Really, I'm sick and need help," one of my patented trick questions, he would get so involved in trying to fake his way thru the answer that he would forget to drop a pencil in front of her desk so he could take way, way, way, too long picking it up while he stared up her skirt. Rhea and I had a connection that was only destined to last a short while longer. Soon, her father would again be transferred. This time to some foreign desolate godforsaken city in a state far away. Rhea was grateful whenever I was able to deflect our twisted science teacher's passions away from her panties and toward the pursuit of science. I however used this spare time to ponder my plans for the future.

My dream back in high school was to one day get a job designing cars in Detroit. This was way back in the day when all the baddest, fastest, most powerful cars in the world were being produced by American union workers in "Motown," and I loved cars. Muscle cars were tearing up the streets and highways of our country and we had the music to go with it. "Jan and Dean" and of course the "Beach Boys" were turning out songs for us to drive to and gasoline was going for 25 cents a gallon. Hot cars were a culture back then and "compact" was a thing your date carried in her purse, it certainly wasn't something you would pick up your date IN. Life was very good for a white teenager back then. If you were a black teen in 1967, well.....probably not so much.

I wanted to be the person who designed the next Corvette or Pontiac with 450 pissed off horses under the hood. I had been reading "Hot Rod magazine" ever since I was a ten year old juvenile delinquent. I didn't have much disposable income at the age of ten so I was forced to use the old five finger discount method of payment for my magazines and cigarettes. They really shouldn't keep those items so close to the front door. This is simply a personal observation.

Due to my dream to be an automobile designer I had signed up for mechanical drawing, drafting, and designing courses all through high school. I had the same teacher (there was only one) for all four years. The highlight of the design class was a year long homework project in my senior year where we were challenged to design a car from the future. The idea was to come up with a car that could possibly be produced within the next few years. I got a grasp of the teachers idea immediately but that didn't stop some of my class mates from creating cars with wings, ray guns and radar antennas. This was, by far, the hardest I had ever worked on a project in my entire school career. I spent two long months coming up with a viable concept car and at least that long perfecting the model.

The year was 1966 and the car that I had created would later turn out to be a perfect cross between the 1969 Pontiac GTO and the boat back, 1971 Buick Rivera. The model itself was perfect right down to the perfect gloss black finish. I had also majored in wood shop and was teachers pet. The chrome work I had borrowed and modified from "Revell" kit cars that had once resided on shelves all over my bedroom. The tires were soft rubber model airplane tires that I had bought with real money because the hobby shop had better security than "NewBerry's." I was so very proud of my model and I was sure that it was going to be my launching pad to a career in the motor city.

My design-class teacher, Mr. De Baca, had a totally different view of my brilliant creation. We had a running competition going ever since we met in our very first class together. Something inspired Mr. De Baca to single me out and make an example of me at every opportunity. At the time I thought he was just being an asshole. He acted like many of the other teachers in my life who hated me for being the only poor kid in class, or because I didn't have a father and my mother's maiden name was the same as mine. This teacher was different somehow. I could feel that in some weird way he was just like me. His mastery of the English language had much to be desired but he was the only mechanical drawing teacher in the entire school system. Good for him, bad for me. I just knew that he had grown up in similar, if not much worse conditions than I had. I believe the reason he hated me so much was that I had thrived on my not so enviable circumstances while he was just hanging on to one of the lowest rungs of the ladder in his chosen field. I had gained some popularity based on a level of success in sports. I know he noticed the girls who would stop by the classroom to flirt with me before class and I suspect he hated me for it. There were a few guys in my class who had similar feelings but they weren't in the position to give me a failing grade.

When I presented my car design to Mr. De baca, he took one look at my model and simply said. "No one is ever going to put a (point) on the back of their car."Yeah? Tell that to the Buick people asshole." Neither of us knew that at the time. I received an "A" on my model but only a "C" on my design. I was the only one who knew just how devastating this news was. I was expecting nothing but praise for my design and yet I still received a crumby "C" for all my hard work. This was a truly important lesson in life for me and anyone else reading this book. "Life sucks, then you die" No that's not right. "Things in life happen for a reason" That's the one. My entire life would have turned out differently if I had been inspired to become a designer for an industry that one day would export my job to some Asian country we had only recently been at war with. All their cars would have odd looking headlights and would exactly resemble all the other cars from that part of the world. I could have spent years in a white shirt and string tie coming up with ideas that would be instantly stolen by my employer. There would have been that, "Last Straw Moment." The gun fire, the police shootout. Things could have indeed gone sideways if I had gotten an "A" on my project. "Thank you Mr. De Baca. You turned my life around."

Note: I have so much respect for the Japanese culture and history. I read both books of "Shike," twice. I am a real fan, however, I'm also an American and until the republicans finally succeed in completely destroying our workers unions, and the middle class, I'm planning to stay and fight for what I believe is the best excuse for a democracy the world has today. If you believe I'm mistaken please convince me so I can start making travel plans. I could thrive in Jamaica but I would really need to work on my tan, or my bob sledding skills.

Following the stunning defeat in my design class I felt this sudden urge to upgrade the list of possible opportunities for my immediate future. As luck would have it, I had recently received a letter of eligibility for a partial athletic scholarship to Connecticut State college for wrestling. I was the first district wrestling champion in our school's brief history and I considered this a genuine option. I had to overcome some real demons in my life to get this far, and the idea of going to college was virgin territory to me.

My young mind up to that point revolved around the very real possibility that I would live the rest of my life with a shovel in my hand earning minimum wage, eating my lunch out of a black metal box and dying from working around toxic chemicals. Now, here I was, contemplating the path of higher education. The problem however, was that my step-dad, Warren, didn't seem all revved up about helping me out in any way. Not that he could if he wanted to. Money, or rather, the lack of money was a major concern. For many of you, life before the internet is just a dark hole in history that probably never existed, like dinosaurs to a born again Christian or the civil rights amendment to a Mississippi sheriff. For many of us who can remember personalities like "Soupy Sales" and "Mr. Green Jeans," when we had a question like "where can I get some cash to tide me over while I go to some institution of higher learning," you couldn't Google grants and student loans. We had to depend on high school guidance counselors or the wisdom of our parents.

My guidance counselor was a perfectly lovely under achiever who had never even heard of me. Her name was miss "Doesn't give a shit" and she couldn't find her own ass with both hands, a flashlight, and a National Geographic ass map. After listening to her advice for about twenty, or thirty minutes I wanted to slit my damn throat. She not only didn't have anything of value to contribute but she kept rambling off on little personal side trips that involved her kids and her handy man who didn't have a college education but was doing quite well for himself and he stayed in great shape working around her house. Just between you and me I think her handy man was possibly doing a little more than cleaning out her gutters if you get my drift.

My parents were quite a few links down on the food chain when it came to having any extra money laying around. Whenever I asked them questions about funding, the answer always revolved around a lawnmower, that we didn't have. There weren't any "Mc Donald's" or "Wal Marts" back then. I took as many part time jobs as I could find but two thirty-five an hour was the best I could do in those days.

Sometimes my step-dad would lay some lame book on me that would guide me down the path of life. "Warren" didn't approve of my choices when it came to reading material. I read "Kon Tiki" when I was in the seventh grade. I was totally fascinated by the adventure of a crew of suicidal Scandinavians who lashed several fifty foot long balsa logs together with "hemp" ropes, and sailed across the Pacific ocean. Warren's imagination was limited only to things that had money or "odds" as the primary subject and he was not impressed by my literary choices. He thought several guys alone on a raft must be gay, even if they were the descendants of Vikings. I bit my lip before reminding him that he had been in the Navy.

I also read the "Autobiography of Lenny Bruce," but again, Warren thought that because the book was written by a "junkie," it must be, well, junk. I read "Leon Uris," "Upton Sinclare," and Sinclair Lewis." My stepfather was reasonably sure that I was going "bat crap crazy." He just hung up fold outs from his Playboy magazine collection in my bedroom to make sure I wasn't batting from the "homo" side of the plate. If he really thought I was turning gay he would have been forced to kill me for my own good. The pinups were actually kind of neat and my guy friends thought I was really cool at the time. I was the only kid in school with pictures of naked girls in my bedroom, who had parental consent. "Fear of the gay" can be a good thing. Unfortunately my grandmother was not on board.

Warren, in his lame attempt to guide me to a higher plane, once handed me a book and told me, "You should try to be more like this guy." The name of the book was "The Autobiography of Willy Sutton." This book was written, in prison, by the most successful bank robber of all time. This was before Bernie Madoff blew the wheels off the bank robbery business forever. I read that whole damn book from front to back and I found it to be quite inspiring. Willy Sutton was the man who, when asked, "Why do you rob banks?" replied "Because that's where the money is." Willy Sutton was a craftsperson at his chosen trade and he was indeed the very best.

My step father told me "It doesn't matter what you decided to do with your life as long as you're the very best at what ever it is." His standard analogy was "I don't care if you become a ditch digger as long as you are the best damn ditch digger you can be." Being the best was all he cared about. After I read the Willy Sutton book I seriously considered becoming a world class bank robber for a while. Soon I realized that I could never live a life of crime. The whole prison thing never really melted my butter. Some of my friends who had been awarded the all expenses paid trips to the "free hotel" were usually seriously screwed up by the time they got out and their lives were changed for the worse, for like…ever.

Note: Prisons are a huge waste of time, and they cost way to much of taxpayers money. Yes, I do believe that violent offenders need to be separated from the general population but "the current way we deal with criminals is a "crime." How can the land of the free have more people locked up in prison than any other country on earth? "They privatized prisons, that's how." It isn't profitable to rehabilitate criminals when someone is going to get richer every time an inmate fails to make it on the outside and returns to their prison.

The point is that my sad little family was broke and financially clueless. When it came to funding any thing more expensive than a large anchovy pizza there was a loan involved. The loan was provided by some guy named Veto or Dutch and the terms were,……well they could involve the breaking or disappearance of certain body parts if you missed a payment.

While we lived in an upper middle class town our weird little family was not a member of a class anywhere near the middle. I mean we were even poorer than the Chinese family that lived downstairs. The hundred year old converted duplex house we lived in was the only rental property in town. Our apartment was maybe 600 square feet tops. My room had a ceiling that was half plaster and half "lath" (wooden slats that support the plaster). The house was built long before someone invented sheet rock. The plaster from the lath side of the ceiling had fallen on me while I was sleeping one night. I thought that the world was coming to an end, at the time. We waited for the landlord to make the repairs the whole time I was in high school but that never happened so we used thumb tacks to cover up the hole in my ceiling with a print sheet. It looked like a bad impression of "Jeannie's bottle." Due to the ramshackle and hazardous nature of our home, I didn't invite very many friends to hang out at my crib. The few guys who did come over were treated to pictures of beautiful, naked, women who all had the same first name of "Miss" followed by a month of the year.

My mother "was" the bookkeeping department and the office manager for a company owner who believed that the less you paid your employees the more you could pay yourself. Never mind that my mother was running the business and being paid in pocket change. "Her boss was the guy who put the douche in selfish fucking douche bag." "Capitalism is a fine idea, but you have to put some controls in place to make sure it works for everyone, not just the giant assholes with the keys to the buildings." Some business owners understand that well paid employees are good for the economy. My mom's boss didn't understand that the more money in the pockets of the middle class the better it is for everyone. Who do they think buys their products? When super wealthy people put their money in off shore accounts to keep from paying taxes, it doesn't help anyone.

My step-dad had a county job and Essex County, New jersey is one of the scariest counties in America. Warren was the head cook in the kitchen of a giant, old, red brick, TB hospital or "sanitarium" as they called them back then. He earned a crappy pay check and he was always getting knives pulled on him by the minimum wage guys from downtown. I heard rumors that he was a real badass with an iron skillet. He had developed a nasty attitude toward minorities and he could go off on just about any race or religion but his own. His spare time was spent sleeping in front of the TV in his underwear or dressing up in his sport coat and slacks, splashing on some lucky "Old Spice" aftershave and heading to the track. Warren wasn't a professional gambler like those rich Texans in one of those stupid poker games on ESPN, which means most of our family money was "gone in 60 seconds," or however long it took for his sure thing horse to fall down and break it's fucking leg.

Spontaneous rant: Hey ESPN, when did POKER become a freaking sport? I mean the Yankees are playing Boston and you guys have a poker game on, and one of the players is wearing a pair of "X-ray specs" that he got from an add in the back pages of Popular Science. Are you kidding me? You really need to fire some of those "suits" you pay to dream up this crap. Who are the shit heads who watch that junk?

Whenever we did manage to save up a few bucks, my less than dependable step-dad, would lose it on a hunch that some dried up four legged bag of fresh dog food "Couldn't lose with a name like Peas and Carrots....Right?"

I spent my summers working for contractors as a roofer, a landscaper, and a brick mason's assistant. The work was back breaking but I would be in incredible shape by time we showed up for football practice in September. I believe these jobs had a lot to do with my abilities on the wrestling mat. Most of the other guys on my team spent their summers hanging out at the town swimming pool or bagging groceries down at the "Shop Right, not so super market." In the winter I shoveled snow and put most of the money in a bank account that Warren would borrow from when things got tight. There was a very loose understanding that he would pay me back someday but we all know that you don't pull the mask off the old Lone Ranger, you don't piss into the wind, and you don't lend money to people who spend all their spare time at the race track betting on the "ponies." I didn't have a choice in the matter as my parents were cosigners on my bank account.

The point to this most recent rant was that I had no visible means of support and if I wanted to attend a school of higher education I would need to find employment in a strange cold place among a totally alien race of people that dress like foreign exchange students and live in the fantasy land of Connecticut. When you grow up in New jersey and have never been further away from your house than the Jersey Shore (yeah that one) you consider places two or more states away as alien as France or Jupiter or... Texas. So much for wrestling my way to the top, or the middle for that matter, besides if I ever put on a pair of penny loafers I think my feet would burst into flames. Those college guys in New England looked like a cross between Richie Cunningham and Pat Boone, and not in a cool way.

Note: Hey kids, some of these references apply to stuff that happened before God invented dirt so please feel free to Google anything that you don't recognize.

The other logical choice in my quest to find the perfect next step in life was an unlikely offer from our New Jersey State senator Krebs to attend the Merchant Marine Academy at Kings Point, New York. I had taken a test at my step-dad's request, just before a football game that I was supposed to take part in. On this particular Saturday morning my biggest worry during the exam was what my coach would do to me if I was late for the game. The test was given by the state of New Jersey and the huge auditorium was packed with about a "million" (vast exaggeration) guys with pocket protectors and tape on their glasses. I realized I was competing with the best and the brightest, super smart kids on the planet. You have to remember this was the same place where Thomas Edison, Albert Einstein, and Yogi Berra hung out. I thought to myself "I am so totally screwed, what the hell am I even doing here."

I nearly got up and walked out but when I started taking the test it was like the lights came on in Yankee Stadium. They had questions on the test for example, if you took this crazy shape with dotted lines all over it and folded it up into something, what would it look like, or what is the next number in this sequence, or if the first gear goes counter clockwise what direction is the thirteenth gear turning. It was like they made the test just for me. Even the algebra problems were easy as they were multiple choice and I didn't need to show how I arrived at the answer. I could do algebra in my head but I could never use the stupid formulas that they forced us to use in high school algebra class. I was always an avid reader and I knew the majority of the answers to the history portion. I mean it seemed so easy that it felt like I was cheating.

I completed the test while the other "contestants" were still figuring frantically away with the mechanical concepts section. This was back before calculators, when smart kids used something called a pocket slide rule to figure out math problems and it was truly a troubling scene. A slide rule wasn't going to help them now. Hundreds of young men doodling problems on scratch paper, erasing, breaking the points off their number two pencils, sweat dripping on answer sheets, bulging zits about to pop, and a lot of muffled cursing. I dropped my test in a basket and ran for the parking lot. I jumped into my two hundred fifty dollar, gold 1952 Caddie, and blasted off to our high school football field. I managed to arrive just in time for the game where I was nearly beaten to death by guys much larger and meaner than me. I only weighed about 145 pounds with rocks in my pockets. Football is a blast and I could catch anything they threw in my general direction but the part where freakishly large psychopaths slam into you at full speed one-tenth of a second after you catch the ball,..."well that part sucked worse than having your balls gnawed off by a rabid wolverine"

One weekend, several weeks after taking the test, we were skating at the local ice pond. The town ice rink was just down the street from our duplex, (I was a decent ice skater). By we I mean just about every teenager in town and a few short people who I suspect were probably children. Personally I was doing my very best to impress an incredibly attractive freshman girl who I was starting to fall in love with......that day. I was a senior and just eighteen and I never really considered the legal implications of hitting on a fourteen year old. She couldn't skate at all but she seemed to enjoy letting me push her around the pond with my hands on her hips. I was enjoying it also and things seemed to be progressing in a very positive direction.

Just then, the spell was broken when my little sister came running up to us, all out of breath and screamed at me that I've got to "get home right away." "Oh for crying out loud." I almost told my sister to go do something horrible to herself, as all I really wanted was to pursue this one sided affair with the attractive little dream girl with the lovely blue green eyes. This fit that my sister was throwing sounded extremely serious. My first thought was that my mom had finally gotten fed up with all my step-dad's stupid racist ravings and had brained him with the three iron from the brand new bag of golf clubs that he had bought with my money but only used once. This possibility also had a bad side so I made up some totally lame excuse to my fourteen year old package of red hot trouble. After shedding my skates and slipping into a worn out pair of "Keds" sneakers, I rushed home to help my mother destroy the evidence.

When I arrived at our apartment, to my surprise, my mom and Warren were both standing in the living room, slash master bedroom, slash den, with completely dumbfounded looks on their faces. They were holding a copy of the Newark Star Ledger between them and I think my step-dad had tears in his eyes. I was partly relieved when I realized that, at least for the time being, there would be no need to mop up blood or pick little pieces of Klan drenched brains off of the already incredibly ugly drapes.

Suddenly fear gripped me as I pondered as many possibilities as my truly vivid imagination could conjure. Had some creature from another planet visited the Pope and were thousands of bible salesmen and evangelist preachers jumping off bridges and tall buildings all across the globe? Had a plane crashed killing the entire cast of "I Love Lucy"? Possibly peace in Vietnam had broken out forcing the CEO's of McDonnell Douglas and Hughes Aircraft and the rest of the military industrial complex to pack up and move off shore to start hiding all their money. I was just getting warmed up when Warren looked up slowly from the paper and stuttered as he quietly informed me that based on my test scores I had been chosen to attend Kings Point Academy on a full boat scholarship. HUH, WHAT, WAIT, HUH?

I wasn't the best student in our school by any means and that was mostly my own fault, but this news really freaked us all out. I'm quite sure I remember our dog, Caesar, doing a double take and making the Scooby Doo sound "Wooh?" when he heard the news.

The appointment had been granted by our good senator. Senator Krebs, as it turned out was going to send me to an academy on state money. I was one of ten students chosen from the entire state to be selected for a free ride to an academy. Sorry girls but this was 1967 and when I took the test I didn't detect one single young woman in the room, and I was a healthy horny seventeen year old young man. I would have noticed a teenaged girl a mile away if the wind was blowing in my direction. If there were women in that room that day they smelled like guys.

Kings Point Academy wasn't my idea but you had to know someone in a very high place to get into one of the military academy's. (West Point, Annapolis, or the Air force Academy.) Unfortunately the most important people I knew were the principles of all the schools I attended whose offices I spent more than a fair share of my academic career in. I mean my step-dad had his own parking space in front of the school for the many conferences he had to attend on my behalf. I was stunned right down to my toes….that, I was just starting to get the feeling back in…..(From the ice skates, remember?) Stay with me people.

As I remember, my entire school experience had been a succession of teachers who put me in the back of the room and saw little need to push me in the direction of college. I had never really excelled in any of my classes save for wood shop, gym, and strangely enough geometry. I did fairly well in English and science however algebra was a complete mystery to me. There was after all always a need for factory workers and roofers. This was back before President Ronald Reagan declared war on the American middle class worker and good union jobs were still there for people who were willing to work. In those days you could work in the construction trades and make a decent living, and knowing the Spanish language wasn't a prerequisite. However this latest revelation was coming from so far out in right field I think I saw Roger Maris. (Old historical Baseball reference). So what in holy hell was I supposed to do now?

I was going through changes on several levels as I struggled with the possible options. I realized if I took the sports scholarship and got injured or flunked out I could get drafted into the Army. I was totally gung ho about the whole war thing at the time but the Army? There is nothing wrong with the Army however in 1967 you joined the Navy, you joined the air Force, you joined the Marines, but you got drafted into the Army. "All four of the guys who enlisted in the Army in 1967 thought they were joining the Coast Guard."

While deeply embroiled in decision making my goofy science teacher asked me, "Does that answer your question mister Peck?" I really had absolutely no idea because I hadn't listened to a word my teacher had said in the last twenty minutes. Pausing, I asked, earnestly, "If that is true, is the light that we see on the television coming to us as a wave or is it a series of particles?" I figured that if Einstein didn't have a definitive answer for that question than neither would our mentally and morally challenged teacher. I was correct as it turned out and while he attempted to explain quantum physics on a first grade level and his breathing became labored, I smiled and returned to considering my options. I could be a real prick sometimes but this guy deserved it.

My young mind was trying to justify the Merchant Marine academy as a real possibility, but somehow I just couldn't picture myself all dressed up in some lame uniform for four years, getting pushed around by my senior classmates, all so that someday I could, at best, wind up as the captain of the Love Boat? (I always thought Captain Stubing was a douche) At the very least I would wind up as the captain of a giant dirty oil tanker. A man who hates his job, gets sloppy drunk, and steers his crappy ship into a topless bar on Miami beach by perhaps less than accidental circumstances.

As it turned out I didn't have enough math and would have to take more algebra in summer school just to qualify for the Academy. This totally sucked. Algebra sucked, and besides I was all geared up to enjoy my summer "down the shore" and summer school just wasn't on my radar. By the end of the science class I had totally talked myself out of the whole college thing especially after watching my teacher, with all his education, totally embarrass himself in front of a room full of young people who thought he was giant waste of fresh air, in a very bad suit.

After returning home from school that day I informed my mother and step-dad that I was considering a third option. I told them I was going to look into joining the Marines. Both of them were really very surprised and disappointed, but I suspect for very different reasons. My reasoning was based on the fact that I knew more people who had been in prison than I did those with college educations. Some of my older friends were already fighting the communist threat in southeast Asia and I had spent a few years on a rifle team and could shoot the balls off a fly if he stood still long enough. I would certainly be wasting my talent by attending some school where I was certain that I wouldn't fit in. Back in 1968, people were dodging the draft by getting into college, or failing drug tests, or pretending to be gay. Of course plenty of the young men and women who were genuinely gay joined the service and thrived. That's a whole other story. There was and is a plethora of gay soldiers and sailors out there, but back then "no one was asking and they weren't telling."

My step-dad had come to realize that once I had made my mind up about something, it was pretty much, written in stone. At this point in our relationship he just didn't have the energy or the inclination to even try to talk me out of my decision. Warren, however was a "ninja" control freak and he chose to use his last card to influence me in a slightly different direction. The fact that I was still a minor in high school and he as my legal guardian would have to sign for me if I wanted to join the service. He had been watching the news and realized that the Marines were getting their asses shot off in Viet Nam, so he said that the only way he would go for the military option was if I agreed to enlist in the Navy.

I really wasn't crazy about Warren's idea but when we went down to the Navy recruiters office they had the coolest poster in the lobby. There was a sailor in a tailored dress blue uniform standing on the dock with a wooden sailing ship in the back ground. It looked like an "Old Spice" commercial. The sailor in the picture was wearing a beautifully tailored dress blue uniform and holding a young boy by the hand. I was impressed and I thought to myself "shit, I could get myself so laid in that outfit." Truly, the reasons young men make the decisions they do is a wonder. My young ill informed brain also reasoned that with my history as an athlete in football and wrestling, and my expert-rifleman medal, perhaps I could qualify for "Seal" training or some other cool outfit where I would get to see some action in combat, as if that would be a good thing.

After some deliberation I signed off on this option. Warren drove me back down to the recruiters office where I joined up with the US Navy. They had what they were calling the 120 day program. No money, no car, no free hair cuts for life, just four months peeled off my enlistment. That was cool with me since three years and eight months was way shorter than the full four years right? Keep in mind I had been totally brain washed by John Wayne and Audie Murphy during my "Wonder years" and to me the military was an obligation and a given destiny for any young man my age. The people who I went to school with took for granted that they were college bound and they were much more concerned with whether they would be accepted by Columbia, Yale, or Princeton. I...on the other hand, believed, "The only reason we hadn't won the Viet Nam war was that I hadn't been there yet." God, I was so fucking stupid, someone should have had me sterilized.

I joined the Navy while still in my senior year of high school. Someone really should write a law to prevent crap like that for Christ sakes. There was already a draft in place cranking out Army soldiers like they were M&Ms. Back in 1967 the whole anti war thing hadn't really kicked in yet, at least not in Cedar Grove. This was New Jersey after all, not San Francisco, and the wheels of the peace movement were only just starting to turn. We lived in a very conservative, republican, part of the country. I had no right whatsoever to be making massively uneducated decisions of this weight at the age of eighteen. I was young and way to deranged to be deciding stuff like this. At this point in my adolescent life I was just starting to get a feel for young woman, so to speak, and trying desperately to get laid, or rather,...and much better sounding "I was trying to develop a meaningful relationship with someone special." The armed forces was still just a cool thing to tell your friends and I had no idea that in many parts of the country there was a real stigma attached to being a soldier or a sailor involved in fighting a really bad war in a part of the world where we didn't belong. Does any of this sound just a little familiar?

Places like Chicago and Memphis were less than wonderful when it came to the treatment of America's fighting forces, but California was the worst place ever to be in the service if you wanted to blend in with the local civilian population. I'll get to this later but suffice it to say, "Momma's don't let your babies grow up to be cowboys or soldiers or sailors or airmen if you want them to be accepted by the younger generation in the middle of an unpopular war." At least cowboys have a horse they can depend on in a pinch." The whole fantasy of wearing a uniform and having women falling all over themselves to get some of that government issue "hardwood" is just that, pure fantasy. Of course there were service people who had plenty of female companions to get them through the night but they were popular long before they ever joined the service. There were many young enlistees and draftees who did manage to find someone to send them off to war but those relationships became the long distance variety early on and very few made it past the first year of active duty.

During the Viet Nam war the vast majority of high school students weren't keeping up with the news issues of the day, and much like today, the schools weren't doing anything to educate us on what was really going on in the world around us. As trained experts on what a gaggle of dead generals did hundreds of years earlier, my schoolmates and I could match up to any other regulated school system in the land. As for current events we were just a big smelly steaming pile of ignorant douche bags/baguettes wearing our lettermen jackets and hanging out at "Bonds" hamburger joint on Friday nights.

There was a discussion beginning in the colleges and universities but then the preppies and penny loafer crowd weren't getting their asses drafted as long as they managed to stay in school. If I had been a smarter wiser 18 year old I would have spent more time in the library learning about the history of Viet Nam and less time trying to get to second base. I swear hormones and religion are the leading causes of war and discontent in the world. Why do young men dress up like friggin GI Joe and run off to some god forsaken third world country to get their balls shot off?....Pussy, that's why. How ironic is that. Here you are, sitting in a rice paddy up to your young ass hole in leaches and land mines in some country that may or may not have oil reserves on it's property. You are starting to realize the whole war is being staged so that the men who run the businesses that sell the planes and tanks and bombs, and fuel, that helps to support our economy get filthy rich. All the while your girlfriend is boinking your best friend in the back seat of your GTO. This is the very same girl that you were trying to impress by joining the service in the first place. Did that revelation just ring a big old bell in someones head? I sure as hell hope it did. (This is why I'm writing this book.)

Let me clarify what must seem to be a sexist slant in this book. Today there are many young women who fight and die or are wounded fighting for this country's oil interests, but in Viet Nam and the wars before it "combat was for the most part a men's club." There were nurses and women in support rolls who got tangled up in the fighting from time to time but for the most part they weren't fighting in rice paddies, flying helicopters, fighter bombers, or driving trucks in hostile territory. Today's all volunteer armed forces provides many more opportunities for young women to experience the thrill of modern warfare and the awesome recovery wards of our nation's VA hospitals.

"RANT ALERT!!!" The crazy murderous bastards who hijacked jet airliners and flew them into the World Trade Center only did it because some creepy old guy in a dress told them there were all these virgins up there in heaven just waiting to….well I don't know what. I never understood that part. I must be missing something but what are all these virgins doing in heaven? If you are a female and you are a virgin when you die, you are either old and as ugly as a monk fish or you died from some terrible disease or a horrible natural disaster, or some dumb fuck wearing a vest stuffed with C4 and marbles blew your ass up. "Either way the last thing you want is to be ghost fucked for all eternity by an endless horde of homicidal maniacs." Perhaps in countries where men throw tents over their women, looks weren't a big deal, I mean you could have a head that looks like an avocado and it wouldn't matter much if you are wearing a burqa. Those same women could very well be the most beautiful creatures on earth but who the hell would know? I have a problem with the whole not letting people dress and act the way they want thing. The other issue I have with the crazy murdering douche bags who think It's just fine to kill innocent people because some screwed up bearded guy in the sky said so.

HEY, crazy murderous douche bags, I only have one question. How good can the heaven sex really be...."WHEN YOU ARE FUCKING DEAD?" I'm no expert but I hear dead people make really crappy lovers. I've never kissed a dead girl, virgin or other wise but I'm sure not gonna blow myself up so that I can see what it's like. I mean that's just plain wrong.....Right?

I personally, feel so bad for the true believers in the Muslim faith. A whole religion was highjacked on 9-11 by a "short bus" load of religious fanatics. Unfortunately not nearly enough Muslim leaders have had the stainless steel, gold plated balls to stand up and denounce the atrocity for what it was. I may be totally off base on this issue because "I'm smart enough to know that I'm not smart enough to know if there is a heaven or a hell." If there is a hell, however, I'll bet there is a special extra nasty corner of it for people who believe that their god thinks slaughtering innocent women and children gets you a golden merit badge in heaven. No offense, crazy religious zealots, but you guys suck. Truth be told, if I ever need someone to "suck start" my pick up truck, I'm calling one of Osama Bin Laden's followers.

I just had a really cool revelation. The next time one of you crazy bastards gets the itch to bang a large group of "ghost virgins in the sky," (potentially huge country hit song title) take this bit of advice. First, you have to dress up in your cutest explosive vest, the one with the woven leather straps and the golden hand grenade accessories would be perfect. Then throw on one of those sweet grey burlap floor length moo moos, and those sweet laced Jesus sandals. (sorry Jesus, that footwear was probably really cool back in the day). Finally invite yourself over to the home of the religious lunatic who drafted you to murder women and children and when he lets you in, just yell "SURPRISE," and press the button on your detonator as hard as you can. You will have to trust me on this but all your dreams will come true. You will get to spend the rest of all eternity with your master and your seventy-two virgins. (once the other martyrs are done with them) You may even get to hang out with his supreme master virgins. If I'm not mistaken that comes to one hundred and forty-four prime grade "A" rosy ripe little virgins. It just doesn't get any better than that. Right? Your crazy assed master will be so surprised, and of course extremely grateful. REALLY. As I said, you'll just have to take my word on this.

Everything was so very different in the sixties. Religion was just a harmless pass time for most people and church was a damn good babysitter I might add. Sunday morning was the only day of the week that my parents had sex. They dropped me and my sister off at Sunday school and then hustled back home for God only knows what. We had to walk home so I know something was going on.

The evening news was so credible that all you had to do to get people to believe something back then was to say it out loud. They told us that Viet Nam was a "domino" and if the puppet government that we supported lost it's power and therefore it's domino then......Well, then......the next domino was California. If I was smart I would have measured Viet Nam on a map and realized that it would take a much larger playing piece to reach all the way across the Pacific Ocean and land on Bakersfield. However the news anchors said it out loud and we swallowed it like a slice of Jersey style pizza. Some of us were raised to defend our sacred shores from foreign invaders, and or, gigantic domino's, whatever the case may be. Think about that for a second. Young men right out of high school were willing to fight and die to protect the American people from DOMINOS. Thank you ABC, NBC, CBS. (That's all there was before cable.) We listened to you and over fifty-eight thousand Americans died. Possibly two million Vietnamese people died along the way but that number never ever gets mentioned in the news because, as everyone knows, American lives are worth at least forty times those of third world countries. Don't shrug this last item off because as a country we fall for this shit all the damn time and people die. Most of the people who die are brown and yellow and black but they are all PEOPLE.

So there you have it. The story of how a destitute, relatively normal, if slightly maladjusted high school student chose to turn down a full boat college education and all the fun stuff that goes with it, for a four year all expenses paid trip to Uncle Sammie's, US Navy fun park. They bust kids for smoking pot which has a zero sum effect on the rest of your life except for the whole drug bust part being on your record for ever and ever. (Thank you Mr. Nixon) Cops don't pull you over for joining the service when you are still in high school and have a college scholarship in your pocket. "Yo society! Where are your priorities?"

RANT ALERT: Here is a heads up for all you boys and girls who may feel that the military is a great way to get a free education and health care for life. First read the fine print. These days the free health care only applies if you get blown up or shot while serving over seas. If you get blown up or shot in Detroit you are on your own. For some young people the service to your nation is a wondrous and honorable thing but be advised, there are some causes that are fought and died for that are not for you to fight and die for. "The United States lost it's innocence at the end of World War II. The Japanese were using wooden bullets by the time we dropped the only two nuclear weapons on them that have ever been dropped on anyone ever, as far as we know. We have not been fighting against any particular enemy as much as we now fight for the interests of the multinational corporations that provide the supplies that make these wars so profitable......"for them."

The word "Plutocracy" comes to mind (rule by the wealthy). Some of you may just have learned something. You can't go starting a war with a country just because some crazy people were trained to be dangerous crazy people on a jungle gym in a desert you can only find if you know how to drive a camel. (Afghanistan) You also can't go to war because your vice president has tons of stock in the company that will get a gigantic contract to rebuild all the shit we blow up. (Iraq)

I was as horrified as anyone after the attack on the World Trade Center. I wanted revenge on the people who did it but they were all as dead as over done hamburgers. It was frustrating, but eventually I got over it when I realized that going to war would result in countless, needless deaths on both sides with nothing to show for it. Then there was the fact that at least one and probably several oil producing nations would wind up hating us more than they already did. I must admit that I wasn't surprised when we went to war with the wrong countries. The hijackers were mostly Saudi Arabians. None of them were Afghans or Iraqis so naturally the Connecticut cowboy and his Darth Vader vice president decided that it wasn't important what brand of foreigner we "lit up" as long as they were brown....and lived on a different continent where most Americans wouldn't care or notice what we were doing to them. There are a few downsides to this idea that we must constantly be in a state of war to make the country prosper, now that multi national corporations run the world.

"The damage these misadventures do to our economy can only be appreciated by what used to be the American middle class." The point that the corporations are missing here is this. They think that by destroying the working peoples unions they are assuring a more profitable future for their share holders. They are madly in love with the idea that by crushing the life out of the middle class in this country will make them even richer than they are now. Here is the fly in that smelly ointment. Who the hell do they think buys all that cheap Chinese crap they are selling. The more money they take out of our pockets, the less we can use to buy their cheap Chinese crap. Our entire economy runs on the spare change of the middle class. The less change we have at the end of the week the less we have to spend on cheap Chinese crap. This is not rocket science people, but then politicians and the CEOs they work for are far from rocket scientists.

The unfortunate truth about what our country has become is that the gears of this great nation are oiled in blood. A fair amount of that blood is shed by brave American service people and a few better paid military contractors. The vast majority of the suffering however is dumped upon the innocent occupants of the third world countries we tend to fuck with.

"I love my country but I'm not crazy about the people who are determined to kill it and sell it off for parts."

So there you have it. Chapter one is officially complete. If you read it all you get an "A." If you glossed over it......you suck. Do you have any idea how hard it is to write a "God Damned Book?" I'm a telephone man for Christ sakes. Give me a freaking break.

CHAPTER 2

Blue Navy Blue

I remember my last day in the "Grove," as we referred to our little piece of paradise there in northeast New Jersey. There was no going away party or a big send off of any kind. My girlfriend and I had spent some quality time together to prepare me for my last night in town. I wondered how long it would be before I would enjoy the soft touch of a woman. I was beginning to have some serious doubts about the wisdom of my decision but it was way too late to turn back now. I didn't sleep much that night, and when I did finally dose off, my dreams were a jumble of old war movies and my reoccurring nightmare about being on a very tall railroad bridge and the train is coming and I have to choose between being squashed by the train or jump off the bridge and be dashed on the rocks far below.

I got up early that morning so that I could have some breakfast and say goodbye to my Mom. I cooked up a stack of pancakes. We ate pancakes with maple syrup we had made from hot water, sugar and maple flavoring, and sipped on sweet "regular" coffee. The two of us just sat and looked at each other. I couldn't comment on what I was in for because I really had no idea. My mom didn't voice an opinion on the matter although I knew she had one. My mother had served in the Navy during World War II. If she was tempted to comment on my decision, she realized it was pointless to say anything at this stage. There wasn't really much to say and neither of us were any good at making "small talk." It was an awkward moment and then all of a sudden it was time to go. Warren was up now and he was good and ready to finally get my dumb ass out of the house for good. I said so long to both of our dogs "Cubby and Caesar." They looked so sad that I wondered if they knew somehow that I was really going away this time, not just leaving for school or work. My mom had tears in her eyes and that made me tear up a little as well as I followed my step-dad down the stairs and out to the green Rambler station wagon where the adventure of my life was about to begin. My sister was sleeping in.

The day was extra gloomy, grey, and damp as we drove down route 3 to 1 and 9 over to Jersey City, thru the Holland tunnel, into New York City, down the West Side Highway to the Brooklyn tunnel and after a blinding number of unnecessary turns and detours we finally pulled into the Brooklyn shipyard where the US Navy had a staging area. My step-dad was quiet and somber as I got down from the car. Warren said, "Good luck Laddy Buck." Laddy Buck was one of the nicknames he had for me, "Laddy Boy" was another but that one always made me feel like a can of puppy chow. Warren was adopted and had never met his parents. He was raised by a strict German family but he had flaming red hair and was so sure his real parents were Irish that he dressed up in a kilt and marched in the Saint Patricks day parade in New York City every year. My honest guess was that he was compensating for his lack of a real heritage by trying to talk like he was from Donnybrook Ireland.

I was cold and numb as I turned and walked into the mad house that was the Naval indoctrination center. The building was an old red brick auditorium of some kind but it reminded me of a prison. I glanced down the street that ran in front of the building and I noticed several Navy ships docked along the pier. Just then an old destroyer, pouring black smoke, steamed past the docked ships in the harbor and "a reality check cashed itself in the pit of my stomach." This new experience promised to be something, but I had a feeling that this something wasn't going to be any fun at all. As it turned out I was very wrong but it would be a while for me to start enjoying all the fun I was in for.

Once inside the building I tried to be friendly toward the other poor, helpless, teenaged, sad sack bastards, as we got our physical examinations. There was the obligatory scene where we lined up in our underwear and turned our heads and coughed while some creepy looking corpsman (Navy for doctor but not really a doctor) groped our junk. We filled out some forms, and got yelled at by people we didn't know. Some ranking officers showed up and they swore us in. There was this strange little ceremony where we pledged our allegiance to our nation and our very lives to the armed services of that nation. The gravity of our decision to serve our country slowly began to sink in. "The sound of hundreds of assholes puckering in unison" is something you don't soon forget.

It didn't seem like much was getting accomplished during our indoctrination but for some reason it took "ALL DAMN DAY." At one point our handlers fed us box lunches of unknown origin and I remember there was a very dry sandwich with something round doing a terrible impersonation of meat centered between two slices of white, stale, bread, and an even drier harder cookie that had live tiny white meal worms in them. I ate some of the sandwich and passed on the cookie although there was probably more protein in that cookie than the sandwich. I was beginning to think that perhaps prison may have been a better choice than what ever this was that I had signed up for.

Several friends and acquaintances of mine had spent time in one, state provided, "Mandatory apartment complex," or another and not one of them were as scary as some of the people I observed around me preparing to protect the United States of America from communism and or out of control peace demonstrators. People wind up serving in the military for many different reasons. It was clear that several of the recruits I was sharing this experience with were only there because they simply wanted to kill somebody.

They lined all of us up and we were marched, or rather shuffled out to the parking lot. We hadn't been taught how to march yet and what ever it was we were doing sure as hell wasn't marching. There was a look of quiet horror in the eyes of some of my fellow enlistees as they loaded us into one of the beat up old grey busses that were quite similar to the busses they use to transport convicts from the court house to the prison. The seats were torn and mended with duct tape. There was a worn rubber mat running the length of the bus with holes worn thru. The metal underneath was polished by the shoes of thousands of young recruits.

We were driven around the streets of New York and eventually arrived at a train station where we were divided up into groups of fifty or so.

Then we were herded onto old scary looking train cars that reminded us of something out of a World War II movie. I felt as if I should be wearing a wide brimmed fedora, a grey flannel suit, and a "Lucky Strike" cigarette hanging out of one side of my mouth.

There were roll calls and head counts and several delays that I think had something to do with one of the wheels falling off of one of our cars. (Seriously, I saw a truck pull up with a giant set of steel wheels on it) I calmly took it all in because I figured you can't be late for the Navy. This was their sideshow and I was just a member of the audience. After an hour or so we coupled up to the rest of the train and rolled out of the train station and out into the very heart of America. I recall our train stopping in several large cities along the way, one of which was Philadelphia. We had stopped to pick up more enlistees. The guys from Philly didn't get into our car, they were already loaded up in their own little train of two or three cars and after some backing up and crashing that loosened one of my teeth eventually they were coupled onto our train and soon we were all bound for glory, eternity, and a whole lot of other unknown shit.

The trip was a long one and some of the guys entertained themselves by playing cards, and throwing some dice. Did I mention that we were from New Jersey and New York? Nothing makes the time fly like a spirited game of "fifty-two pickup" in the aisle of a train on its way to hell. We were trying our best to make the best of a bad situation. I remember thinking about a movie I'd seen when I was a child. The movie was about how Jews in Europe were rounded up and put on trains and carted off to the camps during the Second World War. We were of course no way in that kind of shit. I would never even try to make that comparison but still I felt very alone and totally under someone else's control for the first time in my life.

The problem was that I had volunteered and there was no turning back. There was no way out. I stared out the window of the train car and watched my country speeding by. Occasionally I would see people walking or driving somewhere and I thought to myself that I wished I was going wherever they were going instead of where I was going. This of course was absurd and I realized that those people wandering around in the middle of the night could very well have totally shitty lives. They could be homeless or on their way to buy drugs with the family's food budget. The kind of lives that drive people crazy

Note: If your life has failed you to the extent that you feel all is lost and that you want to end it all, consider this. No matter how messed you and your life are, there are people with flies in their eyes because they don't have the strength to brush them away because they haven't had a decent meal in their entire lives because they live in a place where the people who run their country stole all their nations wealth and kept it. Think about those people and let it sink in. If you still can't find a reason to live then go off someplace quiet and do what you have to do. Please DO NOT make that same decision for a group of people who you think made your life suck. It isn't their fault, It's yours. We are all capable of making our lives less suck-full. The best way to make those feelings go away is to help someone less fortunate than you. Of course, first you have to admit that there are people who have less to live for than you do but are still out there plugging away trying to make their lives just a little better. Hey, it works for me.

The point is none of us really had any idea of what to expect next. We were disoriented and bewildered and missing our friends back home. You start to dream of being in the arms of your girlfriend, or anyones girlfriend for that matter as long as it meant you weren't on that god damned train.

This was the farthest I had ever been away from our apartment in New Jersey and I could feel my lungs starting to clear up halfway across Pennsylvania. The trip lasted all night and part of the next day. Our train finally slowed and screeched to a stop on the "back side of South Bum Fuck, Illinois." Again we were herded onto busses and driven even deeper into the dark smelly bowels of America. Eventually we arrived at the gate of an immensely huge, redundantly gigantic, Naval base in the exact center of freaking nowhere. There were long lines of three story buildings as far as you could see and they were situated around giant paved surfaces called "grinders" where they would eventually teach us to march around like ants on crack. After being waved in by a gate guard our bus driver drove us to a point where we were completely surrounded by the Great Lakes recruit training center (Navy boot camp) located not far from Chicago, Illinois.

From my first week in the Navy I realized that this experience was going to be less like the recruitment poster and more like a Fellini movie. Great Lakes recruit training center is a city of grey. Grey cars, grey trucks and busses, grey office buildings and mostly grey people except for the new arrivals from Southern California and Florida. Of course by winter they would be as grey as everything else.

The screaming started immediately upon debarking (getting off of) our busses. At this point we really didn't know one military rank from another. Instinctively we were sure of only one thing, that literally everyone we met out ranked us. There was a guy wearing head phones and using a leaf blower when we were still riding to our barracks and a whole bus load of helpless enlistees realized that he was much more powerful and had more control of his destiny than we did. I would have switched places with that person in a heart beat, even if it meant learning a foreign language.

This new revelation meant that literally everyone who helped run this crazy farm could yell at us and call us all kinds of horrible but really quite creative expletives all day long, which they did. A few of my new labels were "puke" "shit bird" "faggot" and of course the ever popular "stupid, mother fucking, cock sucking, pussy eating, zit faced, shit bag." When someone hollers that at the top of his lungs with a heavy Bostonian accent, it can be really profoundly, stunningly, humorous. I however discovered that laughing when someone is blasting profanities in your face from point blank range just makes them mad. You'll just have to take my word on this.

The list of colorful name tags was endless and varied depending on the region of origin of your superior. The southern chiefs and petty officers were the funniest. They just drew upon their country roots when they came up with insults like "you stupid pig shit suckin, sister loving, toothless, chicken fucker." Who knew joining the Navy would mean learning to curse like a drunken sailor? That question kind of answers itself I suppose. I had come from New Jersey after all so most of the verbal abuse just made me home sick. It was like an inside joke to me more than it was hurtful, but some of the bible belt guys were in tears as their tormentors zeroed in, on them like they were freshly wounded prey.

Someone with a stripe or two on his sleeve screamed and cursed us into a line and marched us over to a grey building where we were issued a pile of crappy ill fitting clothes that looked nothing at all like the outfit the sailor was wearing on the enlistment poster. The average prisoner locked up in jail got better looking outfits than we did. Again, they lined us up and we were forced to get all our hair shaved off. When the base barbers were done we all looked more like prisoners of war or Nazi white supremacist's than sailors who were destined to have a woman in every port.

The barbershop scene was humiliating and the haircutters were sadists. They would only cut part of your hair off at first so you could look at yourself in the mirror and see what you looked like with half a "Mohawk" or a "Bozo the Clown" haircut. We all suddenly realized that we had been duped and were now utterly screwed and helpless.

They lined us up again and we were given a battery of inoculations that made us ten pounds heavier and sick as dogs for days. They used needles and air guns and pills, I almost expected to be attacked by pigmy's with blow darts. The good news was that we were now immune to everything, like small pox, measles, plague, berry berry, everything that is....except sexually transmitted disease's as it turned out. A large number of our young American servicemen learned this particular lesson just a little too late. In Viet Nam they had a strain of VD that could kill Superman, and there was no shot for it. The discussion between a returning service man and his girl friend went something like this.

Her: (after seeing her man naked for the first time after returning home from his tour in Viet Nam)

"Uh...baby. Where did your dick and nuts go?"

Him: "Yeah, well....about that...They kind of fell off....you know, ...over in Nam."

Her: "What do you mean they fell off? You look like a friggin Ken doll for Christ sakes. They didn't just fall off all by themselves you dumb fucked up mother fucker. You screwed one of those poison pussy whores in Saigon didn't you? You stupid bastard. Get the fuck out of here before I cut your....Well never mind that, just go, and please do not come back,....... ever."

There was a lot more danger in Viet Nam besides Viet Cong soldiers, land mines, RPG's, and deadly snakes. I believe that the very fact that the military separates the sexes, to the extent that they do, is a dangerous mistake. First of all, we are talking about high school graduates who may have had their first sexual experience just a few months before getting shipped off to some foreign land where the only local talent they are exposed to are all professionals. I think many lives could have been spared If corporal "Fresh Meat" could get off work and hang out with private

"Susie Cream Cheese." and maybe have a relatively safe sleep over. I'm just making an educated observation.

Things started to go badly on my second day when I was assigned to a barracks run by a chief petty officer named MacQuinton. Chief MacQuinton at first, seemed to be the very definition of the military man's man. He was the guy we had all seen in those propaganda war movies when we were growing up. This crazy son of a bitch had swagger and he was really loud,...all the time loud. His confident attitude didn't bother me and I kind of liked him at first. He seemed to treat me better than the other young men in his charge. When he tried to intimidate the rest of the recruits he scared the piss out of most of them and they obeyed him like he was God. In spite of his brutal tirades no matter how hard he tried, he wasn't able to break a few of us down.

After years of being relentlessly berated by my slightly to the right of Rush Limbaugh step-dad I had grown very thick skin and verbal abuse had little or no effect on me. The black, and Hispanic city guys just ignored him and went on about their business. The chief and I sort of warmed up to each other and he leveled his fury at the weaker among us while he treated a small group of us like family. Coincidently the other chosen few were the big dangerous looking, inner city, African American guys who could have passed for Mike Tyson's body guards.

The arrangement worked well for the first week or so. I was also able to balance being a teachers pet with maintaining friendships with some of the other men in our barracks. The truth is there were some people who gravitated towards me in an attempt to escape the cruel wrath of our insanely angry chief.

Soon it became apparent that Chief MacQuinton was slowly going mad before our eyes. I noticed early on that the chief could be either deadly as a pit bull on crack or calm and helpful but you never knew which you were going to get and his moods could change in an instant. He was on the fast track to winning a long all expenses paid vacation in a room with very soft walls. Our chief was becoming increasingly mean and abusive towards the slow learners in our barracks. He was punishing everyone for one guys screwup and in turn the vast majority of young recruits would take some form of retribution on the offender. This is an "old school" technique used by the military, sports coaches, and boy scout leaders alike however when actual physical abuse is encouraged by those in control, things can go sideways in a hurry. In our case someone had been hurt badly and it seemed likely that the Chief was directly involved. By this I mean he beat some poor sad sack up with his own hands. The young sailor went to sick bay and the chief was brought up on charges.

Our entire company was put on hold while the Navy found someone to take up the slack, fill in the crack, complete the stack, cover our back, upgrade the MAC. (Oops I got off on some kind of rhyming thing there. I never do that, sorry) In the interim the rest of us were sort of on a weird vacation. We spent the down time writing some very bewildered letters home. "Hi everyone, our company commander went bug fuck crazy and we may be in boot camp for ever. No one knows what's going to happen next. We would all run away but we don't know where we are so we don't know what direction to go. Hope you are all well. See you soon.....or not. Perhaps I'll see you at Christmas or the 4th of July. Shit we don't know."

It took a couple of weeks for our company to be transferred to a new barracks. Those weeks were tacked on to our boot camp experience and a new first class petty officer was assigned to line us up and teach us how "to be all that we could be." The replacement company commander was skinny and pale and looked as though he could fall down and die at any moment. I believe he came to us directly from submarine duty and he was in dire need of sunshine, vitamin D, and muscle tone, as soon a possible. He had permanently watery, bloodshot, eyes that made him look like he was crying all the time. As sad and wimpy as this new company commander appeared he was still much better than that last crazy bastard.

The whole "line thing" is a common theme in the service. Just about each and everything you do in boot camp starts and ends buy lining up "nuts to butts" or "rockets to sockets" with hundreds of other "sorry assed duck fucking douche bags." At this point it's fair to say that all any of us wanted was to be somewhere else. They lined us up to eat. They lined us up to use a telephone. They lined us up to take a dump, and they lined us up get our silly sorry pay check every two weeks. In boot camp we spent literally hours a day standing in those stupidly long lines. Of course, the truth is, those lines were every bit as important as our uniforms. They were a necessary part of this giant well oiled machine that was and still is the United States military. "They were the lines of freedom."

The Ranch

Everything you are exposed to in boot camp has a purpose. We learned that we wore loose fitting bell bottom jeans because in a battle at sea when bombs are tearing your ship into thousands of red hot flaming pieces of metal that can burn right through your clothes, the "bells" let the shrapnel fall to the deck instead of being trapped against your leg forcing you to jump into the ocean. The Navy realized that there would be no "Victory at sea" if all their sailors jumped over board with their pants on fire. Those very same bell bottom trousers could be tied off to make a handy pair of water wings that could keep you afloat when your big grey ship was torpedoed and sank out from under you. This trick only worked if you were lucky enough to be somewhere near the upper deck when your ship suddenly wound up on the wrong side of the surface. Thousands of sailors never got a chance to fashion home made floatation devices during "World War II" because they were trapped below decks when their ship suddenly decided to go on a vertical road trip.

All of this information came at us in a short amount of time. As a group we were sobered by the thought of being entombed in a solid steel coffin for all of eternity. The Navy assured all of us that death by drowning was by far the very best way to die of all because all you had to do was relax, take a big deep wet breath and fucking die. Thanks Navy, we feel much better now that you cleared that up.

I have to say this for the Navy system. They don't give you much time to sit around feeling sorry for yourself. When you did find a few minutes to write a letter home it went something like this.

" Please get me out of here, these people are fucking crazy, and really I'm serious, you have got to get me out of here, please. I think they are trying to kill me so write a letter to president Johnson and tell him I made a terrible mistake. I can't take this much longer. Can you please send me a care package with plenty of gay stuff in it. I'm thinking blond wig, fake eyelashes, lipstick, a pretty blue dress, and, Oops. Sorry I've gotta go and get in line for something very important, don't know what, bye. With love your son.........."

Our bootcamp situation was getting worse by the day and soon had gotten so out of control that there were young American men trying to end their precious lives because of the endless piles of chicken shit we were forced to deal with.

Note: To parents of lonely, misfit kids, who are just not getting with the program, for whom you think the military might be the perfect solution. You may want to think a little longer because there is a very real possibility that...."IT'S NOT!"

One morning while I was making up my bunk, I just happened to look up and see something plummeting past our barracks window. What ever it was...wasn't smiling. I ran to the window and looked down into the concrete area where we hung up our laundry. Poking my head out the window I observed this sorry "shit bird" recruit lying on the ground screaming bloody murder. His reddened face was contorted in pain and he had what appeared to be a very broken leg sticking out from under his body at an angle that you might come across in geometry class but certainly not in the human body. There was some blood on the cement and he had a pile of string in his lap. The string was knotted about every five inches and the unseen end seemed to be attached to something somewhere on the floor above us.

We had all been issued a bundle of eight inch long strings with little metal ends that we used instead of clothes pins. (clothes stops) They were made from very thick strong government issue string. We had to tie our shirts and jeans and "skivvies" (under shorts) on the steel cable clothes lines with the little strings and they had to be in perfect rows and the knots had to be perfectly symmetrical. We had a two hour class to learn how to hang up our stupid ugly fucking clothes. This is one of many things we, sailors to be, referred to as "chicken shit." The Navy as it turns out is made up of one giant steaming grey boatload of chicken shit after another.

Our troubled recruit had spent the whole night after lights out going to every ones locker and stealing all the clothes stops he could find and then he tied them all together. When he was done he tied one end of his "rope" to his "rack" (not his man boobs, but his steel bunk bed) then he tied the other end around his neck and lofted himself out of the freaking window. He was on the third floor, I was on the second, so when he went flying by our window with that puzzled look on his face he was still picking up speed, which he did until the precise second he hit the pavement. He traveled about 25 feet and hit the ground with a terrible thud. I don't know exactly how fast he was going upon impact but you can ask a physics student if you are curious. The sailor's plan was perfect except for the string rope being about a hundred feet too long. This guy was from one of those states down south where his whole family only had about four teeth between them and his cousin was his sister and his other sister was his mother or some such country song. I imagine he wasn't real familiar with buildings with two or more floors and way over estimated the number of clothes stops he needed to weave into his plan.

Directly following our human meteorite's fall to earth. By that I mean in a real damn hurry. Like one minute he was sprawled out on the ground, screaming like a monkey with his nuts on fire and the next minute he was completely and utterly gone. In his place there was a detail of recruits cleaning up the blood. The Navy doesn't waste a second in an emergency, situation. My guess is that they carted his dumb country ass off to the base medical facility somewhere that had a fully staffed mental ward. The poor, sorry, broken recruit was never seen again in boot camp. There are rumors that he moved to Texas and was instantly elected governor.

Did I mention that I have some issues with Texas, the state of, and Texans, the residents of that flat, god awful place? I don't have a problem with all Texans of course. Janis Joplin, Willie Nelson, ZZ Top, Steve Martin, Nora Jones, Beyonce, Lyle Lovett, Bonnie and Clyde and Bobby Seale are cool but that's pretty much it. Oh yeah and Eva Longoria, sorry Texas but most of the rest of you all just suck. And what's with those gigantic cowboy hats? Do you realize how small they make your heads look? I'm just kidding, many of my very best friends are from Texas. Please don't get me started on the crooks in Houston politics, that's a whole other book.

The attempted suicide incident helped me adjust to life in the Navy. I figured that there were people around here who had problems much scarier than mine and I reveled in that fact. From that day on, whenever I noticed some screaming idiot go flying past the window….I just smiled knowingly to myself, and looked forward to spending just a little less time in that line at the chow hall.

The Navy teaches you absolutely everything you need to survive on board a ship at sea. We had to work in the chow hall, where I learned how to make a tasty breakfast for four thousand men out of real and not so real eggs and a huge shit load of potatoes. You quickly became very proficient at cracking eggs and peeling spuds. Most of us could peel potatoes all day without cutting our fingers to ribbons, but some people were never born to use anything sharper than a tooth brush. Mashed potatoes aren't meant be pink in color but in boot camp sometimes they were. Similarly some guys just could't get the hang of breaking four eggs at once, two in each hand. This explained the plethora of egg shells in our breakfast from time to time. There is something special about being in a room with a thousand other mostly grown up people who are all spitting out little pieces of white, crunchy, chicken placenta wrappers. It was kind of like an indoor snow storm, with sound effects.

The instructors taught us how to put out a compartment fire in a steel room filled with burning oil and so much smoke you couldn't even see the blazing inferno just a few feet ahead of you. The door you came in through is closed behind you so that your only choice is to fight the fire until you get it out. It's scary but you learn to overcome your fear and let the adrenalin take over. Your hands, face, and lungs are coated in a greasy black glaze when you finally exit the building. One of our brother recruits showed the rest of us how not to chew gum during the fire exercise by choking to death in the fire room.

There were a few accidents and a couple of suicides but the vast majority of us made it out of bootcamp alive. All things considered I emerged from the experience smarter and wiser but basically undamaged by basic training. This made me quite happy as I recall.

The most rewarding aspect to life in the service and boot camp in particular is the human zoo of people you meet there. One day you are in high school and most of your friends are from the same place you are. When I was young I could have ridden my bike to the door step of every one of my schoolmates.

When I enlisted I was suddenly surrounded by a carnival of characters from all over the country and many places that I never really would have guessed were part of the country. I always knew that Puerto Rico was a protectorate but we had someone from Guam and even a guy from Utah. Are you kidding me? Seriously?.......Utah?

I found that the majority of these fellow recruits were as fascinated by me as I was by them. When we had a little down time we would question each other in detail about what it was like to be from Mississippi, or Arkansas, or California. Being from New Jersey meant that the first question everyone asked me was did I know anyone in the "Mafia." I denied knowing anyone "connected" mainly because I didn't want one of the New York guys writing a letter home about this "Jersey douche bag who was spreading rumors about his family." That and the fact that at the age of eighteen I didn't know many gangsters besides a bookie or two and a few street corner hustlers from Paterson. One girl in my high school class did have a father who tripped and fell on several bullets over in New York one night and woke up with a terrible dead ache.

I really liked learning about other people and places but some people and their places were much more interesting than others. We had a big strong baseball pitcher from Tennessee who had signed a major league contract but was badly injured while driving a tanker car full of moonshine whiskey. His car was a big Buick with specially welded compartments for the highly flammable product. The bumper had been replaced with six foot sections of railroad track. He told us the story of one getaway where his car tore right through a police roadblock and that front bumper turned two cop cars into shredded piles of scrap metal. His accident involved a bridge, a fire, and months of rehab in the hospital. He lost the baseball contract but got to keep the scars. He was a good guy and a I respected him as a friend but looking at his face took a little getting use to.

My closest friend was from Thibedoux Louisiana. His name was Adams and he was a Cajun. That still doesn't explain why French people use so many god damned letters to spell simple words. Adams told us stories about working on oil rigs in the gulf of Mexico and showed me some Voo Doo tricks including terrorizing our RPOC (recruit petty officer) with a doll that he fashioned from scraps of cloth and some arm hair that he claimed to have shaved from the RPOC in his sleep.The poor guy didn't get any sleep for weeks.

Once Adams asked if he could borrow my high school ring. We were friends and I agreed without giving it a second thought. Adams reached into his pocket and pulled out a two foot long piece of thread and quickly ran the thread through the ring. He pulled the ends together and let the ring hang suspended for a few seconds and then he softly said watch this. He spun the ring with his free hand and it twirled perfectly in one place. Then he told me to watch the ring until it turns into a baseball. I played along with the trick and sure enough after ten or fifteen-seconds the spinning ring became a baseball before my eyes. That's all I remember. I blinked my eyes and the ring was back on my finger. I realized that some time had gone by when I noticed that my bell bottom jeans were on backwards and everyone in the barracks were suddenly standing around the bunk and they were all laughing. I had never been hypnotized until then but I knew better than to ask what had gone on while I was "away." Stuff like that can screw you up for a long time.

"In this life, the trick to survival and well being is, you have to get yourself in a groove. You can deal with almost anything once you understand that everyday is going to be a mind blowing adventure on some level, the rest is mostly a matter of making the appropriate adjustments. This strategy works well most of the time but some incidents are so disturbing that it takes a long while to get all the spiders out of your brain."

One overcast afternoon we were returning to our barracks after one of our daily "drills on the grinder." We had just learned how to perform an "oblique turn" as a unit. This means that eighty men, while marching in step, turn off at a forty-five degree angle at exactly the same time. It took all afternoon to get it perfect but we were all very proud when the drill was over. This maneuver was so cool to see and we would be the company to bet on to win the marching competition and a coveted silly yellow flag of glory. After marching for hours all we wanted to do was jump in the shower and get ready for our march to the chow hall for dinner.

When we entered the huge room where eighty of us bunked together, we were stunned to find that all of our racks (bunk beds) were flipped over and our lockers were dumped out and everything we were responsible for, our clothes, bedding, personnel belongings, everything, was piled in heaps all over the room. None of us had the slightest idea what the hell was going on. I had never heard of a tornado forming on and only on the second floor of a building. I remember thinking. "What in the high holy fuck could have possibly caused all of this destruction?" After surveying the devastation for ten or fifteen minutes our first class petty officer, company commander, came barging into the room, all revved up and yelling about the inspection that had been performed while we were gone. He was a man possessed and his face was bright red as he ranted on about the three "gigs" (points off) we had received for violating the skivvies folding commandment.

We had been issued three pairs of the ugliest, ill fitting, boxer shorts the world has ever seen. They were the kind that puffed out in the back and would make anyone wearing them immune to getting anything close to laid by anyone or anything. Personally I believe that perhaps this was the Navy's way of preventing a sudden outbreak of homosexuality. That and the "saltpeter" that rumor had it was going into the imitation scrambled eggs. There was, after all a practical reason for everything we were exposed to in boot camp. They gave us a training session and we were shown how our ugly shorts had to be folded and stowed in our lockers. Some poor, sorry misguided soul, had accidentally folded his shorts left over right instead of the proper, Christian, military, right over left approach and he alone was responsible for the entire company having failed our barracks inspection.

Our company had spent the entire weekend spit polishing our club house and it was spotless. Everything looked perfect from the floors which we had buffed with our wool blankets, to the toilets that we had cleaned with someone's tooth brush. We didn't tell the guy we borrowed the toothbrush from, but somehow I think he knew. Every piece of metal was shined with "Basso." The windows looked like mirrors and we dusted every square inch of wall, giving special attention the tops of the lockers. All our shoes looked like patten leather and our belt buckles shone like the sun. We were all so proud of our work.

Some ruthless underwear folder had destroyed our perfect inspection and now we would not be able to graduate boot camp with the stupid little yellow flag that you get for passing the inspection. Our main competition was a company we had lovingly nicknamed "The Evil Scouts." The Evil scouts had already won every flag and every other meaningless, piece of shit award that you could win. When they marched to the chow hall they looked like a float in the Rose Parade. As one, we all thought, "How sweet it would be to have just one lousy banner to march around with." Besides that, now we had to spend the rest of the day and evening putting everything back together. I was aware that all this underwear bullshit was just one more way to grind crazy Navy crap into our brains. Despite realizing how incredibly stupid all of this was, we still were forced to deal with the consequences.

The really shitty part of this story was that the company commander chose to inform all of us who the unfortunate person was who had screwed up his shorts and was thus responsible for us not getting to march around with a yellow flag on a stick. For some unknown reason the vast majority of our company was so outraged at this poor bastard for his crime against underwear that they were determined to exact revenge against him in the most painful way possible. I could not even imagine being that pissed at something so contrived. There must be some form of mental illness that transforms a person into the perfect cut of meat that can be ground up to produce a good obedient military hamburger with extremely shiny shoes. I was seemingly immune to this brain ailment and one day it would prove to be my downfall, or my salvation depending on your point of view.

Later that night the majority of our company threw the young sailor a blanket party. For those of you lucky enough to never have experienced or witnessed one, the guest of honor at a blanket party is held down by several people using his own blanket. Then he gets to lie restrained and motionless in his bunk while the remainder of the group wails on him with fresh bars of soap wrapped in tube socks. There are undoubtedly variations on this ritual but the out come is always the same. Some poor unfortunate mothers son winds up all beaten, bruised, and bloody for absolutely no good reason what so ever.

Our particular, tried and convicted, party guest was coincidently also our religious petty officer. He was a farm boy from Iowa or Nebraska. I don't know but it was one of those flat states you drive through and all you see is corn. Our farm boy was from someplace with tons and tons of corn, cows, chickens, and a 4H club, but no rules about proper underwear care. He had come to us from a world where if you got most of the sheep shit raked up before dinner time you were having a good day. The victim kept an old worn bible with him everywhere he could. The poor naive goof would read scriptures to us every night, whether we wanted him to or not. He was really a very nice person and although I could easily have done without all the preaching I enjoyed listening to his farm tales that I think somehow revolved around how lonely a farm really is and there are all these animals around and how a sheep's vagina looks just like a human one. He never came out and admitted to bestiality so I won't go there.

The Ranch

I tried my best to calm down the mob but they were determined to trash this dastardly fiend with all their self righteous might. I was at least successful at bringing a few of my friends over to the not so dark side and we refused to join in on the beating of the unfortunate childlike "nowhere man." Four or five of us lay in our bunks while the others drummed away for what seemed like hours. When they were done beating him they dragged his black and blue ass into the shower room for something called a "GI shower." Someone found a bristle push broom and they used it to remove any dirt along with the top two or three layers of skin while he lay writhing on the floor. The screaming and yelling was so loud that I was sure that someone would come running in at any moment and break it up. No one came of course. Our superiors had stationed some third class petty officer to be on duty in case of a fire or perhaps a revolt, in each of the barracks facilities. There were people in authority who heard the riot but no one responded. This was all part of some sick plan to put the fear of god into us and the sacrifice of one poor farm boy was a small price to pay for discipline. God alone knows what would happen if we were suddenly attacked by the Russians and one of us had our underwear folded incorrectly. It would surely mean the difference between victory and defeat. The American people would all be eating beet soup, drinking vodka by the quart, and chain smoking incredibly nasty cigarettes, if it weren't for all those perfectly folded boxer shorts.

I was concerned that they had killed our unfortunate, farm boy, but the following day he was still alive, all beat to shit but still alive just the same. Imagine putting someone in a laundry bag and throwing him down the stairs,......of the Empire State building. It was sort of like that. Our religious petty officer was never quite the same after his special training session and I don't remember him saying another word other than "yes sir" and "no sir"...ever again. He just went through the motions with his head down and mumbling what I assume were bible verses but then it could have been lines from the Rolling Stones song "Paint It Black." I personally am not a big "god guy" but I could have used a few good lines from the book of Rudy or who ever it was who preached that we should forgive those who trespass against us and or those who don't fold their undershorts correctly.

My tiny crew and I felt terrible and wondered if there was anything we could have done to prevent this monstrous inhuman act. In retrospect

I should have pulled the fire alarm. This would have at least delayed the attack long enough to alert someone in authority to the situation. Of course this particular strategy probably would have backfired and I would have put myself in jeopardy. When the water dried up, the blood thirsty band of brothers would still have terrorized our lonely recruit. I know this sounds self serving but I was still in awe of the mysterious power these people had over us. The military is a strange well thought out combination of fear, peer pressure, and meaningless rewards. The stupid little yellow flag that we would never earn or have been allowed to keep even if we had won it is the perfect example.

After the blanket party / GI shower incident I was never quite the same either. I realized that this madhouse was something that I would have to either learn to deal with or else start planning a midnight escape from the base. We weren't that far from Canada but winter was approaching and we hadn't been issued our sweaters and "Pea coats" yet. One cold morning they found one of our recruits frozen to death. He had died while on watch because he was wearing a light jacket on a night when the temperature was 10 degrees. He was still in the empty dumpster that he thought would keep him warm. By regulations we weren't allowed to wear our warm winter gear until some arbitrary date had passed. This was clearly no time to go AWOL and risk becoming a blue eyed government issue vanilla popsicle.

I decided to suck it up and stick it out. The good news was that I was gradually getting really good at all this crazy Navy stuff. I had the fastest time on the obstacle course in history. (as far as I know) I was getting excellent grades on all the tests and I was so awesome at the shooting range that when the black Marine instructor with the prosthetic leg, fresh back from Viet Nam, noticed I was putting all my shots through the same hole in the target he asked me "what the fuck are you doing in the fucking Navy dick head? You should be over there sniping the shit out of gooks with the special forces dudes." I wasn't totally clear on what a "gook" was at the time but I think it meant he liked me and he wasn't going to hit me in the head with his cane like he did to just about every one else. In boot camp stuff like this was like a promotion and my fellow sailors treated me with a new level of respect from that day forward.

Note: Just for your general information. If you remember the movie "Officer and a Gentleman" the part where Richard Gere gets over on his

The Ranch

fellow midshipmen by polishing shoes and belt buckles for a profit. Well, that trick was invented by enlisted men in boot camp well before his dumb ass did it in the movies. Only difference…we didn't get caught.

The finely tuned, if at times misguided, machine that is the US military works because of millions of tiny details. These helpful hints have been learned through out the years by mostly enlisted and or drafted personnel who sometimes payed for those lessons with their very lives. Did you know that Chapstick (a petroleum product) and pure oxygen like the kind that is delivered to our pilots through their face masks don't mix? By gosh neither did I, until an unfortunate pilot who must have fallen asleep during that class, nearly blew his face off. I believe there was a cigarette of some kind was involved. This type of explosion requires oxygen, fuel (Chapstick), and some kind of spark or heat source (joint). Sorry to be so clinical about some pilot's unfortunate mishap but, funny is funny. There was no U-Tube back then but I wish there was.

Note: I believe that the education young men and women receive in military boot camps, and service schools, as well as on the job experience should be counted as college credit when they get discharged. No wonder so many discharged personnel wind up pan handling and living under bridges like well trained trolls when they get out. Few people realize what great employees ex-GI's make. They are just a group of barely educated high school kids when they go into the service. The only thing most of them are really good at is masturbation and….well that's about it. After the military assigns them a MOS. (military occupation specialty) they are very good at least one more thing. That thing can be driving giant diesel powered vehicles or rebuilding them. Service people are trained to operate nuclear powered submarines as well as giant ships the size of small towns. There are radio, radar and electronics specialists and these days the computer networking people should be guaranteed instant jobs when they get discharged. Unfortunately this is seldom the case. Their training seems so specialized that it is considered worthless when they get out. The part employers miss is that in the military you learn how adapt. You learn to adjust to circumstances that can mean the difference between life and death. These people are all trained to take and give orders without question. Treating our veterans like they were candy wrappers should be a crime. They don't start these insane wars. They do their best to finish them.

I easily sailed through boot camp from that point on, and before you know it, the boot camp odyssey was suddenly over. There was a big fancy graduation ceremony with a band and a few high ranking officers dressed up with all their medals and gold braid. We proudly showed off our newly acquired marching skills, and even though we didn't have a useless yellow flag on a stick, somehow we all graduated just the same.

Toward the end of boot camp they made us take one last test and I scored high enough to be assigned to attend an "A" school near Memphis Tennessee where I would learn how to work on jet aircraft. This was considered an exceptionally cool school and a "guaranteed path to employment" after the Navy. (big freaking fantasy as it turned out) I remember feeling a little dejected by this news because I had put in a request to be considered for a slot in special forces, which In my case meant the "Seal Team." I was never informed why my requests were ignored but I believe things sometimes happen for a reason and I also believe that if I had wound up with the Seals the outcome could have become a genuine tragic opera.

I had many of the skills needed to become a Seal team member but not the temperament and certainly not the politics. By that I mean I was developing political views and felt a need to voice them from time to time. When you are on a special forces team there is no room for politics whatsoever and special forces is a whole other world with no need for personal views of any kind. You must have a mentality like, " An Arab, a Jew, and a white supremacist walk into a bar. It's your job to go in there and eliminate them…and make it look like the Chinese waitress did it,….. by accident." I just wasn't cut from that cloth. Personally I don't think I could eliminate someone, If it was my job to do such a deed, I would go into the bar and buy the three "targets" plenty of drinks, take a few steps back, and simply wait for them to kill each other.

Seal teams are among the most highly trained and well equipped forces on earth. Members of these teams work together as one and everyone is an expert in everything. They have to react and improvise. If there is a need to learn a language, they learn a language. They know how to identify and use any weapon they may come across during their mission. If they lose a member of the team, the remaining members pick up the slack on the run. Everyone has to know each others job as well as their own. When the mission is over they start all over move on to the next hot spot. These guys get the hardest jobs and perform those jobs flawlessly, as far as we know. There are no other people who are as competent at their jobs than seal team members, as far as we know. I am a real fan. I am also aware of my own limitations. Faced with a situation where I had to end the life of a young boy or girl holding an AK47 attack rifle, I might hesitate to contemplate the motivation of the young combatant. That hesitation would give the little third world youngster the opportunity to blow my nuts off and that could put the lives of the whole team in jeopardy. That could put the entire operation at risk and that, in turn, could put some of the wealth of the people who sent us on our mission in the first place in the pockets of our enemy's wealthy people. Wars are complicated, the people who fight them are not. Soldiers do what their superiors tell them to do.......most of the time. There are times when our young warriors feel the need to go off script but the job at hand always gets done. If this were not the case we Americans would all be driving around in Japanese and German cars...... Wait, that was a really terrible example. The point is that people in the US armed forces are willing to sacrifice their very lives for the better good of their nation. The people who send them on endless dangerous adventures all over the world do so for the better good of their Swiss bank accounts. If you feel the need to comment on my opinions you can Email me at www.blowme.com.

CHAPTER 3

J.E.T.S...Jets Jets Jets

When we finished our boot camp training, The Navy allowed us a few days leave to go home and pack for our respective school and or ship assignments. We had a chance to hang out with our friends and girl friends for a couple of days. I remember visiting the high school I had recently graduated from wearing my dress blue uniform and it caused quite a fuss. They kicked me out for creating a disturbance and I realized I wasn't in Kansas anymore. We weren't in boot camp anymore either and we would be allowed to wear our civilian clothes (civvies) off base. My civilian clothes were nothing to brag about but were still better than the ugly crap we had been issued by the government. I must say however that our dress blue uniform was fairly cool. It looked damned good, once I had mine tailored. I especially liked the bell bottom slacks with the 13 button flap in front. (one button for each of the original colonies) They were dark Navy blue and made of heavy wool material. One handy feature was that they didn't show the tell tale stains if you spilled a drink on yourself. They also came in handy at bars when you had a few too many beers and couldn't get those thirteen buttons loose in time. Generally, when I was out and about, among the general population, I preferred to dress like someone who had never been near a Navy uniform.

After my brief visit and a few solidifying moments with my ex-wife to be, I boarded a big airplane bound for Tennessee. The "A" school was

The Ranch

located in a suburb of Memphis, Tennessee near the town of Millington. (This is a scary idea all on it's own) The base was situated on the grounds of an old Army base that was probably built during the Second World War and our dorm was an old fire trap army barracks. The dilapidated two story wooden buildings were built of old, dry, hard as nails, lumber and were structurally very sound but tended to burn up in a matter of minutes when one of them caught on fire. Just such a blaze had taken place sometime before my arrival, and scores of young sailors had been trapped and died in the middle of a dark cold night on that base. The buildings were wide open on the inside and drafty so that people would bring in cheap electric heaters in the winter. It was a recipe for disaster as the ancient wiring would heat up and ignite the tinder that had accumulated in the walls of the old buildings.

The year was 1968 and we were in Tennessee so they divided us up into separate black and white barracks. This sounds incredibly racist when you think about it but it was Tennessee in 1968 for crap sakes and this segregation shit was all new to me but those people down south had it down to a science. My Mom never brought me up to treat people differently because of race or religion or the color of their sox, but some of these southern folks had a whole other belief system. Southern hospitality means people will be sweet and helpful and charming to you.....If you're white and Christian. I'm sure it's totally different down there these days.

I remember one weekend, getting a haircut in the tiny town down the road from our base. The place was sort of like a little, dirty, ugly, Mayberry. In this twilight zone version Andy the sheriff was a fat, loud mouthed, douche bag. He was sitting in the other chair getting his buzz cut trimmed while spitting brown goo into an old coke bottle as he rattled off these long winded rants accusing the "Jews and the niggers and long haired faggot hippies" of everything that had ever gone wrong.....ever. I'm not Jewish nor am I African American so right then and there I decided to become a long haired hippy as soon as circumstances would allow.

Forty years later this very same sheriff could have been a broadcaster for Fox news, or a sit in for radio host Rush Limbaugh. The guy playing "Floyd the barber" was ex-military, had a ridiculous comb over haircut, and didn't understand me when I said, in plain English, "just a little off the top sir." He just kept cutting and cutting and agreeing with everything the sheriff had to say. It was a nightmare and reminds me now of the scene from "Easy Rider" in the diner. Jack Nicholson, Peter Fonda and Dennis Hopper start to realize just how deep in " Southern fried shit" they really were. I hadn't seen that movie yet and was just beginning to notice the loathing and ignorance I was surrounded by, not to mention the shitty haircut I was exposing myself to.

I hadn't seen the movie "Deliverance" yet either so if someone had suddenly told me to squeal like a pig I would have responded with a sincere, heartfelt, "Blow me fuck face!" I did however realize that I was in some kind of dangerous alternate universe where all signs of reason and intelligence were replaced with fear, hate, very bad breath, and not nearly the normal number of teeth. They had strange music coming from an ancient RCA radio that sat on a shelf between two deer heads that served as hat racks. The music was sad and all about heartbreak and being broke and drinking. Sometimes they threw in a dog or a train or a girl friend who banged everyone when you weren't around. It sounded like the blues sung by cowboys and out of work tractor mechanics.

Before we get off the redneck train I would have loved it if "Billy Jack" had walked in just then and kicked the ever loving shit out of those cracker pricks with his bare feet. Nothing but blood and hair and a tooth or two flying in all different directions would have been just the perfect end to that crappy day. Without going into further details, I never went back to "Dingleberry Ville" ever again. My hair thanked me profusely when I assured it that I was so sorry and that it would never happen again. I of course was lying out of my ass because I was still in the Navy and had a few horror show haircuts in my future. Don't even get me started on what I did to my poor bewildered hair in the 80's. Just think, "White afro" and you will begin to understand what a cruel bastard I was to the top of my head back then. I'm amazed that my hair cut has stayed with me all this time.

Our "A" school instructors were a combination of Navy and Marine veterans who had served in at least a war or two…or three and were killing time while they built up their retirement. After that they would wind up as disgruntled postal workers, or working at a local Veterans Hospital, or possibly shooting at people from the top of a tower somewhere.

The classes were very technical and we learned way to much about every screw and nut on the jet engines that powered the carrier based aircraft of the day. The "F-8 Crusader," the "A-4 Sky hawk," and the stupid powerful "F-4J Phantom" among others. They even let us climb into the cock pit of an old Saber jet fighter left over from the Korean war and we learned how to turn up the engine. Sitting in a jet plane with the engine turning at 80 percent is a real rush as you can imagine, especially when the engine you are turning up is twenty years old and could turn into a blazing fireball at any moment.

There is a lot more to flying a fighter bomber than taking off and landing. There is also the bomber part. The more I learned about these weapons systems, the more I began to appreciate what it must be like to be the people on the ground in one of these poor underdeveloped countries that we decide should be divided up into bomb, don't bomb, maps. Some people are just born in the wrong place at the wrong time. Viet Nam was definitely the wrong place and the 60's and 70's were totally the wrong time.

As for the Navy schools, most of the instructors were very efficient and professional. The amount of technical information that they were able to instill in us in such a short amount of time was astounding. The training was so effective that I still remember most of the jet engine theory classes and the operation of the fuel control system in those amazing jet engines. That is saying something when you consider all the pot and alcohol and other mind altering substances that I've consumed since I took those classes. That is indeed another story.

The Navy had to retrain us in math and science because many recruits came from high schools in parts of the country where science and math were considered superstitions. If god had wanted you to know how much 3 X 222 was he would have tattooed the answer on your forehead, right? Wow I'm starting to get good at this. Steven King you are toast.

Our math instructor was a Marine combat veteran who made such an impression on me that he literally changed my life forever. I've mentioned that at the time I was totally convinced that the war in Viet Nam was the only thing that was keeping America free from the communist threat. None of us was quite sure what communism was but we all knew it was something bad, very bad. We had all been sold a bill of goods by John Wayne, Audie Murphy, Ronald Reagan, and our fathers about how war was this glorious adventure and to become a man you had to baptize yourself in blood, death, and honor.

Our generation had been brainwashed to become righteous warriors. We were taught that whoever it was we were fighting were subhuman evil monsters. The military does a thorough job of dehumanizing the enemy to make it easier to pull a trigger or push a button that will end a life or a whole town full of lives as the case may be. All feelings are removed from the equation and you are trained to react to orders and not emotions. When soldiers are given the order to attack a village full of other human beings and burn it down with the people still in it, ninety-nine, out of one hundred soldiers will do exactly that, and they will kill anyone who tries to stop them. Occasionally, however, there is someone who says to themselves, "Hey, this is fucked up. These are real people we're wasting," and he resists the order he was given and puts himself at odds with the entire military structure that surrounds him. I'll get back to this later in this book.

We were assigned to a math class with a tough Marine sergeant named Vogel who had recently returned to the states after three tours of duty as a side door gunner on a Huey helicopter. He was the guy you see in all the Viet Nam movies and news reels blasting away at the jungle as the pilot maneuvers his aircraft just above the tree tops and brass shell casings fly from the ejection port on one side of his M60 machine gun with a tin beer can spot welded to the other side to keep the cartridge belt from jamming. Seriously, you would think with all the money that the American taxpayer pays for these machine guns that they could spot weld the beer can onto the ejection port in the damn factory for Christ sakes. Beer cans were made of heavy duty tin back then. You couldn't pull off that trick with the aluminum foil cans they have today.

The good sergeant's job in Viet Nam was as full of danger as you can imagine. The Viet Cong after years of practice had become very proficient at shooting down our helicopters and the flight crews had an extremely short shelf life as a rule. The ones who lived were lucky and the ones who volunteered for three tours were just plain nuts. Good old sergeant Vogel was one of the craziest Marines of all time. His favorite expression was, "Gun time is better than bed time." This was a person who literally enjoyed ending other peoples lives more than he enjoyed making love. I was "young, dumb, and full of cum" and to me this mindset just didn't register in my eighteen year old brain one little bit.

If you saw this person you could only imagine the quality of the female creatures he was forced to settle for, or pay for. Perhaps blasting people with bullets WAS more fun to him than making love or what ever it was he did to the women in his life. If I had let my vivid imagination wander in the direction of sergeant Vogel's love life it probably would have involved a gun, handcuffs, duct tape, and a blindfold. I'm going to stop this drift right here because I just threw up in my mouth a little.

At first our sergeant's stories were exciting and interesting to listen to. They gave us a realistic idea of what it was like over there. His accounts were full of details and color but as his memories unfolded they became so twisted and over the line that I began to feel dirty just being in the same room with this maniac. He told us of dropping fuel drums from his chopper with incendiary grenades attached with tape and timed to detonate above the thatched huts of a village. When the Vietnamese occupants scrambled out to escape the inferno he would open up on them with his beloved M60. His reasoning was that if they were running away they must be Viet Cong. If they were children they were simply short communists and had to be executed before they could grow up to be slightly taller communists. If they were women they were breeders of the evil menace and they had to be exterminated like cock roaches. Our crazy assed instructor hadn't the slightest shred of humanity. To him the people of Viet Nam were merely moving targets like the ones at a carnival arcade only they were much more fun to shoot up than the arcade variety because they were full of blood.

The good sergeant told us the story of a pregnant farm girl who started waving a wooden rake at his helicopter because the noise and rotor wash was scaring all of her animals. He quickly determined that she posed a threat to the American way of life and he cut her in half with several bursts of machine gun fire and her baby was sort of born in that moment but was instantly shredded to pieces in a cloud of red fog and high velocity bullets. He was gleeful as he told the gruesome tale and the look in his eyes sent a jarring chill down my spine. He was a sick, sick man and I couldn't imagine this piece of human garbage trying to assimilate back into society with normal people as neighbors and god forbid have an Asian family move in next door to him. As far as I knew I had never met anyone like sergeant Vogel. The disturbing part is our world is crawling with veterans of various wars and very few of them want to tell the story of what they saw and did over there. I wish these people would open up and get that stuff off their chest. Trying to keep memories like that locked up inside is where PTSD comes from. Being the people who get sent to fight wars is hard. Coming home from those wars can be harder.

Sergeant Vogel was a raging racist who made Hitler look like Jesus so naturally he had the two black marines in our class sit in the back of the room which is where I also chose to sit as well. I just wanted to be as far away from this creepy vile scumbag as was humanly possible. The three of us became very close friends and we shared jokes under our breath whenever the instructor was facing the blackboard. One day, as Vogel was ranting away on the orgasmic pleasures of destroying nonwhite people, one of the black students, "Mike," was drawing something on his scratch pad. The sergeant asked him " hey boy, what the fuck are you drawing in my class." Without hesitation Mike testified "I'm drawing a white man." Obviously pissed Vogel exclaimed " a white man? What is this white man doing?" Mike followed with " he's just hanging around," and he paused, "at the end of a rope, like some kind of strange fruit." he exclaimed as he turned his head to the side, sized up the teacher and made a few finishing strokes with his pencil. Our teacher didn't get the Billie Holiday reference but he did get the joke.

I froze for a second as I evaluated the situation that Mike had inserted himself into. Sergeant Vogel was a sadistic control freak who held the lives of his students literally in his deadly hands, especially the marines in the class. He was able to decide which students should be passed on to further training in their field and who should be forwarded directly on to duty stations overseas. In 1968 this clearly meant an all expenses paid trip to the sunny and wonderful land of Viet Nam. I suddenly felt obligated to do something to buffer the wrath that was brewing to the surface before my eyes. I wanted to say something but there was no time to come up with the perfect quip that could quell the wrath of the evil monster in our midst. I did the only thing I could at the moment and I began to laugh. I tried to be as sincere and boisterous as possible to deflect the steel cold hate I saw in sergeant Vogel's eyes away from Mike and over to me. The laughter slowly became contagious and soon the whole room was roaring with glee and the insane pressure of the situation started to drift away.

My ploy worked to perfection and I was rewarded with an opportunity to show the entire class how good I was at doing push ups. As it turns out I was very damn good at doing push ups and I even did them the marine way where you clap your hands between each one and catch yourself just before your face kisses the deck (floor). When I was done with some crazy amount of "marine push ups" I jumped back up with a big grin on my face and the sergeant winced and just said, " What in the holy fuck are you doing in the Navy, puke?" Puke was a term of endearment that was bestowed on only the truly outstanding and I smiled and I said, " I failed the sadism portion of the Marine test sergeant." More laughter from the class made the bastard start to shake a little bit.

Vogel instinctively hated the black students but now he hated me even more for befriending them. You just didn't do stuff like that back in his dark, unlit, corner of Mississippi. From that day on I got more than the normal amount of practice doing push ups and sit ups and pull ups and just about every kind of "up" you could imagine. The good sergeant and I were at war for the remainder of the class and the tension was so thick at times I could hardly keep myself from blasting Vogel in the mouth whenever he started reciting his racist rants but I reasoned that if any one should retaliate against this twisted prick it should be Mike or Keith. Keith was the other black guy in our class. Keith was from Chicago and was a champion swimmer (so much for that stereotype). Keith was also smart and this fact pissed off our sergeant to no end. I'm certainly not a religious person by any means but if anyone should have a reservation at the "Hotel Hell" it was our butt crack math teacher. I was also exposed to a brief but crystal view of what life in America must be like for a black man or woman. I will not pretend to fully understand the African American experience but my level of respect increased immensely because of this series of events.

Note: Growing up we didn't have a single African American in our little middle class town in New Jersey. That meant I got to be the minority because we were so damned poor. In my senior year the first Black family moved to town. This is terrible but I thought, "finally someone else can share in the weight of unspoken prejudice that existed in town. I only got invited to one party in High school and that one was sports oriented and I was obligated to go. The only problem was that the new kid's dad was a well to do doctor. He was also an excellent athlete who quickly became one of the most popular guys in school. Ah well it was his turn and I would have to wait to get a shot of self confidence, the military would give me that.

The experience with my math instructor was a real wake up call. I began to question my own belief system, like what in the holy hell was this war about and how exactly were we helping the people of Viet Nam buy blowing them up setting their villages on fire and murdering their people. I also wondered why was it so easy to justify the destruction of an entire culture as long as that culture was yellow or brown or red or black. I began to study up on the ages old conflicts between Viet Nam and the many other countries who at one time or another had tried to impose their will upon this truly amazing country. The Chinese, the Japanese, the French among others had attempted to invade and enslave these very brave and resourceful people. Now Uncle Sam was trying to save our god fearing nation from the scourge of communism by killing as many of the home team as possible with the most expensive weapons the world has ever known. Of course Viet Nam was a convenient place to fight a proxy war against our real cold war enemies, the Russians and the Chinese. The problem was, and is a fatal flaw in the way the United States views third world nations. When we start dropping bombs on people, we think we are somehow subduing them and turning these unfortunate residents into good, Christian, freedom lovers. In reality we are creating a whole new inspired enemy in the relatives of the people we slaughter in the name of Democracy.

I found myself imagining how I could possibly deal with having my family murdered by a foreign army who had taken over my country. This idea is hard for a young American to get his or her mind around. Slowly I was beginning to sense the feelings of the average citizen in one of these far away places where we get to test all of our fancy military hardware. I totally believe in a nations right to defend itself from foreign invaders,….. only in Viet Nam, we were the foreign invaders.

The truly weird thing that really freaked me out was that Ho Chi Minh the leader of the people we were fighting, or "Uncle Ho" as he was affectionately known to his friends on the cocktail circuit had been an important ally to the United States. General Douglas McArthur had acknowledged him for helping to save the lives of American fliers who had been shot down by the Japanese in southeast Asia during the Second World War. Uncle Ho, who lived in the United States for a while had also been inspired by the story of the American dream and had studied Jeffersonian democracy to the point that, as rumor has it, he fashioned a document considered by some to be the Vietnamese version of the Declaration of independence as a blue print for his country's future after he chased the French imperialists back to Paris. Ho also lived in China and became a communist so his politics were a bit complicated.

Unfortunately following the siege of Dien Bien Phu and the brilliant defeat of the French by the out gunned Vietnamese, the United States chose to side with the fairer skinned, and much better dressed French. After that war the US began to devise a giant case based loosely on those "giant communist Dominoes." The plan was that we had to begin dropping thousands of tons of expensive fiery ordinance on every living thing we could see and plenty of stuff we couldn't see. Conveniently there were defense contractors lined up around the block to help us do just that.

The main problem our soldiers experienced in Viet Nam was that they couldn't see much of anything at first because of the lush green forests that existed every where. The geniuses at the Pentagon decided to have our clever chemical companies develop this shit stew called "Agent Orange" that could make all the leaves fall off the trees. This brilliant strategy would leave nothing but large groups of enemy soldiers standing out in the open with silly looks on their faces and then we could shoot them, lots of times, with our really cool guns and stuff. Looking back the whole idea of naked trees seems like it was thought up by a class of second graders with some unnatural inbred fear of leaves.

This not so well thought out plan also assured that any human being exposed to this magical potion would over time develop some form of damage to their central nervous system. The victims included our own troops on the ground, and pregnant Vietnamese women who didn't have to wait long at all to see the wonderful side effects of Agent Orange on their new born children." It amazes me that the people who call an abortion murder are the same people who vote for the maniacs who think this crazy shit up."

Note: To all self righteous douche bags and douche baguettes. "POST birth abortions are just as bad as the pre birth variety." Blowing up a pregnant woman by accident while you are trying to kill an enemy soldier in his own country is an abortion as well. This could also be considered murder by someone related to the unfortunate mother to be, thank you very much.

Agent Orange also worked its magic on the "privates" of privates and corporals and sergeants. Strangely it didn't work nearly as well on Generals but that may have something to do with fact that generals spend more time on golf courses than they do in rice paddies and defoliants and golf courses don't go together as a rule.

Please! Would someone just once try to put yourselves in the shoes,...... or sandals, of the people whose homes we destroy and the relatives of those people who just happen to be in the proximity of someone that we consider our enemy. If our citizens were forced to endure random bombings and our homes and cities were being attacked on a regular basis by a superior fighting force from a country half a world away we would go crazy. I mean rednecks with totally ridiculous arsenals of weapons would rise up and kill every foreign looking person within range of their 50 caliber sniper rifles. (that's really damn far by the way).

The point of this ramble is that after much discussion and research I could find no rational reason for our sending troops to a country on the other side of the planet that had no way of harming me or my girlfriend. I mean Viet Nam had been trying to purge itself of colonial super powers long enough and was desperately trying to experiment with self rule the best way it knew how. They had home field advantage and they were very clever at finding ways to defeat much more powerful enemies.

Note: I believe that governments are a necessary evil and just how evil depends on the character of the residents of the country they represent.

From the day I graduated from the Navy Jet school I decided to seek out a different yet appropriate way to serve my country. I realized that at some point I would need to take a stand against the madness of war but it would be a while before I figured out exactly how, and just what shape that stand would take. In the mean time I had yet another plane to catch. Much like the Beverly Hillbillies I was on my way to California. Unlike the Hillbillies of Beverly I wasn't worth fifty bazillion dollars that they got from shooting a hole in the ground in some hick town down south somewhere. I could shoot at the ground all day long in New Jersey and all I would hit were the corpses of prematurely deceased Italians.

CHAPTER 4

California Dreaming

The flight from New Jersey was long and tiring but this was back in the day when most of the "stewardesses" (my computer hates it when I use gender specific words like stewardesses) were goddesses and all of them were women. The fact that they didn't ask to see an ID card for service people back then made the trip an enjoyable one. After one of the scariest approaches you can imagine we came in for a landing next to San Diego harbor. We had skimmed just above the roof tops so close to the ground that I could read the license plates on the cars below. I've heard that pilots are required to have a special certification before they are allowed to land at the San Diego International Airport.

After debarking from the aircraft I grabbed my sea bag from the luggage carousel and wandered out into the late afternoon warmth of the San Diego bay area. All things considered I think San Diego must be one of the most perfect places in the country or at least it was in1968. There were giant, grey, Navy war ships and cute little white sailed, sailboats flirting on the water and dense clusters of homes climbing the surrounding hillsides. The first major difference I noticed about southern California was that they have freaking palm trees…everywhere. Back in Jersey the palm trees were all painted on the walls of strip clubs.

I started taking snapshots with my "Brownie Instamatic camera" the second I got off the plane. Every picture I took had at least one spectacular palm tree in it. Most of the pictures also included a representative of the California State police department, complete with reflective sunglasses and riding boots. You literally can't spit without hitting a cop in southern California. I wouldn't try it however unless you don't mind being beaten to death with fifty night sticks. The temperature was about 75 degrees in March and the sky was clear and blue all day long. The brown polluted air of Los Angeles was visible up the coast but it was no way near to San Diego....yet.

The nights were cool and comfortable. I was totally sold on the climate and the scenery but not the economic requirements of living in California. Even back then home prices were way above normal, and there was the sense of police state in the air but I tried to ignore it in hopes that it would go away.....(it did't)

My new duty station was the Naval air base at Miramar just north of San Diego. Miramar was, and is, a flight training facility, AKA "Fighter Town." The gigantic airbase was built for training Navy Pilots how not to kill themselves and others while taking off and landing on the decks of enormous floating cities like the USS. Constellation and the Enterprise. If you've seen the movie "Top Gun," well than you know a little tiny bit about Miramar. The scene in the movie where Tom Cruise and Val Kilmer fall in love with each other in slow motion during that steamy shirtless volley ball game? Yeah, well that was my barracks in the back ground. In real life the pilots would never be caught dead within a mile of the enlisted men's quarters. There were, after all, rules that prohibited officers from fraternizing with enlisted personnel, but then in Hollywood any thing is possible.

In the real world one of the few times an officer and an enlisted man would interact out side of the confines of a ship at sea or during regular working hours on base was when an officer would arrive home unannounced and find his beautiful, darling wife, in a passionate embrace with the here to for mentioned enlisted man. This happened quite often and generally involved large amounts of naked sprinting and gun play. I personally would never be caught dead in a situation like that.....I was much to quick and dodgy.

California was just like every beach blanket movie I had ever seen. I imagined Annette Funicello was lying just down the beach with her bikini

The Ranch

top untied. (Annette was the first of many Mickey Mouse Club hotties and I had a huge crush on her when I was a young Mouseketeer). From my first day on the base I decided to volunteer for the night shift so that I could spend my days enjoying the amazing climate and stunning scenery. In the mean time I spent all my week ends in or very near the ocean. I became friends with a surfer named Bob who was once an Olympic prospect swimmer. Bob had this mint condition, yellow, rag top, MG sports car that we rode to the beach in with his surf board hanging out the back. Bob's nose was always coated in zinc oxide to protect it from the suns rays. That took a lot of zinc oxide because his nose was the size of a door knob. I used Copper Tone SPF 0 to insure a rich dark tan. It also insured pounds of peeled flakes that I left behind everywhere I went until my New Jersey skin turned from white to red and finally dark brown. Back then we were oblivious to the harmful effects of the sun and the word "melanoma" wasn't on anyone's vocabulary list. Today the list of stuff that young people know nothing about would be endless. No one reads these days unless it's a "text" or the instructions on the condom box.

Our beach was La Jolla shores, a world class destination for ocean lovers. I was totally blown away by the sheer beauty of the place and the atmosphere was incredibly perfect. The long wide beach curved north from a cove and went on forever, all the way to Alaska. Just south of the swimming and surfing area there was a fancy assed hotel where the soon to be president Richard Nixon and his family hung out. One of my beach buddies was always bragging how he was banging Julie Nixon, but this individual had a bad habit of grossly overstating his sexual adventures so I usually took his stories with a whole shaker of salt. I wasn't in the same bedroom with him and Julie so there is no evidence that he ever really nailed the future presidents daughter.

Just southwest of the hotel a sheer cliff rose above a shallow coral reef. This area was alive with every kind and color of fish you could imagine. This natural wonder curved out to a stunningly beautiful cove. The reef had become a snorkelers port of call. Jutting out towards the breaking surf was a natural sandstone arch, back then. That arch is gone now after it was destroyed by giant waves during a storm in 1977. I could barely tear my self away and head back to the base after spending a day in La Jolla. The other guys in my "cube," (Small, separated living area with three bunk beds and six lockers) hated me because there was always sand from the beach and flakes of dead skin on the floor after my return from one of my all day tanning sessions. The guy in the bunk below mine said it was like a sandstorm followed by a snow storm. I was sorry and tried to adjust my habits by showering and applying moisturizer before entering our cube and I enlisted the help of several friendly young women in bikini's to keep my skin well oiled. I was happy to return the favor. It was the least that I could do. These concessions weren't nearly as painful as they sound.

The weekends were my own unless I had duty once a month or so. The remainder of my time was spent swimming, body surfing, and getting to know some of the golden brown California girls who were in complete and total control of the beach. The "Beach Boys" would have you believe that the guys with the bushy blonde haircuts and surfboards were in charge of the sand, but they would be off base by a mile. Those girls had cast a spell over us and they knew it. I don't remember complaining and was just happy to be part of this new amazing life style. You must remember that, where I came from, the only girls who had a tan all year long in New Jersey had relatives in countries much closer to the equator.

One of my first California girl friends was a lovely, seventeen year old native American who had the improbable indian name of Judy. I don't know why but I was expecting something more exotic like "Princess who walks on water. (she was a surfer after all) Judy's mom was Navajo but her dad was a hard ass Navy commander who I only met once when I went to her home for dinner. He caught us kissing on the couch and he immediately drove me to the highway and dropped me off in the middle of nowhere. I wound up sleeping under a bush in a school yard. Judy and I remained close friends but I never went back to her house.

This lovely young native American princess gave me some kind advice early on in our relationship. Judy told me "grow your hair, lose the East coast accent, and don't tell anyone you're in the service, if you want to get along down here." I was a little stunned but Judy was an extremely savvy, beautiful young woman and I trusted her judgment. I started wearing a ball cap at work to cover my blond hair that was getting longer and blonder every day. I dialed back on the "F" bombs and tried to sound as if I had been born in El Segundo. The phrases, "Dude" and "far out" became part of my vocabulary. As for the service thing, I was starting to understand the whole antiwar movement and I began to feel concerned about the part I might have to play in this very bad idea that was the Viet Nam conflict/ police action/ WAR.

Note: Viet Nam was a war. The men who were drafted to go off and fight and die there would agree. Afghanistan is a war. Iraq is a war. Korea was a war. Any time you drop bombs on people's homes it's a war. Whenever you whip out the B-52s it's a war, or at least a devastating concert. Young Americans have no idea what it's like to live in a country like Viet Nam, or Iraq, or Afghanistan. For a visual aid try to picture a universe where everyday is September 11, only it goes on for ten years at a time. We lost less than 3000 people on "9-11". The country of Viet Nam lost over two million citizens during our "conflict," Now start counting to two million and take notes on how many times you pass 3000. You can get back to me on this because I'm guessing it will take a while.

I hadn't been in California very long before I met my first "Hippies." Most of the people who frequented the beach were members of the surf crowd but there were always a couple of vans or VW micro busses parked out in the corner of the parking lot with flowers and peace signs painted all over them. They had tie dyed curtains in the windows and I noticed there was always a strange sweet aroma whenever you walked near one of them. One fragrance, I learned later was Patchouli oil, but there was another sweet smell that I would learn much more about in the very near future. One particularly outrageous van had a beer keg strapped to the roof of the cab and a piece of surgical hose running from it down into the drivers side window. There were paintings of naked women dancing around a bonfire, anti war slogans, and a sign on the back door that said, "Don't laugh, your daughter may be inside." I'm guessing that they would get pulled over by California's finest about every twenty feet if they ever tried to drive that van out of the parking lot.

I was intrigued by the giant brass balls these strange people had. In 1968, California cops made Nazi storm troopers look like Cub Scouts. These people however were unfazed by the police state and were flaunting themselves for all to see. It was all so crazy and yet I felt I needed to get to know more about them.

One fine day and quite by accident I met this incredibly beautiful girl who had a band of pink and yellow flowers in her hair. She was wearing a long cotton print dress, there was no evidence she was wearing any other clothing under that dress. She was barefoot with several tiny brass toe rings on her perfect little toes. Some of the guys from the base were tossing a football around and one of them threw the ball and hit the young girl right in her perfect little head. For a brief moment there were flower petals floating around her face and she looked like an angel. Her beautiful blue-green eyes were slightly crossed at that moment. Impulsively I ran over to her and asked her if she was OK. She was a little stunned but she blinked and smiled at me and assured me she was fine and I think I fell in love a little right there. She told me her name was "Moonbeam."

I picked up the football and threw it in the ocean. The surfer who had beaned my new friend started to give me some shit but I shot him the patented "New Jersey Look," the look that says, "fuck with me asshole and I'll hit you so hard your dogs nuts will fall off." He paused and shook a little and then he backed away and marched off to rescue his ball. Most loud mouths and show offs are also cowards. The trick is in the ability to figure out which ones are and which ones aren't. In this case I had guessed correctly and therefore I would not be forced to battle someone just to impress a beautiful young girl. I was also smart enough to know that those battles always end badly and the girl who is being fought over is seldom still around by the end of the fight.

Moonbeam and I began talking and she told me she was some kind of model who had a part time job working for the Sears teen catalog. We soon became friends and would take long walks down the beach just talking and enjoying the ocean and the amazing weather together. We would bring along a blanket for us to relax on at the end of our little journeys.

One day, the two of us walked way up north past the Scripps pier, almost to "Blacks Beach," where all the naked folks hung out. We found a cave out of the sun, spread out the blanket and set up a little camp site at the entrance to the cave. About then, this lovely young girl pulled a painted leather pouch out of her giant woven bag. Then she removed a few items and began to roll up a cigarette. I was naïve but not totally stupid and I surmised that this was going to be my first experience with the dreaded herb, marijuana. I suppose I could have refused to join her when she lit up her "fatty," but one look at that innocent face with that silly little grin and I just relaxed and went for it. Did I mention I was nineteen years old and she was a beautiful Sears model? Some things are just not under our control, nor should they be.

I have no regrets and some of you may not believe this but I had no craving for crack, or heroin, or airplane glue, or spray paint afterwards, however I did have this incredible urge for a Big Mac. Moon Beam, of course, was a vegetarian and I had to keep my need for greasy mystery meat to myself. She was way ahead of me and whipped out a bag of "Cheetos Cheese Puffs." The magical snack was gone in a few minutes. We had orange stains on our hands and smiling faces and we laughed every time we looked at each other. I wanted to kiss that orange right off her face but I was in fear of being shot down....like Bambi's mother. My demons prevented me from trying to take our relationship with someone so clearly out of my league to the next level. Yes, it's true you are reading a book written by someone who was once a cowardly douche bag. Now after many years I may still be a douche bag but I'm no coward.

This experience proved to be a profound turning point in my life. For one thing I was crossing a boundary that I had set for myself a long time ago. I had convinced myself in high school, "Never get involved with illegal drugs." I had fallen for all the propaganda. This marijuana stuff however, just seemed so innocent and natural. I hadn't done my homework on this subject and all I knew about weed at the time was what I had been told by my teachers and my step dad during his crazy tirades. I for instance, had no idea that one of the main reasons for the ban on pot was the direct result of a giant campaign paid for by Patty Hearst's insanely wealthy and influential grand pappy, William Randolph Hearst. (Patty Hearst was a famous heiress who had inherited some of her grandfathers great wealth and was kidnapped at gunpoint from her college dorm by armed members of the Symbionese Liberation Army in 1974. After some thorough brain washing she helped rob a bank and did some time but President Jimmy Carter let her go free. Most of her captors were obliterated in a fiery gun battle with hundreds of LA's finest.

William Randolph Hearst was a newspaper and magazine giant who owned entire forests full of those big tall things they make paper out of. Just for those of you who didn't know, marijuana has another name and purpose. Hemp is one of the strongest natural fibers found on earth and was used for thousands of years to make incredibly strong rope and yes, you guessed it, paper. (I've been told that the original copy of the Declaration of Independence was written on hemp paper. This is probably one of the main reasons that this important document is still around) The sentiments of this document were discarded long ago.

What does a super rich guy with thousands of acres of wood pulp do when he learns that someone has just come up with a machine that separates hemp fibers at a super fast production rate? This machine was to hemp what the cotton gin was to cheap T shirts. A machine that could put trees out of the paper business for good? Well, for starters Hearst cranked up these crazy but very effective fables about young white teenaged boys who smoked one marijuana cigarette and instantly turned into mad drooling maniacs who raped and murdered lovely young innocent white girls. Once you smoked that first doobie you were hooked on hard drugs forever. Do you know how he spread the news? Yep you guessed it. (You people are so smart) He printed it in his newspapers and magazines on his own paper. Reportedly he also used his newspapers to help start the Spanish American war. You can look all this stuff up.

It wasn't long before movies like "Reefer Madness" appeared in theaters across this great land of ours. (if you have never seen this huge steaming pile of propaganda, it is a hoot) The United States government fell right in line. (Hearst owned more politicians than the Koch brothers) Our sold out politicians passed laws prohibiting the possession and production of this natural substance that can grow "anywhere." (Trust me on this fact) The first people to be affected by these laws were of course poor black folks who had smoked reefer for eons and perhaps a few white trumpet players in blues clubs in our nations cities. Once the publicity of the anti marijuana laws began to kick in, the youth of America created a whole new industry that is still alive and well today.

Now of course the illegal drug trade has grown to a point where the murderous capitalist bastards who have taken over the sale and distribution of marijuana and other illegal products have more money than most countries. The least these scumbags could do is say thank you to the United States justice department for creating an atmosphere where their enterprise can thrive and grow. It's all tax free, and they didn't have to become a religion or a charity, they simply said, "if you want our stinking taxes, come and get them." The Mexican cops who tried to end the drug trade in their country are all dead now and no one is lining up to take their place.

The United States is a nation based loosely on the idea of personal freedom, and the people of this country think they should be free to do what ever the hell they want, as long as you aren't hurting anyone, and when you tell them suddenly that they can't do something, it makes them crazy and they just want to do it even more. Many times when that something possibly had never even occurred to them in the first place. Our wise and benevolent government once tried to outlaw alcohol. In doing so they created a huge underworld network of crime families and a giant lawless culture fueled by the immense profits that prohibition provided. They also increased the budget of law enforcement agencies and prison systems all across this great land of ours. Absolute pure fucking genius.

Note: Thanks to the war on drugs. We as a nation are going broke trying to enforce unenforceable laws and we now have more people locked up in "for profit prisons" than any other country on earth. We taxpayers pay incredible amounts of money to feed and keep millions of people fed and housed in those for profit prisons. When these formerly law abiding, employable, citizens finally pay their debt to society they find that it is nearly impossible to find work with a prison record so many of them return to the drug trade and a life of crime and the beat goes on. The vast majority of these people are black and Latino and their crimes are considered felonies. Now they don't get to vote. Hmm, a whole bunch of mostly brown and black citizens being deprived of their right to vote. Who could possibly profit from a law like that? Hint: Black and brown voters vote for democrats as a rule, except for that black guy who they put behind Trump at all his rallies. Why don't the networks interview that guy?

Note: learning from the past is not a natural trait here in America. The next time someone asks you if you think we should continue this mad adventure known as the war on drugs, "Just say NO."

Perhaps if we let the DEA lead us down this road a while longer, Mexico or Columbia could become the next great super power. A super power controlled by the scariest bunch of crazy mother fuckers the world has ever seen. I'm picturing Nazi Germany with dark hair, porn star mustaches, and nuclear submarines that deliver shipments of cocaine hidden in torpedoes and ballistic missiles.

Moon Beam moved on soon after our uplifting experience together. I think she wound up traveling to New York to pursue her modeling career. I suppose I should have been sadder but it's not like we were lovers and there was no shortage of beautiful young women in San Diego. I, however, will always be grateful to Moon Beam and her little bag of happy dreams because in many ways she helped to change the general direction of my life. If I could, I would thank her for opening up my mind and for letting me enjoy her beautiful spirit and that wonderful knowing smile for that brief moment in my life. Oh, and those Cheetos were amazing.

"The American people have been driven down some winding roads by our corporate controlled government but none so harmful and costly as our war on drugs. Of course if you run a privately owned prison, you're all good, right?"

My world was never quite the same after the experience in the cave. It was as if certain people knew my little secret somehow. Those certain people were the ones who also were getting high at the base. Some of my fellow workers on the flight line started to feel me out and before long we were all best friends and were enjoying a little bit of natural god grown goodness on a fairly regular basis. There was no shortage of good old Mexican weed, and the Navy base was the perfect place to get the more powerful varieties from Panama, Hawaii, and of course Viet Nam and Cambodia. We were just having the time of our lives. The next couple of years were a series of winding, strange, yet very humorous side trips from the very straight line that had been set before us by the Naval establishment and the United states government.

Back at the base I discovered that there was some kind of parallel universe that, until then, had been invisible to me. I don't know if it was always this way or if the madness of the Viet Nam war just fostered an atmosphere of rebellion, but those of us who had begun experimenting with banned substances became part of a very elite and special group of democracy defenders. We didn't hang out at the enlisted men's club on base or the USO downtown in San Diego. We didn't get drunk and get into bar fights. When we did go to a bar it was In Tijuana, and we didn't go to the "donkey show" where women perform unnatural sex acts with animals. (those are the same donkeys that they dress up during the day and let you and your kids sit on by the way) We also didn't go to the clubs in the "red light district" because we didn't relish the idea of getting shots of penicillin for weeks to come, besides the marines were lined up at those places like they were giving away free beer. They only gave free beer to their best customers.

My friends and I spent our "Mexican nights" at the "Oasis club" or the "Blue Note" and we danced all night long. We were in awe of the very talented live bands who couldn't speak a word of English but could perform "Proud Mary" on a par with "Ike and Tina" and "Creedence Clearwater Revival" would have walked out of the bar in shame when they heard these guys play their music. This was another defining moment for me. I was just starting to realize that talent of all kinds existed beyond the borders of the United States. As Americans we are brought up to believe that we invented everything worth inventing and produced everything worth producing, but there is a very robust economy out there that we would be forced to deal with in the future. Many people in our country just didn't understand this fact. Cultures in countries like China, Japan and Babylon were thriving thousands years before Americans ate their first "Jumbo Jack," or stuck their first flowered, plastic, hat in "Mrs. Potato Head's" plastic head.

Our little extended family attended concerts and a couple of "love ins" with groups like "Jefferson Airplane," "Canned Heat," "Richie Havens," "Taj Mahal" and "Buddy Miles," to name a few. We once went to an "Ike and Tina Turner" concert. This was before Tina finally got tired of having the crap beat out of her and took her solo act on the road. My friend Mario and I were the only white men in the audience. There were many white girls in attendance and it was sort of like an episode of "Soul Train." There weren't any chairs on the floor of the auditorium but that was just fine because everyone in the place danced to every song. We had an amazing time and were treated like family by the others in the crowd all night long.

One fun evening we dropped a little acid and went to see Arlo Guthrie. (For those of you who have never tried it, there is no such thing as a little acid) Arlo sang some of his fathers songs and I was close to jumping on a night train to Oklahoma by the end of the concert. We hardly noticed that neither Alice nor her restaurant were represented at the show.

Note: Yahoo/Google "Woody Guthrie" / the "Great Depression." Don't hurry, I'll wait………..Cool guy, right?

After the performance we returned home to our apartment. Woody only knows how we found our way back. My "1956" blue and white Buick had an excellent auto pilot. After relaxing for a while I decided to walk down to the local Circle K for something to drink and pick up a greeting card to send to my girlfriend back home. I was about a block from the store and the store was two blocks from our apartment. I'm sure there is some algebraic equation that would tell us exactly how far I was from our rented house, but it certainly wasn't to fucking far. I was walking slowly with the words to "This Land is Your Land" playing in my head when I heard the siren and was blinded by the search light on the City of San Diego police cruiser. A lone officer exited the vehicle and ordered me to put my hands on the car. I was still a little wired but I wisely persuaded myself not to try to escape. Running away from a California cop is just another term for suicide so I did exactly as I was told. The officer patted me down and asked me to show him my ID. I did my best to explain that my home was a block or so away and that my wallet was back at the apartment and all he had to do was drive me or follow me there so I could show him my drivers license and Navy, ID card. That was when he started to go a little crazy.

It seems that this police officer had a brother serving in Viet Nam. The cop freaked out when he realized I was in the Navy. The truth is that the person standing before him wasn't dressed like a good little sea scout. Admittedly my attire that evening was just a teeny bit over the edge. I was wearing a pair of tight denim bell bottom jeans with colorful patches and bare feet. I was also wearing a leather vest with long hangy down things decorated with wooden beads, and no shirt. There was a peace sign on a leather string around my neck and tilted slightly on my head was a beat to shit floppy denim cap with some flowers stuck in a hole in the side. And I had a better tan than Halle Berry. The cop's eyes were tearing up as he went off on me for daring to look like I did while his brother was off in a land far away, defending my freedom. I considered pointing out that the way I was dressed was part of the freedom that his brother was defending, but he looked and acted like he wanted to shoot me in the face, so I just let it go.

The officer radioed in to his dispatch center and told them that he had a sailor who he thought was AWOL, (absent without leave) and to have the shore patrol come and pick me up. I wasn't high any longer, now I was pissed off. This was total bullshit but I had no choice. I just had to adhere to the program. My other choices were get brained with a long black night stick, or get shot in the face. Sometimes I think that the whole Hippie movement was just a way for young white people to expose themselves to something similar to the black experience without going through the actually being born black thing.

After what seemed like an eternity the shore patrol van showed up and two fat, nasty smelling, tobacco chewing, red necks, from Alabama got down and started in on me.....again. You would think these assholes had never seen a stoned hippie, third class petty officer, with some slightly wilted flowers in his cap before. They literally picked me up and threw me into the back of the grayer than grey, shore cop van, and drove me downtown to the brig. "Brig" is a big fancy Navy term for jail. When we arrived at the brig / jail, I expected to be booked or notated in some fashion but it became clear that I was only there for the amusement of the nitwits with the SP armbands on their fat, pork rind enhanced, biceps.

After throwing me into a large holding cell, one of the guards, (I think his name was Billy Jimmy Bobby) ran to the back office to get a Polaroid camera. He came back all grinning, showing a few of the nastiest teeth I'd ever seen outside of a zombie movie. The other fat goober started pointing and yelling instructions like he was directing a "Chuck Norris movie. "Get that there hat, get them there flowers, damn get that there peace sign and that there hippie vest." I felt like Brad Pitt with all the flash bulbs going off in my face. They taunted me for a while but ran out of words early on and had to repeat themselves. "Hey peace freak faggot, you sure look awful pretty in that fag hat you stupid fag peace lover faggot." I was tempted to ask the dumb turd if he had some kind of issue with his own personal sexuality but I thought better of it and just stayed quiet. I showed so much restraint that night I could have been the center fold in the latest copy of Bhudist monk magazine.

My tormentors grew tired after a while and left me alone to consider my situation. As it turned out I wasn't exactly alone. There was a black sailor sitting silently in a corner wearing his neatly pressed, dress blue uniform, sharing the oversized holding cell with me. I was locked up for being out of uniform. He was locked up for being black, in uniform, on "Alabama night."

Ship board sailors were required to take turns being on shore patrol duty when in port and our "southern fried heroes" had paired up to raise a little government supported mayhem upon hippies and minorities who also happened to be serving their country. For them, it was just like being back home.......except they weren't allowed to burn crosses or hang people from trees for looking at white women. The following morning we were released. The charges against us weren't dropped based on the simple fact that there never had been any charges.

Back at the base I was about to discover a brave new world that I never dreamed existed. The strict Naval environment was evident on base. There were American flags flying everywhere as well as cannons, and a retired jet aircraft or two, adorning the grassy parks that were scattered around the campus. The underground was less pronounced however, and very secret. There was a building right on the flight line where the sailors who loaded the rockets and bombs on our aircraft showed up for work. The "ordinance shack" was a three room quancet hut, and the ordinance technicians or "ordies" were feared and respected by everyone. You didn't want to piss off people who could blow up your car, your dog, or your hat....while you were still wearing it.

I was invited into their "ordies shack" one day by some new friends who I had recently smoked a joint with down in "Happy Valley," near the base. I entered the building and the front room was all very clean and ship shape. There were several pictures of aircraft loaded with bombs, flying over the jungle. There was the obligatory picture of our then President Nixon and plenty of grey furniture and of course an ash tray made from a bomb casing with a squadron insignia painted on the side. The room was well guarded by a sailor with a neatly pressed uniform and very shiny shoes. After checking me out and getting the OK from my new friends we continued through a heavy blue wool curtain into a second store room of some kind. Every thing was in perfect order and ready for inspection.

Just outside the window, less than fifty feet away, there was an F4-J Phantom jet taxiing out to the runway. The deadly looking plane was loaded up with bombs and rockets, all ready for a practice run at the Arizona test site. We stepped down a short hall way and came upon what appeared to be a pad locked back door but when we went through the door (the pad lock was a fake) there was another heavy black curtain and a bead door. I pushed the curtain and beads aside and entered a third room. It was dark, but as my eyes adjusted, I could make out pillows and people lying all over the floor. The strong smell of grass was overpowering. There was a filtered exhaust fan but it didn't help much.

This was such a mind blowing scene that I couldn't believe my watering eyes. There was a huge water pipe with smoke rising from a full bowl and someone invited me to hit on one of the three tubes attached to the base of the pipe. I settled onto one of the pillows and after breathing in a couple of deep tokes of the sweet smoke I coughed a couple of times and settled in for the afternoon. There were posters of "Janis Joplin" and "Jim Morrison of the Doors" and brightly colored Peter Max posters and peace signs all around the room. I mean this little building was in the epicenter of one of the most famous Naval air stations in the country and here we were, stoned, listening to "Frank Zappa," and munching on potato chips and "Milk Duds" for Christ sakes. I seriously wonder how Alice would have handled it if there was a place like this in Wonderland.

I started to get to know some of the other sailors in the room, at least the ones who were awake and this was when I first met "Smacks." There was this tall, athletic looking African American with a huge, fully blown, perfectly round, "Afro" and a tie dyed scarf wrapped around his forehead. He had on an extra large pair of dark sunglasses and looked a little like "Sly Stone," of "Sly and the family Stone" who was very popular at the time. We smiled and exchanged introductions, fist bump, high handshake, and a five on the side just to seal the deal. Smacks was a little hard to communicate with at first as he tended to drift off track from time to time. I could tell that Smacks was under the influence of more than just some grass. We talked and laughed and we both had big stupid grins on our faces for I forget how long. As it turns out I forgot quite a lot stuff back then, but now, years later it is all as clear as day. Curious. I kept wondering how Smacks was able to function within the boundaries of military life. I learned our friend with the spectacular "fro" had been discharged months before and was simply residing on the base when he wasn't living down in Tijuana with his prostitute girlfriends. He somehow managed to hide the natural haircut beneath an oversized, navy issue baseball cap when he was wandering around the flight line. Just in case any of you were wondering, afros are retractable.

Smacks was sleeping in a bunk in our barracks but no one in authority knew he was still around. His free accommodations came to a sudden end one day when a fleet of "shore patrol" trucks pulled up to the barracks and a dozen "turtle heads" (how we lovingly referred to the navy police in their tiny grey plastic helmets) poured into the building. My friends and I had just rolled into the parking lot after downing a few Big Macs over In Claremont, a small town just south of the base when all the excitement started. We instantly decided to hold off on the going inside thing and opted to wait and see what would happen next. The building itself was three stories tall with large ledges that ran the length of the building above the first and second floors. (as seen in the aforementioned movie Top Gun) The ledges made frequent window washing relatively safe and easy. As the drama unfolded, we all realized what was going on. Someone had finally "dropped a dime" on our friend Smacks.(this was back in the day when a pay phone call cost a dime) (This was back in the the day when there were in fact pay phones)

We sat in my Buick Road Master, like we were at the drive in movies, passing around a big fat doobie. I had carefully parked downwind and we were being carefully discreet since there were pissed off men in little grey helmets and "Billy clubs" running all over the place. As we watched the scene play out before our eyes I looked up to the third floor just as Smacks climbed out of one of the windows and onto the concrete ledge. Looking cool and relaxed he backed up to the edge of the ledge and took one short step back. At first we all thought he was committing suicide but as he dropped he simply and gracefully caught the edge of the ledge with both hands as if he did shit like this every day. He then dropped him self gently onto the second floor level where he repeated all the same moves again and deposited himself into the garden at the corner of the building. At this point our friend just simply disappeared. I had played football with Smacks at the beach and he was scary fast and could just jump right over the guys who tried to tackle him so I wasn't surprised when he was there one moment and gone the next. The poor silly shore cops searched for an hour before giving up in disgust, and what I assume ended with some vengeful retribution against the poor misguided snitch who had ratted out the unwelcome house guest.

The incident with Smacks made us all realize that the crushing weight of power and control, that until that moment, we thought the Navy had over us, was a bit of a sham. If there had been a big red curtain handy I would have cast it aside and there would be our base commander standing in his underwear with food on his face screaming for us to ignore the man behind the curtain. As we watched the mob of make believe cops depart in their crappy little grey pickups, all we could do was smile. Truth be told, after all the pot we had just disposed of, the earth could have been on fire and the most we could have done about it was perhaps cook us up some "jiffy Pop Popcorn" by sticking it out the window of the car.

CHAPTER 5

The Job

I took a jet aircraft related proficiency test that was all about the million or so things that you could do wrong that would ultimately result in a very expensive flying machine falling from the sky. I must have done well on that test because I was promoted to "Plane Captain" about four minutes after completing it. Being a plane captain means that you are trained to know every thing there is to know about your plane. I didn't just know my plane, I was madly in love with my plane. My aircraft was the super powerful F4-J Phantom jet fighter bomber made by our friends at McDonald Douglas. Someone representing McDonald Douglass blew somebody way up top in our government and got a huge contract to build a shit load of these incredibly scary, flying destroyers of other peoples stuff. I thought It was by far the coolest combination of metal and fire that we had at this point in our human evolution. The Phantom could burn up more JP-5 jet fuel in a few seconds than any other aircraft of its kind. This made the oil people happy and that is, after all, what it was all about.

The F4-J Phantom jet held all kinds of records in it's day. It could fly faster and higher than any other combat aircraft in the world back then..... as far as we knew. It was as close to the SR-71 (space ship that looks like a jet) as you could get, at the time.....as far as we knew. For those of you not familiar with really cool stuff this means that the Phantom was just a few thrust pounds short of being able to fly into outer space. The F4-J was just plain bad and it knew it. If a machine can have attitude this one had a severe case. It also could take a licking and keep on ticking. These crazy stupidly well built planes would come back to the same ship they left from with all kinds of bullet holes and stuff shot off of them and they were still ready to take off and fly more missions.

The pilots were ready to get back up there as well. Combat is indeed a drug and the more dangerous the mission, the greater the need to return to the action. The veteran pilots were amazing and had bravery stenciled in their underwear. They also had a way of dealing with what they were doing that was a tiny bit disturbing. I once asked one of our pilots how he could drop napalm bombs on a village full of human beings only some of whom may be the enemy.......or not. He looked me right in the eyes and told me.

"I make believe there is nobody down there. It's the only way any of us can deal with the power of life and death that we have when we climb into that cockpit." This brief interaction with a "superior officer" made me realize that, "I was his enabler, his accomplice." "I was the guy tuning up the get away car for a crime against humanity."

"War is madness on steroids, with a super fat wallet" The Viet Nam war was heavily financed by the most powerful nation the world has ever known. (At the time) The Vietnamese people never had a chance in hell to survive victorious,......except for the part where they didn't know how to loose a war. These very same people had turned back the Chinese, they had kept the Japanese at bay during World War II and they had kicked the shit out of the French who had attempted to enslave their people to help harvest the huge rubber plantations that France was betting on to make them a super power again. This of course was just on the cusp of the plastics revolution that would soon turn rubber into clay. Oh well, France still has a better health care system than just about everyone except perhaps Cuba.

"The French conundrum" How can a country so full of themselves and so hostile towards any poor bastards who don't speak French be so good at stuff like health care, and eating food the rest of the world would never even think of? I mean sautéed snails? Are you kidding me? Yes, I'm just screwing with you France. I love French cooking and I am crazy about "quiche." I remember back in the day there was this author named Bruce who wrote a book titled "Real Men Don't Eat Quiche." He published his book in the early 1980s and He used examples like "John Wayne," and said that the "Duke" would never eat "Quiche" because he was a real man. "Hey America! Now hear this." If you are a real man you eat any fucking thing that tastes good. You can eat "quiche Burritos" with a spoon if you want because real men don't give a shit what four foot tall "Munchkins" in "Buddy Holly" glasses, say, or think, or do. So there, blow me. (note: call my lawyer and see if I can get sued for any of that) (just kidding Bruce. I'm sure your very popular book was written purely in jest and that you also thought that John Wayne was a Hollywood, government, front man, who was being used to sell patriotism to the youth of a nation whose leaders (the uber rich, and their paid for politicians) had decided that perpetual war was the best way to proceed into the twenty-first century. George Orwell was off by a few years but he had it right. (google 1984) Then read the book…please.

My Navy job revolved around these super cool, super dangerous birds of prey. The F4-J Phantom jet fighter bomber was the sexiest airplane built since World War two. It was my mission in life to know how they worked and how to make sure that if one of them did happen to fall out of the sky,…. that my name wasn't on the paperwork. As a plane captain it was my job to inspect the Phantoms before their missions and sign a form that roughly said if the plane blew up it was my fault. The pilot could drink a bottle of Southern Comfort and fly his plane into the side of a fucking mountain and it would still be the plane captains fault. The theory of plumbing was adopted by the military. Shit does indeed flow downhill and as a plane captain it was my mission to stand at the bottom of the hill and dodge all the giant, flaming, stinking, turds that were headed in my direction.

One of the other functions of a plane captain on the flight line was to climb onto the wing of the aircraft and make sure that the pilot had strapped himself into the cockpit correctly before take off. If you found your pilot had slid himself into his ejection seat facing the tail of the plane it was your job, indeed, it was your duty to turn his dumb ass around. The next thing plane captains had to do was to pull all thirteen safety pins from the ejection seat and place them in a red plastic bag and show them to the pilot so that he knew that his seat was armed and "HOT." The giant, J79 jet engines, were already running so everything we did was translated by hand signals.

One morning, an (EID) "extra intelligence deprived" rookie pilot, who was trying way to hard to look like he had a clue, jumped onto the wing of one of my jets. He stepped up into the cockpit using the spring loaded shoe door ladder. Then, the pilot to be, ducked his head to avoid braining himself on the canopy and slid down into the seat (facing forward) and I began to get the straps and buckles ready to fasten him into the plane. After securing him safely I removed all thirteen safety pins from his ejection seat and placed them in the red bag. I tapped him on his flight helmet and showed him the bag. He nodded like he knew what I had just communicated to him. About then he started playing with all the cool dials and buttons. I watched in horror as he began to pull on the ejection seat handle. This is quite similar to playing with the trigger of a really big loaded hand gun while the muzzle is in your mouth. I was leaning over him at the time and if the seat had fired he would have launched himself one thousand feet into the air...with MY severed head and shoulders in his lap. I recoiled the best way I knew how. I slammed his head into the other side of the canopy with both hands and arched my back and fell backwards onto the wing. His flight helmeted head banged back and forth a couple of times like a bell clapper and this dramatic move put him into a state of shock. An enlisted man had just put his hands on a superior officer in a very aggressive manner. By all rights I should have been on my way to the brig, but the expression on my face and the appropriate hand gesture made it abundantly clear that if he even considered turning me in I would be forced to kill him and all of his relatives and their associated pets. I will always remember the outright look of fear in his eyes as he sheepishly settled back down into his rocket seat and tried real hard not to look at me or that yellow and black striped ejection seat handle.

I finished prepping the pilot for his mission and then jumped down onto the runway. I went through my set of hand signals to test the various components, before take off, as if nothing had happened. I fully expected to be court marshaled for assaulting a superior officer but no such order was ever issued. I think that after some time in the air with the image of my bloody face in his crotch, the pilot must have decided that discretion was the better part of valor, and he let me go on about my business. This was probably a very wise move on his part. I was just beginning to get really tired of all this toy soldier crap and my patience with officers was wearing quite thin indeed.

Chris Peck

"THE ACCIDENT"

One beautiful southern California day, we were seated in our countries finest military restaurant enjoying a fine lunch of steak or lobster or possibly both. Miramar really did have the best damn military chow hall in the world. Seriously, on lobster days it was all you could eat and some guys went freaking nuts. Empty claws and broken shells were flying everywhere. Melted butter sprayed in all directions and sailors were sliding across the floor while trying to get more sea spiders on their plates. It was sheer delicious madness and, oh man, so freaking good. I was doing all I could to keep from falling into a dark pool of guilt while also enjoying every last savory bite of our wonderful, tax payer provided, feast. There were certainly people in far away places, starving to death at that very moment, and here we were stuffing our faces with perfectly prepared deep sea delights. We were blissfully enjoying food heaven when the whole building suddenly shook. Within a second there was the unmistakable sound of a thunderous series of crushing explosions. I glanced around the chow hall to see a giant room full of people who had no idea what was happening. In southern California earth quakes are as common as breast implants but this was something very different.

Everyone rushed out of the dining hall and into the parking lot just in time to see a small dark object blast through the roof of the now fully engulfed hanger number three. We didn't know what it was at the time but I had this terrible feeling that the flying object had a face and a name. The hanger was situated on the flight line up the road from where we were standing. Giant bright orange flames bellowed out of the east and west doors of the hanger as that small dark object arched over the hot desert landscape and landed in a puff of dust. That object turned out to be some one's young son. He was a sailor who had been working on the ejection seat of one of our aircraft when a F8 crusader jet came blasting in through the open doors of the hanger. Somehow the seat fired during the first explosion and launched the young sailor right through the steel roof of the building.

I watched in horror as the deadly inferno grew more intense. As we took in the whole scene someone noticed there was a single lonely parachute with what I had to assume was a college graduate in a flight suit hanging from the straps. The parachute floated safely to the ground at the end of the runway. Small explosions continued to tear up the inside of the huge metal structure. Our hanger was awash in smoke and flames and death.

We had no immediate means of transportation available and my big Buick was parked back at the barracks parking lot. We started running toward the plume of smoke in our loose fitting navy issue work boots (boon dockers). We were more than a half mile away and it took us about six or seven minutes to reach the flight line. Let me say this. The Navy teaches it's sailors to be excellent fire fighters. On board a ship at sea, every second counts and every sailor becomes a firefighter in a heartbeat. By the time we arrived a small army of men who had survived the initial fireball and the subsequent explosions had gotten fire hoses up and they had the worst of the fires under control. The young brave sailors were performing rescue missions into the smoking aftermath. There had been sixty sailors working in or around the hanger when the F-8 came flying through the doors and crashed into the planes inside.

There were several stories about what exactly had happened. One of my friends said that the plane's engine was running at full throttle as it entered the building and it sucked a mechanic through it's engine just as it hit the ground. He said there was a cloud of red vapor just before the first giant explosion. My friend fell to the ground when he saw the plane coming directly at him and this is what saved his life. He was just out side the hanger and the screaming, pilotless, jet passed just above him before tearing into the line of parked aircraft and working sailors.

There were so many of us who showed up all at once that the shore patrol had to hold us back to prevent more people from getting hurt. Helicopters arrived to transport the injured to Balboa Naval hospital. We felt helpless and noticed that there were a few blackened corpses laying on the pavement. Most of the dead sailors were people we knew. One of them slept in the next bunk in my cube in our barracks.

All of us were wondering what in holy hell we had just witnessed. Eleven young men died that sunny day in Miramar and I don't think very many people outside the base ever heard about the horrible event. The news was tightly controlled during the Viet Nam war. Everything had to go through the government. I didn't watch much TV back then but I asked some of my friends from off base if they had heard about the accident and they hadn't. There is of course the possibility that the story made the nightly news but most of my friends were busy getting high and had totally missed it. There were some news paper articles written at the time but not nearly enough to cover the scope of this "accident." I say accident because I don't think the pilot deliberately flew his plane into a hanger full of very expensive military aircraft and other associated support equipment, not to mention the young offspring of ten American families (two of the fatalities were brothers) from all over the country.

They estimated the damage at around twenty-five million dollars. This was a fairly large amount of money back in 1969. The most expensive jets we lost that day only cost two or three million each. Today our military fighter aircraft go for fifty times that amount.

There was some sort of formal military inquiry and the pilot made a statement and testified that his aircraft had shut down after his engine flamed out and had lost all power, forcing him to eject. In theory a pilot isn't supposed to bail out of a running aircraft if they are flying over a populated area but rather they should try to direct their plane away from buildings and people and try to land the best way they can. If the pilot happens to get killed in the process at least his family knows he died trying to spare the lives of those on the ground.

I can tell you that we knew this pilot's memory of what happened must have been clouded by a sense of self preservation. We knew his story about his jet engine shutting down was just that. We had little sympathy for his less than heroic deed that day. I don't think they took the statements of the line crew under consideration since the word of an officer always trumps that of an enlisted man. The pilot was transferred to a new duty station for his own good and was rumored to have caused another costly "accident" when he clipped the wing of another plane while flying in formation. This time however only two planes were turned to rubbish and no one was killed as far as we know. No one knows what happened to the sorry assed pilot after that. I'm guessing Texas politics.

I was slowly developing a deep seated dislike for the "Roger Ramjets" of the world. "Rogers" was a nickname I had given to our pilots. I arrived at this catch phrase based on one particularly "assholeified" jet jockey that we all had learned to live with.

This pilot bravely sauntered around the flight line in a pair of custom made suede flight boots. He was a character in his own movie and he always had a silk scarf wrapped around his neck with the tail hanging down the back of a very cool decked out flight jacket. He looked and acted like a movie star but treated his flight crew like we were his key grips. I was his plane captain and he ordered me around with a look of distain on his chiseled face. This is like pissing off your waiter on a busy night in your favorite restaurant. If you don't want someone spitting on your mashed potatoes or jerking off in your soup…respect the wait staff. I was more familiar with his plane than he was and he knew it, but he tried extra hard to look like he knew what he was doing in the cockpit so he tapped on all the gages with authority and played around with the joy stick between his legs like it was his dick.

The pilot had heard the story through the grape vine about me and the other misguided pilot who had played around with one to many brightly painted gadgets in the cockpit so he knew not to go near that ejection seat handle. I caught his eye at one point and glanced over to the handle as if daring him to grab that black and yellow baby just once. He blinked at me a couple of times and I knew that I was now the one in control. I swiftly showed him the red bag of safety pins and stowed them down beside his seat. I tapped him on his glossy flight helmet with the cool screaming eagle decal and gave him a thumbs up. He nodded and I jumped down off the wing, grabbed my light wands, and took up my position about thirty feet from the nose of the F4-J Phantom. At my signal the pilot ran up the engines slightly and we went through our preflight dance. I instructed him to turn on his lights, I gave him another signal and the wing flaps raised and lowered and I swiftly ran from side to side to verify their correct operation. My crew of two scampered beneath the belly of the jet and checked the belly gages to verify that the hydraulic lines were fully charged. That means 10,000 pounds of pressure by the way. DO NOT have your hand or head inside a hydraulic door when it snaps shut. This would be an extremely unfortunate life choice.

After a couple of minutes all the tests were complete and both of my guys pulled the wooden chocks from the tires and we all stood back to allow the plane to taxi out to the runway. On this occasion however I made sure my crew was all lined up perfectly at attention and we began to sing the theme song to the cartoon show "Roger Ramjet." We were singing quite loudly "Roger Ramjet he's our man hero of our nation etc.") but of course no one could hear a thing over the roar of the two screaming General Electric J-79 engines. The pilot looked down at us in wonder, waiting for my signal for him to continue to the runway.

I finally sent him on his way and we all snapped a perfect salute as he pulled away. He knew we were "goosing" him and so did everyone else on the flight line but there was really nothing he could do. At any rate, that is where the term "Roger" came from when referring to our beloved pilots. Small victory's were rare for enlisted personnel but I gained a few points among the other plane captains that day. As it turns out I also drew some wrath from one particular second class petty officer.

CHAPTER 6

Crime And Punishment

There was a small building we called the "Line shack" situated just across from the flight line where our aircraft were parked, ready for inspection and launch. The line shack was there for the plane captains and our crews to hang out between launches. We had a dispatch area in the front of the building where we received our assignments and flight times. We were expected to have all of our "birds" inspected and ready to fly. As plane captains, we signed off on each of them. The signature meant that if anything at all went wrong with the plane it was our ass. There was a whiteboard with all the days plane numbers and columns where they checked off the status of each aircraft.

On a typical day each plane captain would get two or three aircraft to inspect. We would launch our "birds" that same day as long as the flight wasn't cancelled or if they decided to have a night launch. Everything was very organized and ran better than the New York City subway system most of the time. We spent our down time in the line shack, drinking coffee and listening to record albums on my GE stereo portable record player. We played The Beatles, Simon and Garfunkel, and the Rolling Stones. Country music was against the law in California back then, although Johnny Cash was just starting to gain some popularity, probably because of the whole Folsom prison thing. Willie Nelson was sort of a crossover artist and had a certain amount of "street cred" on the left coast because of the whole pot smoking thing.

As plane captains we found it necessary to come up with some games to play to pass the time after launching our birds. I rummaged through our spare junk area and found some three foot long pieces of half inch tubing and fashioned some very effective blowguns. I made the darts from sharpened sheet metal screws and duct tape. The next step was where we would have to choose items around the office to use as targets. The ugly assed black and white picture of President Nixon never had a chance. One evening after an exceptionally vigorous game of blow darts we were surprised by the sudden dramatic entrance of petty officer Billy. Billy was his last name, not his first, and he came from the swampland in a state somewhere....where they have swamps. We had swamps back in Jersey but they were full of people. The people may not have been alive but they were people just the same. We called our swamps Meadowlands so we could fill them in and build sport complexes on them. Mr. Billy came from a swamp that had real prehistoric creatures twelve feet long as permanent tenants.

Petty officer Billy was a second class petty officer (he out ranked me by one class) and he went absolutely bug fuck crazy when he saw the "Tricky Dick" picture with a big hole where the center of the face used to be. I really thought he was going to start killing people. Billy began screaming and just wouldn't stop. He stormed about the room, waving his arms like a mad man. He must have been secretly in love with president Nixon. I think he was speaking in tongues there for a while. After way to much time, way out on the dark side, he settled down long enough to take all of his pent up rage out on his favorite red headed stepchild. He knew damed well who had instigated this horrid act against his beloved war criminal. His face was about an inch from mine as he told me to be back at work at zero seven hundred sharp (That's 7:00 AM) for special duty. My eyes were stinging from his dragon breath. After he stormed out of the room I tried to wipe the smelly spit from my face. Billy's teeth were spaced like a picket fence and he always had a hard time keeping the nasty stuff in his mouth where it belonged.

I spent that night trying to figure out what I had done that was so wrong, I mean Nixon was a monster as far as I was concerned. Most of my associates hated the fact that such huge flaming asshole was running our country, everyone except petty officer Billy that is. Billy had a serious crush on Nixon and all things Republican. If he is still alive Billy's probably at a Tea Party rally wearing a MAGA hat carrying a sign claiming that president Obama is a communist, gay, Nazi, Muslim, Mexican, illegal alien, eskimo, who was born on the Greek Island of Lesbos.

When I showed up for duty the next day Petty officer Billy was standing in front of the line shack with several cans of sort of green and sort of grey paint. He also had an old wooden milk crate filled with brushes, rollers, red rags, and a gallon can of turpentine. The paint was left over from World War II and had the skull and crossed bones sign on the back with a long list of ways the fumes from this deadly potion could kill you or leave you permanently brain damaged. The EPA hadn't really kicked in yet. Did I mention that there was a republican President in 1969? To be fair Nixon had a decent record when it came to the environment. Today he would have been run out of the republican party like a convicted union member.

I caught on right away and realized that I would be spending the rest of the day painting the line shack and perhaps the rest of my life if I wasn't real careful with the whole ventilation issue. I resigned myself to the punishment and began planning out the project in my head when petty officer Billy started off on me, again. He had several hours to compose a speech and he gave me the swamp version of the Declaration of Independence and accused me of being a communist and a fascist pacifist. I probably had a few socialist views at this point. I mean Social Security and Medicare sounded like good ideas. Having a fire department when your space heater sets your house on fire is a plus as are roads and bridges. The peace sign that I wore on my jacket was a dead giveaway but fascist, communist? That seemed just a little on the harsh side.

Note: Damn it people. Before you start accusing people of being this or that, read a god damned book for Christ sakes, or these days all you have to do is Google the crap you are calling someone so you don't sound so fucking stupid. Just so you know, like in case you live in a swamp. Fascists believe in corporatism, where corporations rule the state and wars are a means of keeping the country strong and the investors money coming in. Sort of like what we have today. Actual communists believe that we are all responsible for each other and we need to work as one for the common good. Nothing like what we have today.

I tried to explain all this to petty officer Billy but his eyes were starting to bulge and glaze over in a fit of righteous indignation and he screamed at me to "just shut the fuck up and start painting, you stupid fucking commie, faggot, bastard." This was a classic last straw situation and he had finally pissed me off.

After petty officer Billy stormed off I began to devise a plan of attack that would be appropriate to his level of "Swamp thing behavior." There was a one inch piece of molding about four feet up the wall of the line shack that ran all the way around the room and the room was sort of green above the molding and sort of grey below it. My orders were quite clear. Petty officer Billy had said during his rant that he wanted every thing above the line to be green and every thing below the line must be grey. He planned to be gone all day and warned me that, "You had better be done when I get back or there will be all kinds of holy fucked up hell to pay."

This last statement was disturbing considering that the person who was going to make my life "HELL", came from a swamp. Hell is a relative thing and when you had to live with snakes, alligators, and close relatives who were only connected to the human race by a thread, Hell must be a really scary place indeed. Right then and there, I resolved to paint that damn building EXACTLY as I was told and that is what I proceeded to do. Not only did I follow my orders to a tee, I finished with time to spare, including cleanup.

When petty officer Billy returned late that afternoon, he marched into to the line shack with a big shit eating grin on his face thinking there was no way I had completed my mission on schedule but when he took one look inside the building his eyes got as big as pizza pans. I had painted every inch of the room grey or green just as I was told. Everything below the line was grey including the table, the chairs, the floor, half the door including the door knob and, the bottom four feet of the refrigerator, front and back. I painted the trash bucket as well as the salt and pepper shakers on the now all grey table. Above the line I didn't miss a thing. The windows were green now and the room was quite a bit darker during the day as a result. The clock on the green wall was green but it was still seventeen thirty (5:30 PM) under that green paint. At least I was reasonably confident

The Ranch

it was, but you sure couldn't tell by looking at the fucking clock. I had painted the clip boards that hung from little green hooks, as well as the papers clipped to the clip boards. At one time those papers contained more than enough useless government gibberish that some douche bags in Washington had deemed so terribly important that none of us ever read, with the obvious exception of petty officer Billy. My crowning glory was the brand new picture of President Richard M. Nixon that had been hung that very morning to replace the one with the big hole where Nixon's nose had been. That creepy picture had always made my skin crawl and I gave it three coats.

I was just as proud as proud as can be. There was a knowing smile on my face because I had followed my orders to the letter, without question or hesitation. Finally I turned to face petty officer Billy and was shocked to see his face nearing critical mass. He was turning bright red and he had a huge vein bulging out of his pimply forehead. His eyes were darting around the room like he was counting mosquitoes and I backed up a step just in case that big old ugly head of his exploded. This time there was no speech, "Swamp Thing " just stuttered something , not words by any means, just odd sounding noises, grunts, and a gag or two. and then he suddenly turned walked into the door frame, bounced back and forth and then staggered out of the kind of green kind of grey line shack.

I was positive I was totally going to get sent to "Ice Station Zebra" or some other government facility near the arctic circle. I had opted "to push the envelope all the way back to the post office," and now I would have to pay the price for my gesture. I spent that evening trying to imagine all the horrible, possible duty stations I could be carted off to, not the least of which was of course an aircraft carrier stationed off the coast of Viet Nam. As a trained plane captain, my job aboard ship would be to help launch our planes, loaded down with bombs. The bombs themselves were a potpourri of death and destruction. We had bombs filled with high explosives to blow shit up. We had bombs filled with napalm to burn shit down. We even had bombs that were filled with hundreds of little baby bombs that sometimes didn't explode until some child came along and thinking it was a toy, played with it. The village clinics handled many unfortunate civilians mostly young kids who made this deadly mistake. One particularly nasty prick of a bomb was invented by a scientist of the sadist faith and was filled with white phosphorus. The phosphorus bomb, when exploded sent white hot droplets in all directions. When these droplets of burning liquid metal landed on a human being they burned into his or her skin and just kept right on burning.

Bombs don't have feelings or a conscience but the people who decide who we drop them on are supposed to. For the first time I began to contemplate what I would have to do if my orders came in. I clearly had to give my decision some serious thought because to disobey an order while in the service to your country could very well involve prison time. I mean the kind of prison time where the keys get lost forever and your relatives get a letter saying you died serving your country. This may be an exaggeration but none of us knew what would happen if we refused an order once it was given.

I showed up for duty the next morning expecting the absolute worst. I just knew petty officer Billy would be there with an officer of some sort and probably some men in tiny grey helmets with side arms. When I arrived at the line shack, however, there were cheers and handshakes and plenty of laughter as guys from all over the base showed up to check out my artwork, but there were absolutely zero swamp people. It seems petty officer Billy had some sort of break down and was being sedated downtown at the Balboa, Naval hospital by the park. He didn't have many (any) friends and everyone else was just happy to see him gone. As for me, I was suddenly a hero and the other guys on the line treated me like I was Dorothy and I had just squashed the wicked witch with my sort of green, sort of grey line shack. The remainder of that day went surprisingly smoothly, mainly because we didn't have a supervisor trying to tell us how to do our job. We all knew how to do our fucking job.

The following day, just like Voo Doo, we had a new first class petty officer running operations on the flight line. Our new boss's name was Doobie. We didn't know if that was his first name, his last name, or just a very tricked out nick name but we figured anyone was better than petty officer Billy. Doobie turned out to be an extremely cool supervisor. Doobie didn't hassle us at all because he knew, that we knew, that we could perform our duties perfectly well without his supervision. This is the sign of a superior manager. He also knew that his experience was mostly on aircraft with propellers in an entirely different war (Korea) and his hands on supervision would probably result in some level of pain and or death, and lots of severely bent aircraft. From that day on we mostly lived in peace and harmony.

Note: Management is tool that people in power use to keep track of the people who work for them. "Seldom do managers need to manage anything if their people are properly trained. Unfortunately this doesn't stop some of them from trying."

Our new boss was one hundred percent better than our last, but he was just a tiny bit off plumb. By that I am implying that he was as crazy as a monkey on heroine. There was this very weird habit that Doobie had where he would tell us that if we took off our shirts and we let him pop out the blackheads on our backs he would let us have the afternoon off. I thought this was more than a little creepy, but it was California and the beach was so close, and besides it was comforting to know that there was nothing but tan on your back while you were getting to know your new best friends in bikini's. As for the whole "gays in the military" thing. There always was, there is now, and there always will be. It's probably just closer to the surface now than it was back then.

People are people and I have always believed that those who have the biggest problem with other peoples sexual preferences, usually have serious issues with their own sexuality i.e. Mike Pence. Good old Doobie was gayer than an Easter basket, or queer as a football bat as they say, he just didn't know it yet. I for one wasn't going to be the one to tell him. I don't really know how someone who has denied his feelings for a lifetime comes to that kind of realization. Perhaps when you are going through your record/CD collection and there are mostly soundtracks from Broadway shows, or maybe you notice that you have ten to many pairs of colorful cowboy boots in your closet. At any rate it must come as a shock to some military men's-men who wake up one morning with a giant hard on and a really strong urge to rub some sun tan oil on the cute recruit in the next bunk. There are as many views on how to live a life as there are people. I love the fact that we are all different and we can all live side by side once we learn to cut each other an inch or two of slack. All to many people aren't smart enough to see diversity as a positive thing. To bad.

CHAPTER 7

The "A" team

People in the military have friends, or at least know people who are so dependably scary that that the guy from the "Elm Street" movies wouldn't fuck with them. While serving in the military I was friends with several of these people and I looked upon them with great respect. Also I knew enough not get anywhere near their bad side.

The most obvious of these awesome mutant ninjas was a not so gentle giant I will refer to as Stan. Stan was a heavyweight Golden Glove boxing champion from Montana who was one big solid muscle with a head. When he worked out on the heavy bag at the gym the whole building shook as each devastating blow lifted the 150 pound bag several inches with either hand and then came crashing back down on its chain that was suspended from the roof of the metal frame building. The first time I walked past the gym while Stan was working out I thought we were having an earth quake.

I first met Stan when I pulled a night watch in our barracks. We took turns minding our home away from home and saw to it that everyone was awake for their shift at the appropriate time. If the place caught fire it was our job to wake everyone up and make sure they got out of the building. In an ideal situation the night watch was the last man to get out alive. We worked from a wake up sheet on a clipboard that everyone who needed to be disturbed from their wet dreams had filled out the previous day. I took over my first ever graveyard shift at midnight and the guy who I was relieving handed me the clip board with all the names of each sailor and their wakeup time. He then handed me a mop handle minus the mop. "What's this for?" I asked, with an unknowing look on my face. "That.... is for Stan, my friend." He was careful to let me know just how important this nugget of information really was. "Stan is on the first floor, cube six, bottom bunk, on the left. You use this mop handle to wake him up. Just be out of sight when he opens his eyes." "Are you just fucking with me?" I asked. "Is this guy someone who I need to be concerned about" My mentor advised me that the last person who neglected to use the mop handle found himself in the garden outside Stan's cube covered with shards of glass and he also had a broken jaw to show for it.

"So, you want me to poke the monster with a stick?" I asked in disbelief.

"It's either that or Stan will hit you so hard when he wakes up that your grandmothers tits will fall off."

I had been warned and was careful to use the mop handle as I was told. At the dreaded moment that was noted on my wake up sheet I leaned around the corner of the cube doorway and peered at the darkened bunk that held the sleeping hulk of the deadly giant, Stan. I noticed that his back was easily twice the size of any other normal human being I had ever met. His back could have been used to project movies on, although I wouldn't advise this option to anyone.

Carefully I took the mop handle and gently tapped Stan on his ridiculously huge shoulder. Nothing happened so I tried again a little harder than the first time but again he did not stir an inch. The third and forth tries were increasingly violent in nature but were still not providing the desired results. This was truly a predicament that had to be overcome. It was a Monday morning, Stan had spent the previous evening at the "EM (enlisted mens) club, over drinking and if he was late for his shift it was going to be my ass that would pay for it. I decided that I needed to take some sort of aggressive action and it had to be sooner rather than later. I took the stick in both hands and after calculating the proper velocity and angle I hit Stan squarely in the head with a blow that could have killed a lesser man. At first I thought Stan might not wake up ever again but he soon stirred and after rubbing his head he turned and looked me in the eye and simply said, "Thanks man, you really know how to wake a guy up."

We became friends soon after because Stan was well aware of his prowess and he knew that I was taking my life in my hands when I hit him that hard in the skull with a stick. Guys are weird.

Soon Stan and I were drinking Red Mountain wine by the gallon and cooking "Jiffy Pop" popcorn over a campfire down at La Jolla shores with some of the girls who spent the better part of their lives at the beach. This is what you did while waiting for the morning fog to burn off. As it turned out Stan was a poet as well as a deadly fighting machine and while it has been way to many years ago to try to remember his poems, they were very heartfelt and stirring. I could make something up but it just wouldn't be right, besides Stan could still be alive and I wouldn't want to do anything to piss him off. I do remember shedding a tear or two after hearing him recite one of his poems. His voice was oil well deep and it sent a chill down your spine. I wiped the tears from my eyes innocently but I think he noticed and he lowered his eyes and broke out with the least bit of a proud smile. I never told anyone this story before now and neither did he. It was like that warm man-moment between the Japanese scientist and Godzilla.

One quiet night I was wandering back to the barracks from the bank of pay phones where I had just spent a pocketful of quarters talking to my girlfriend back in New Jersey. As I approached the barracks I noticed a loud conversation coming from the far end of the building. I jogged to the corner of the barracks where I found Stan getting yelled at by a huge loud person with a thick southern accent wearing a super big cowboy hat. Stan was a big man but not all that tall, perhaps six feet with his shoes on. The southern gentleman was six or seven inches taller and he was brawny and dangerous looking. Stan stood his ground as the cowboy got louder and his twangy voice was scaring the chickens. I personally didn't see any actual chickens but if there were any chickens nearby I'm sure they were shitting all over themselves. The one sided discussion revolved around something Stan may or may not have done with his own mother. I was starting to get interested because I was aware of how this particular conversation was going to end. Stan could take a certain amount of bad mouthing but you just couldn't say anything that involved his mother, that was the rule.

Just then I noticed the Corona beer bottle in Stan's hand drop to the ground. When the first right uppercut landed on the offender's square jaw his big old cowboy hat shot straight up into the cool night air . The guy's chin shot up also, just like in a Popeye cartoon. He was looking straight at the sky but I doubt he could see the full moon we had that night. The next four blows sounded like a short burst from a machine gun. The poor stupid bastard was sound asleep in a twisted bloody pile before his goofy hat came back down. When it did Stan ground it into the dirt with his BF Goodrich sandal and hurried off into the night. I also didn't wait for the shore patrol to arrive because of the bag of weed in my pocket. I didn't pay to see that brief fight.....but I sure as hell would have.

Another person on my "people never to fuck with list" was Larry. I met Larry while running along the beach at La Jolla shores one beautiful sunny day. I was jogging near the waters edge. The surf was high and I was just trying to keep a step away from the waves as they came ashore. The wet sand was firm and easy to run on. All at once some guy comes blasting by me like I was made of extra strength slow motion. Being young and competitive I stepped up my pace to try to keep up with him. I slowly caught up but was feeling the burn in my lungs when I noticed something that freaked me all the way out. This runner who wasn't even breathing heavy was kicking a "pinky ball" between his feet as he ran. Shit, I was about to have a stroke and he was bouncing this little pink ball perfectly with every stride. I was astounded and I stammered something stupid like "Where are you from, Mars?" It was the best I could do at the time because my brain was about to shut down. He slowed to a trot and laughed at my feeble attempt to keep up. Want to try it, he asked as he kicked the stick ball in my direction. The ball flew past me but I caught up with it and I was able to pass it between my feet a few times and that was at little more than a jog. I was tired and discouraged as I kicked the ball back to this Zen master of beach runners.

Larry as it turned out was also stationed at Miramar and was a mechanic in my squadron. I was fairly new on base at the time and didn't know many of the guys who worked the hanger on the other shifts. We talked briefly and he told me his name but not his story. We ran together back to the park and I stopped but Larry just kept right on going. I was cooling down when one of the plane captains I worked with came up and asked me how I knew Larry. I told him that we had just met and that he seemed like good guy. "Jesus man do you know who that guy is?" my friend exclaimed. "How would I know who he is? We just met." He told me that,

Larry was the most dangerous mother fucker on base." This was sobering news because I had seen "Stan" in action and that was a thing of terrifying beauty. My coworker explained that Larry was some kind of martial arts expert who could kill you with nothing but his feet. He had trained in the art of "savate" or French foot fighting for eight years. He was a master and everyone knew him by his reputation.

As the story goes Larry traveled to Tijuana one night with a couple of sailors from the base. Larry's buddies got drunk in a bar and started a fight with a superior number of Marines. The argument moved out to the street where Larry's comrades ran off like scared school girls, leaving a quiet but very aware sailor in the center of a circle of eight or nine pissed off "jar heads." The two cowardly seamen got to a corner and turned around just in time to see the first Marine's head fly back violently followed directly by the rest of his body. One by one the highly trained soldiers lunged toward Larry and one by one they were dealt a blindingly swift foot to the head. At some point Larry had removed his shoes and stood on one bare foot while he spun like a top and put all but one of the Marines to sleep on that dirty Tijuana sidewalk. The last guy just took off.

The story was hard to believe mainly because of Larry himself. This guy was so calm, and he always had a smile for those of us who he considered friends. I did some homework and verified the story with some very convincing eye witnesses. Stan was the one who sold me for good when he told me that he made it a habit to never mess around with Larry. Stan didn't stay clear of anybody but Larry was his one and only exception. Larry and I hung out with many of the same people and when we were together we got along great, however I knew enough not to push his button. I wasn't totally clear where Larry's button was but I sure as hell didn't push it or anything that looked like a button when I was around Larry. That would have been a huge mistake. "Huge." "Like trying to use a hair drier in the shower Huge."

Commentary on violence:

I have only been in a few fights in my life and they were all purely defensive. Sometimes I was defending myself, sometimes I was defending someone else but I never picked a fight with anyone. I came out on top in almost all of my battles, almost. On one occasion, however, I got my eleven year old ass kicked by three friends who all knew me separately but none of them were aware that the other two also knew me and considered me a friend, until that day. If this doesn't make sense please read it over until it does. Thank you.

It was a crazy cold winter day and I was dragging my beat to shit, second hand, "Flexible Flyer" sled back home after a day of "hair on fire" sleigh riding on a local iced over hill that was only slightly less steep than a sheer cliff. I was tired and wet and cold and I could have taken a shorter route home but I took the long way home because I was in stupid love with an impossibly unattainable girl who lived on Bordick Road. Lynn was my dream girl and I took every possible opportunity to walk past her house. Lynn was dating guys in the Navy when she was in sixth grade. She was so hot that she could have given the Sun a hard on. You see where I'm going.

I dragged my sorry sled a half mile out of the way for a chance to possibly see Lynn in her yard but of course that did not happen. I kept on going because of "fear and loathing" of what would happen if I was ever brave enough to walk up to Lynn's door and ask the people inside if she was at home. After trudging past the house of the girl I had this mad, ridiculous crush on, I continued down the hill toward the old two family house that was my home. "Young boys have serious brain damage caused by young girls who are perfectly aware of this medical condition that they have caused."

I was probably about a half mile or so from the relative warmth of the house when I saw three guys coming in my direction. You need to consider the fact that our town was small enough that everyone in town knew almost everyone else. I knew these people and they knew me. At first I recognized "Russ" who I considered a very close friend. We had spent countless hours watching the "Three Stooges" on the TV in his parlor together with his brothers. We played baseball in the large lot next door to his dad's bar. We hung out with his big Italian family and I had helped him build his clubhouse on a piece of his family's property along side their home that had the town tavern downstairs.

Next was "Okie" who was more of an acquaintance but still someone who I considered a friend. "Okie" was a small person who held a certain amount of respect because he came across as cool in a "James Dean" kind of way, except for the cowardly punk part. Okie wore black everything. His shirt was black his pants and shoes were black, and I'll bet his underwear was black but I didn't really know him that well. He was wearing a black leather jacket with the collar turned up like Marlon Brando in "The wild One." (ask your parents).

Last but far from least there was a fat, loud Jewish guy named Scott who had a big fat chip on his shoulder that had something to do with him being big, and fat, and Jewish. He was always blaming everyone else for the "Holocaust" and because I had blond hair and blue eyes I'm fairly sure he thought I was of Nazi decent. I'm English-Irish but that didn't matter on this day. Scott was clearly in charge of his small band of brothers and I was all alone and had no clue what was about to happen.

We came closer to each other and I noticed the three were talking amongst themselves but looking at me slyly as they approached. When we were at arms distance Scott moved around behind me and grabbed me around the chest pinning my arms to my sides. Suddenly Russ and "Okie" started punching me in the face and stomach. Scott was twice my size and I was helpless to defend myself so I resigned myself to the beating. The good news was that besides being cowardly punks Russ and Okie were also weak and sucked at punching stuff, like my face. I was wearing a heavy winter coat that absorbed the body shots nicely and by moving my head from side to side I was able to make most of the blows to my face glance off without much damage. There is a trick or two involved in getting beat up and this was my first lesson. If you are able to outlast your tormentors they eventually get tired. Punching someone repeatedly is lot of work and when your victim doesn't cry or scream for help it takes much of the fun out of the experience.

After my beating Scott let me go and the three misguided assholes marched off like they had just defeated the Germans in WWII. I, on the other hand, used some snow to wash the blood from my face and to sooth the pain in my swollen cheeks. The journey home was a long and lonesome walk of shame. All I wanted to do when I got to the house was to take a warm shower and eat something, anything. Believe it or not, getting my ass kicked had made me extremely hungry.

As I slowly climbed the stairs to our tiny apartment my step dad saw me and immediately noticed the smeared blood and bruises on my face. He sternly looked me in the eye and asked "What the hell happened to you?"

I started to explain how three guys had beaten the crap out of me when he instantly grabbed his coat and he exclaimed "Let's go." "What? Go where? Can't I just take a shower and try to forget this shit ever happened?" "No" my stepdad roared. "We have to find them god damn it, NOW." I never made it to the top of the stairs. Warren grabbed the collar of my ugly, green, hooded, blood spattered, winter coat and pushed me down the steps. Warren disappeared around the corner of the house. All to soon he came back with an eight foot long 2X4 white pine stud that he had brought home for some reason but he never figured out what to do with it. Warren wasn't a carpenter. Warren wasn't a plumber or an electrician either but that didn't stop him from trying and he very nearly killed himself on several occasions. Yeah, so now we had a big long piece of wood and he had some twisted idea that we would find the guys who had fucked me up and he was going to hold them while I hit them over and over with a beam. This made zero sense to me but it made perfect sense to Warren and he was driving.

Warren and I drove around for an hour and we passed several groups of guys including the very same kids who had trashed me. Each time he asked me "Is that them? I just said, "Nope." Yes, I was pissed and sore and hurt in more ways than I wanted to think about, but these guys were school mates. I just couldn't imagine showing up at homeroom on Monday after putting three of my classmates in the hospital, with a 2X4 stud. I'm sorry but that wasn't something I was prepared to deal with. We continued our search for what seemed like a lifetime but we were almost out of gas and Warren, thankfully, had forgotten his wallet. We finally drove home and I stumbled out of our piece of shit Rambler and headed for the shower and a cold plate of spaghetti from a can.

I didn't have very many good days when I was young and this certainly wasn't one of the good ones. Now I had to deal with what I should do about the fact that three people I knew had beaten me like a drum. Two of these people I could expect to see in school on Monday. My options were limited because everyone knew and liked Russ and Okie. I briefly thought about calling my friends in Patterson but they were much to dangerous to let loose on these douche bags. I was considering some sort of revenge but the boys from Paterson might kill someone and I figured that would be a wee bit over the top. I was mad but I wasn't homicidal.

I decided on the course of least resistance. I knew Russ and Okie were afraid of me now and they say that a coward dies a thousand deaths. The plan was simple. Whenever I passed Russ or Okie in the hall I just looked them in the eye, frowned, and shook my head, or I would ignore them until the last second and then I would smile knowingly and walk on by. It didn't mean anything but they didn't know that. They knew they had fucked up and now they would have to wait to see if I had a plan to deal with them. Russ and Okie were aware that I was friendly with a really scary crew from Patterson and that alone was enough to give them ulcers. The best part was that the big fat kid, Scott, had disappeared. I guess his parents moved him to a better town, whatever, we never saw him again. This was fine with me, Scott was an asshole and now his partners in crime had no one to defend them. Russ and Okie stayed out of my way from then on. I felt no need to escalate the situation. War was averted and the threat of destruction was all I needed to let me sleep at night.

My friends in Paterson would have called up their troops and my two tormentors would have spent the next three months in intensive care. The Paterson boys had put some poor kid in a drier at the Laundromat for two dimes (twenty minutes) just for visiting some girl from their neighborhood. I never really fit in with those people but my stepdad was lifelong friends with the father of one of the guys from the "candy store." Literally we all hung around the same corner store that sold a variety of things that included hamburgers, shakes, candy, and they had a real soda fountain that made the best black and white sodas and egg creams. They also sold airplane glue but you needed a note from your parents to buy it. I was the best athlete in the group when we played baseball, stickball, and street football. There was a game called "hot leather" that involved a thick black belt, some running, and of course red welts on the person who finally got cornered by the guy who found the belt.

I mostly minded my own business and hardly ever got into fights, although I had to jump in to prevent someone from being severely damaged on several occasions. Once in a while I just stood back and let one of those someones take a beating when they deserved it. If you provoke a bigger, more dangerous thug into kicking your butt, you shouldn't expect others to jump in and get their knuckles all bloody because of your large, mouth.

"Violence is forever," and people tend to seek revenge upon those who do them, or their loved ones harm. This is not always the case but the "turn the other cheek crowd, is a small and select one.

Note: People who believe that peace is the answer, (John Lennon is dead, that leaves me, Yoko and some guy named Lenny). People who believe that peace is the answer should never be confused with Christians, or people of any major religion for that matter. Bhudist's seem peaceful enough but I think it's because they fast all the time and don't have enough energy at the end of the day to do any harm. Give one of those bald guys in the saffron robes a couple of hamburgers and a couple of six packs and I'll bet they would go all "Kung Fu" on anyone who gets in their face. And forget the Jews and Muslims. That old testament god was a real prick.

Some of today's Christians, define hypocrisy. More people have died in the name of Jesus than anyone else ever. The new testament is loaded down with story's of Jesus doing good for the weak and the poor and the sick but many of todays Christians have become selfish assholes who don't believe in paying taxes for education, welfare, or health care. These very same people don't seem to have any problem with military funding, however. Is this just a little contrary to the stuff Jesus was trying to teach his followers. or am I missing something?

I simply must remember to ask Glen Beck the next time we're doing shots of "Patron" together. "Glen, if Jesus was in the Air force what color bombs would he drop on his children? This question would probably make his crazy little eyes spin around and his head would explode all over the inside of that oversized NAZI helmet that he always wears when he is downing shots with his progressive friends. Of course this is a trick question on many levels. First, Jesus could never actually get into the US. Air force because of the whole beard and long hair thing, not to mention his views regarding the bombs v. children issue. As for the color of the bombs, everyone knows that you drop blue bombs on little boys and pink bombs on little girls,......duh.

Just for the record Glen Beck doesn't do shots with anyone anymore. Only a dry drunk could come up with the crazy ass shit that he does. (with the possible exception of another ex-alcoholic, ex-president, who starts wars he can't finish and put's them on MY credit card.) Some nut case recently killed a bunch of innocent kids at a camp in Norway. The camp was sponsored by a leader of the labor party. Mr. Beck suggested that perhaps the kids had it coming because they were attending some sort of Hitler youth camp. Glen, there is a huge difference between the NAZI party and the labor movement, but you wouldn't know this due to the fact that the only people with smaller more damaged brains than yours are the morons who listen to the crap you spew on your TV and radio programs. Sorry Glen but sometimes the truth is a hard pill to swallow. The good news is the truth will also set you free. You have a choice here buddy. Have a nice day,

CHAPTER 8

The Transformation

All was quiet on the western front (coast) for the time being and things went smoothly on the flight line and off base as well. I had a girl friend back in New Jersey who was as close to a fiancé as you could get. She would one day become my ex-wife, but I was nineteen she was three thousand miles away, more or less,.....and did I mention I was nineteen. There were many conflicted feelings when I met and dated California girls. A man can rationalize anything when there is a beautiful young girl in a tiny swimsuit who is in need of a fresh coat of suntan lotion. For the first time in my life I was at ease around young women and I was comfortable talking to and getting to know them. The most astonishing part was they really wanted to get to know me as well. I didn't take this newborn popularity lightly. I realized how fleeting something like this could be and that set me apart from those chosen few who had been created to be loved by women no matter what they did. The best part was that I really enjoyed the young women I was meeting. The California girls were very different from the "Jersey girls" I had grown up around. Not better just different, I was slowly maturing and learning how to be attentive to their stories and feelings.

It was around this time in my development that I met a beautiful young girl named Aileen. Aileen was visiting her wealthy dentist uncle and was in town for the summer. She was only sixteen and I was careful not to let our relationship get out of hand but she had an old soul and was very deep in her understanding of the world around her. We talked for hours and she told me how she felt about the war and of how she would often cry while she watched the evening news. She was so sincere when she spoke from her heart you could see the feelings in her lovely eyes. I had never met anyone like her before.

I was enchanted with Aileen and I began to try to enhance my knowledge of the world around me. I suppose I might possibly have done this to impress her. No....I was definitely trying to impress her, I was a little crazy about her in spite of the huge difference in our ages. When you are nineteen and a wonderful young girl of sixteen comes along there are laws in place that make those three years a real "Berlin Wall" to young love. I was aware of this and refrained from committing a "statutory crime" with Aileen but from that point on I began to read the news papers and started watching the news on TV. Slowly I began developing a deeper understanding of the mess we had gotten ourselves into in southeast Asia. Aileen was gone by the end of the summer but I will always be thankful for the influence she had on my life and my world view. "Thank you Aileen, I hope you've had a wonderful life and I sometimes regret not trying to follow up but, partly thanks to you, my life became very complicated after you went back home."

I started showing up at concerts and rallies for the causes of the day. I went to Caesar Chavez rallies for the farm workers union. I gave spare change to the Black panthers, and the socialist workers party. One night I attended a concert put on by the "Viet Nam Veterans against the war" and for the first time I was sincerely hooked on the peace movement. I really had no choice since Jane Fonda was in attendance and I was a big fan ever since her movie Barbarella. Dick Gregory, Peter Boyle, and Donald Sutherland also made impressive appearances. There was also some gorilla theatre and music that altogether made me feel like I wasn't the only one who shared my feelings. The following day there was a march down town and several people in the crowd tried to urinate on veterans with purple hearts in wheel chairs. Unfortunately brains come in all sizes. I didn't agree with those who spat on returning soldiers and called them baby killers. There is the fact that wars kill babies and anything else that gets in their way. Wars suck but the young guys who got drafted to go off and get their nuts shot off didn't deserve to be treated like criminals when they got home.

My friends were partier's and pot smokers but none of them were politically minded by any stretch. I seemed to be the only one on base that was venturing off in this direction, with the possible exception of "Smacks" who I would run into quite "by accident" at these gatherings. Smacks was an enigma and he lived in some kind of parallel universe. There were times when I secretly suspected that he was some kind of super, deep cover, agent. There was no real explanation for the fact that he never got busted for any of his outrageous behavior other than blind luck. Of course people must have thought the same thing about me, I suppose. I really liked Smacks partly because when I was hanging out with him it was like having some kind of crazy, magic, get out of jail free card, I realized however that when the time came for me to make my stand against all this military madness, I would be on my own.

I was already working the night shift when I was promoted to third class petty officer. This promotion gave me the option of moving off the base and into an apartment with a couple of roommates and one of their girlfriends. (it's not like I was going to buy a house on four hundred fifty a month) My friends were both fellow east coast guys who liked to smoke a little pot and party in Mexico. Mario was an Italian guy from Trenton, New Jersey and Eric was from Boston.

Mario's girlfriend was a native American from the "Nez Perce" tribe. Her name was Sunny and she was one crazy little Indian girl. She was all about "whites and reds" (uppers and downers) Sunny was so much fun to be around, and when she was speeding her personality was just magnified. Sonny was very cute and she really had a cool sense of humor. Her laugh was infectious and she was the life of every party. She was the kind of person who could get everyone at a funeral to jump up and start singing and dancing. We all loved Sunny, even when she was a little "amped up.

There was only one little problem with Sunny" You really didn't want to be around when she was doing "reds". She was a totally different person on downers. Her eyes looked like they were nearly closed and she would loose her temper with no warning or provocation. No one was safe from her wrath when she was "droopy." Sunny wouldn't do downers very often but she seemed to use them to give her the courage to go off on the people she was pissed at. When she was really mad at someone she wasn't afraid to call in the troops from the reservation. Sunny could summon up some very scary native American gangsters when she needed them. Sonny called up the reserves (young thugs from her tribe) sometime later when she and Mario broke up. Mario was caught off guard and took a bad beating. I felt bad for Mario and I was saddened because Sunny broke up with all of us that day.

Before she left Sunny had taught me all about her tribe and their history. The most interesting part was the story of Chief Joseph and his running battle with the US cavalry in the late 1870s There is a whole movie about him so I won't bother you with a history lesson, however Chief Joseph was one of America's greatest warriors. (if you google him his occupation is listed as warrior) He was a truly brilliant military leader but you probably will never read about him in school books unless you attend West point.

Note: We Americans may not get to read about Thomas Jefferson either if the "Christian Cracker Barrel Congress" down in Texas has anything to say about it. They want to write Jefferson out of the history books because he believed in the separation of church and state. Just so you know, a large amount of this countries school books come from Texas. The same state that gave us George Bush, Dick Cheney, Tom Delay, Enron, Halliburton, and the war in Iraq, is in charge of dishing out faith based education to the youth of America. "There is a reason that there just happened to be a school book depository in Dallas in 1963." If this last reference went over your head I apologize. There may be some young people out there who don't know who John F. Kennedy was and that he went to Dallas one day to smile and wave at people and was blasted into eternity by some really bad people in front of a school book depository.

Note: President Obama (or who ever is president by the time I publish this damned book. The next time Texas threatens to secede from the union ….Let them.) I would help the Mexican workers build THAT fence.

Back at the apartment we had a sweet little house hold going on. All of us had different schedules so there wasn't much of a problem with the fact that there was only one bathroom. There was only one bedroom as well. Mario and Sunny got the queen sized bed, Eric and I took the bunk bed, with me in the bottom bunk and Eric in the upper bunk. Sometimes

Eric would have a sleep over with one of his girl friends. I was OK with the bunk thing, I mean I'd been sleeping in one since boot camp and this was still a much better deal than living in the barracks on the base. There was a certain fear factor however when Eric was pounding away with his girl friend and I was trying desperately to get some sleep while fearing that the bed was going to collapse on my face.

While I was working at the base at night in the hot brakes area on the flight line I noticed that there were three guys pulling and packing drogue chutes after the Phantoms returned from their training flights. I had worked with the hot breaks crew while working the day shift and I had grown quite proficient at the job. No one could pack chutes faster than me and my chutes opened when they were called upon. Many of the chutes packed by less talented line crew members just popped out in a tangled mess or never made it out of the bag. I fashioned a deal with my chief. I would do the job of the three men allowing them to return to the flight line as plane crew members and in return I could go home when all the birds were on the ground and the chutes packed. The job was a challenge but it kept me busy and the time just flew by. The returning jets would land and we watched to make sure the drogue chute had popped out of the tail cone and opened properly. The chute helped slow the plane enough to remain on the two mile long runway before turning back up the taxi way on it's way back to the flight line. If the chute didn't open the pilot had to use extra brakes to slow the speeding aircraft. After one of these landings the brakes would get so hot they could cause the magnesium wheels to catch fire. Magnesium fires don't go out, they burn out, and you don't want to be the person who tries to put out a magnesium wheel fire with water. The resulting explosion will send you to heaven or hell or France for ever.

As the one and only member of the hot brake crew I was by default the crew chief. I gave the rest of my crew, and by that I mean me, a large number of fringe benefits. Whenever we (me) landed a flight of phantoms and packed their chutes I let my crew (me) take a nap. A drogue chute makes a perfectly soft pillow and the concrete runway was like sleeping on a cloud for someone as tired as I usually was. The F4s made plenty of noise when they came in for a landing. When I heard the scream of those J79 engines I would turn my head toward the runway, open one eye, and watch the tail of the incoming jet to be sure that the chute door opened, the pilot chute popped out, and the main chute deployed. If these things happened in the correct order most pilots could slow the plane down without burning up the brakes. Most but not all. After the aircraft taxied back from the end of the runway It was my job to stop the plane by crossing my light wands so the pilot could see them. Once the plane stopped rolling I would dart under the fuselage and tap each wheel with the back of my hand. If the brakes were safe the skin on the back of my hand would still be on my hand. If they were to hot some of that skin would be stuck to the wheel with strands of smoke that smelled like, well...fried flesh. If the brakes were really hot they would glow red and I would bail out from under the plane in a big hurry. Those wheels could go off like bombs and kill anyone near the plane.

The wings, where the landing gear (wheels) were mounted, were also fuel tanks so we had to evacuate the plane to the "hot break area." The hot brake area was about a couple of hundred yards from the flight line and I would signal the pilot to get his plane over there ASAP. He would alert the base fire team from the radio in the cock pit. Sirens would sound and the fire truck would arrive in a minute or two to lay down a special fire retardant foam and the pilot, and the RIO could be rescued if things got out of hand. The pilot is the one in front and he flies the plane. The RIO is the radar intelligence officer, he sits in the back and flies the bombs and rockets to their targets. It takes both of these people working in perfect unison to perform a successful mission. PS. A successful mission is one where a group of people on the ground who were alive yesterday are, let us say, a little less alive today. This also applies to the pigs and chickens.

If the returning jet's brakes passes the skin test I would run to the rear of the plane and try to grab one of the cords of the drogue chute and pull it to one side. I would then wave my wands to signal the pilot to release the chute and gun the engines to pop open the spring loaded chute clamp. This maneuver worked usually but there were times when I had to pull the chute loose by grabbing several of the chute cords while standing directly in the Phantoms powerful jet wash. I would pull with all my might to free the "D" ring from it's clamp. The "D" ring was a heavy piece of metal that was attached to all the chute cords and you had to be careful to get out of it's way when it came loose and flew directly at your face. I saw a sailor get hit square in the forehead with the "D" ring and the chute wrapped around his body while the jet wash rolled him down the runway like an unconscious nylon burrito.

Note: Military personnel don't earn enough money and they deserve a much larger benefits package when they leave the service. The men in suits who work for the corporations, and by that I mean our politicians in Washington, don't appreciate the young men and women who loyally serve our country. They constantly come up with new and totally useless reasons to put our service people in harms way. Even the non combat jobs are dangerous and people get injured or die every day and OSHA isn't there to insure a safe workplace environment. The people in Washington are there to make money and give tax breaks to the people who paid huge amounts of cash to get them elected. These very same people don't give a shit who has to die to ensure we sell more ships and jets and tanks. We fight wars to secure access to someone else's oil reserves. If the sons and daughters of poor families across the country get killed or wounded in those misadventures it doesn't concern them as long as the shareholders are collecting dividends and paying as little tax on those dividends as possible. Most enlisted military families live below the poverty line.

I had to find myself a part time job as a greens keeper on the base golf course. I also had a job working down at the port of San Diego as a part time non union dock worker. (The only non management Anglo worker) Usually during the week I was only at the apartment long enough to sleep and shower. On the weekends we would go out dancing in Mexico, or sometimes we would attend reasonably priced concerts in Balboa stadium and afterwards hang out in Balboa park. Across the road from Balboa Naval hospital.

Note: For a ships captain who sailed around the world "discovering" places that already had people living on them. (Sunny's tribe was thriving in Oregon long before Balboa "discovered" the West coast.) Vasco Balboa sure had way more than enough stuff named after him. I'm just making an informed observation here. I'm not judging the guy, although for a man, he sure wore some silly looking outfits. In the paintings I've seen he looked like an Easter basket with skinny legs in black tights and a hat that resembled a fancy French pastry.

Short Colonialism Rant: A typical communication between an explorer and his King would go something like this. Assuming, of course, that the King and his explorer both had cell phones.

Explorer: "Um, uh, your majesty, I sort of just discovered a totally new world while on my way to India.

King: That's great Vasco, did you find any gold? We sent you over there to find gold.

Explorer: Yes there is gold here. But there is one small problem as I see it. There are millions of brownishly colored people living here already and they have all your gold."

King: Uh yeah, that is a common issue. "Can't you just kill them?" Usually we just kill them and the problem isn't as much of a problem in the morning.

Explorer: "We can't kill all of them, did I mention there is like a million of these darkly shaded, mostly naked, indigenous people all over the freaking place? They are deadly accurate with their bows and arrows. We would need a lot more of that grey powdery stuff that my soldiers put in their long shooty things and a shit load of those little round metal balls." (This particular explorer had majored in business.)

King: "OK, how about this for a plan B. Just kill a few of them. Start with the strongest and smartest ones so there won't be any Mandingo's (look it up) to muck things up. Enslave everyone else and send me all the really attractive ones on the next ship. Boys, girls, whatever. I'm really not particular. Oh yes, and this is very important. Shove the church as far up their ass as it will go. Nothing subdues a native population faster than a pissed off deity. Oh, and by the way, you're welcome. That's why I'm King.....douche bag. Well, I've got to go now, you're breaking up, mainly because they haven't invented cell phones yet. Oh and please don't forget to bring back all the gold your ship can carry on your way home. Thanks."

The Ranch

OUR FAVORITE DESTINATION

While living in our San Diego one bedroom mansion, Mexico was by far the grand daddy of all our favorite haunts. After one of our infamous adventures in "TJ" (Tijuana) some serious down time was required afterwards. A typical trip to Mexico involved all of us jumping into my Buick and heading for the border. We would cross the magic, not so invisible line with all the agents and cops. The Mexicans checked you on the way in, the Americans checked you on the way out. We would then drive to the down town area of Tijuana. This was a short but visually stunning ride where we were always astounded by the stark difference between the United Stated and a real, hard core, third world nation. We would drive past piles of oddly shaped structures assembled from a variety of building materials that included plywood, corrugated steel, cardboard, tar paper, and discarded cinderblocks. A few random telephone poles here and there provided power for television, hair driers, and toasters.

Fires were frequent and often deadly. Within these piled up shacks there were no real streets but simply hundreds of dirt alleys that wandered off in various directions. One friend of mine who had joined us for the first time once asked " how do these people get their mail." Sonny responded with her sly grin. "You're kidding, right? Do you see a fucking mailbox anywhere?" His question was reasonable coming from someone who had grown up in a country where the government could mail a tax bill, or Ed McMahon could send an entry form from the publishers clearing house to just about anyone, anywhere. For those who chose to ignore the first letter from the IRS there was a second letter that simply said. "Go directly to jail, do not pass Go, do not collect $200.00."

While exploring the back streets and side roads on the poor side of Tijuana we would often notice children in rags running down the alleys on their way to beg quarters on the busy streets downtown. Sometimes simply beautiful young women with long raven hair dressed in simple yet lovely white, black, and red dresses would emerge from the rubble on their way to work in the bars downtown. It reminded me of the song "A rose in Spanish Harlem."

We would gently roll down the torn up pavement on my not quite bald, $5.00 tires, onto a side street and park a few blocks from the center of town. Here we would unload any long haired hippies who were hiding in the trunk. These travelers were mostly hitchhikers who would have been denied admittance into Mexico without a little help. The Mexican government had a big stick up their ass when it came to hippies. They didn't like any Americans who didn't have enough money to spend in the clubs or pay off the police. We never accepted any payment for our taxi service. That would have been a crime. Were we breaking the law? That subject was sort of up for debate. This is what some would call a "grey area." Dark grey perhaps but the crimes being committed by our government at the time were much more harmful to humanity than someone getting free transportation in the trunk of my Buick. "Rationalization is a gift from the gods and I've always been quite religious in that respect. If Jesus had owned a big fat Buick I'm sure he would have done the same thing. Amen."

After debarking our riders we would walk down to the "Blue Note" or the "Oasis club" and dance and drink cheap beer all night long. Sunny and I loved to dance and Mario and Eric liked to drink beer and listen to the music Sunny knew her way around town and she would hook us up with a friendly cab driver who would supply us with a "roll of whites" (mild speed tablets). Sort of like real strong coffee but you didn't need to go to the bathroom as often. For a couple of US dollars a tin foil roll would last all night. We often stayed well into the morning and just as often there would be a frantic search for my car afterwards. The beat to shit streets all looked alike in the daylight. Nothing looked the same in the bright morning sun as it did in the dark of night when we had parked my giant nasty pig of a car. Once when we finally found my ride in some shady area off the main drag, we would have to excuse ourselves to the young Mexican couple who were trying to steal my radio.

A typical road trip to Mexico usually ended with an affordable breakfast of Huevos Rancheros and plenty of coffee at the "Chock full of Nuts" all day all night restaurant. In downtown TJ. By 11:00 AM we would be wide awake and ready for the trip back to San Diego. After the short drive we would arrive safely back at the apartment. Sleep was the only cure for the way we felt after the all night ordeal. I would shower when we got back just to get the smell of beer, cigarettes and burnt tires out of my hair. The sky's of Mexican border towns are generally brown with the smoke from tires and cable insulation. It is the easiest way to get at the steel cords in the tires and the copper in the cable. You don't see many documentary pieces about air pollution on "Telemundo." At least not back before the dawn of time.

Our other downtime destination back then was Los Angeles. The trip would take somewhere between one and three hours depending on how lost we got along the way. My Buick Road master was always the mode of transportation and in 1968 it didn't have a GPS system. The president of the United States didn't have GPS. All was fair and good with the world. I would take care to visit the junk yard in Murphy Canyon before a long road trip. The tires were used but they had plenty of rubber and I generally only paid about five dollars each. I didn't mention this fact to my passengers. They would chip in for gas but I figured that the overall safety of the Buick should be kept on a need to know basis, and they didn't really need to know.

One memorable trip to LA began when a friend told us about a concert being held at the Shrine Auditorium featuring the monster group of the day, "Iron Butterfly." Our excitement grew throughout the week as we prepared for the road trip. We made a short list of stuff to buy and things to do. There wasn't a Ticket master back then so we asked around to see if anyone had scored extra tickets but no one had even heard about the concert yet. We were undeterred and decided that worse case we should be able to get tickets at the door. The Shrine was a huge venue that was built before Columbus discovered America We had been there before and cheap tickets had never been an issue.

We would need a baggie of "Mexican mind widener" for the road. We hooked up with our local "Pot Mart" distributor and ten bucks later we were all ready to listen to some good old fashioned rock and roll. It wasn't old fashioned at the time but whatever it was we were ready to get down to it. We stopped by a small local super market and picked up the chips, Cheetos, and little white doughnuts that were an important part of our journey. As I recall there were a couple of quarts of "Superman Orange drink" in our bag of goodies that evening. We never drank alcohol on road trips.

We got off early from work that Friday and threw on our concert attire. I generally wore a denim cap and tight brown plaid bell bottom slacks and a black print silk shirt. Today this outfit might be considered a little on the hairdresser side, or something out of Saturday Night Fever, but in those days people thought I looked cool. At least I sure hope they did. The hippy culture was everywhere at the time. The girls would be wearing long flowery dresses of cotton and lace with colorful floppy hats, tie dyed scarves, and sandals. There would be a few mini skirts and just the right amount of tube tops and see thru blouses. Denim bell bottom jeans and T-shirts were of course always in style for either gender.

We all loaded up into the big blue and white "Road master" and after stopping to fill the monster car with twenty-five gallons of regular, or about $7.50. Gas was going for about $0.30 per gallon. What in the holy hell happened?

Rant alert! In those days most of our gas came from places like Texas instead of Canada and Mexico like it does today. We do get oil from the middle east but not as much as they would have you believe. I still don't understand what all the fuss about the middle east was about. Other than it being a good excuse to crank up prices every time there is unrest in places like Libya or Iraq. This translates to every other day for those of you keeping score. Wall street has screwed us so hard and in so many ways we should all feel like rape victims by now. The "price of oil" scam could bring this country to its knees, and some politicians want to give these vandals more tax cuts? Are you kidding me? People this corrupt used to go to federal prison and now they get millions of dollars in bonuses. Where did we go wrong? Oh yeah, right, we started electing bad actors and oil men from Houston to run our damn country.

Soon we were on route 5 and headed north toward Los Angeles at a high rate of speed. Because of the fact that my tires were all different sizes I couldn't tell you exactly how fast we were going but the speed limit was 55 miles per hour so my best guess is somewhere between 95 and 100. We had a plan to attend to. Our plan involved smoking up all of our reefer before we got any where near LA. We feared the police in San Diego but the cops in Los Angeles were like something out of a horror movie. Rodney King had an opinion on this subject. You would have to go all the way to New Orleans to find scarier police than the "blue crew" they had in Los Angeles at the time. We had a little rolling machine and the guys in the back seat were turning out joints like they were union workers in a Carolina cigarette factory. Before long we had to roll down the windows just to see the highway because of all the thick sweet smoke in the car. Cheech and Chong would have been proud of us as we cruised north with a white fog pouring out the windows. My copilots had carefully stashed a couple of doobies for the ride home as we entered the land of hopes and dreams.

Note: I don't condone smoking and driving. I did it, I was wrong, and I'm sorry but I'm glad I wasn't drinking Bourbon or I wouldn't be here writing this book today.

After a few wrong turns and a few requests for directions we arrived in front of the famous Shrine Auditorium. We were amazed that we hadn't wound up in Arizona or Alaska. I was getting excited but yet something seemed very wrong as we circled the parking lot looking for a space. Everyone we saw was dressed up in black suits and gowns like they were going to the "Oscars." We found the answer as we passed the bill board that announced in big red letters that the butterfly showing that night turned out to be a Madame and not an Iron one. We all spun around and glared at Mike who had told us about the "Iron Butterfly" concert. In unison we all declared "Madame Butterfly? Are you fucking kidding me."

We were stupefied! After having just driven a huge amount of miles, stoned, and now we had no where to go in a really scary city, a town without pity, this was so shitty. (sorry, I lost it a little there for a second) At first I was really pissed off at the situation and the absurd nature of Mike's error but before we knew it, slowly we started to smile and soon we were all lost in a sea of ridiculous, pot induced, laughter. This went on for a while until we had snot bubbles on our noses. All was good with the world.

Slowly we decided that one of us had to come up with another plan. We were way to wasted to consider driving back to San Diego. Driving wasn't the problem but my car was so ridiculous it was a moving target for the state troopers and I just wasn't looking forward to having an extremely uncomfortable conversation with one of California's finest at that moment in time.

The first bright idea came from yours truly and I said lets go find a party. It seemed reasonable at the time but we were in LA. We drove around for a while and wound up in a part of town called Watts. The windows were rolled down and we could hear music so we just followed the sound until we were outside a large building with a stairway leading up to a second floor club of some kind. Everyone was yelling at me to keep going but I saw some very attractive young women going up the stairs and I was driving. We exited the blue and white Buick starship and climbed the stairs. The music was getting louder but I still couldn't say I had heard any of the songs before. Fact was, I couldn't understand any of the words either. When we got to the top there was a landing with a very large man in a suit taking money at the door. He had a thin black mustache. The door man asked us for ten dollars each in a very heavy Spanish accent. We all noticed at about the same time that we were the only Anglo faces at this party and a crowd of young well dressed young Spanish teenagers had gathered near the door waiting to see if they were going to let us in. We also noticed that the girls were all very young and a big neon sign that said, "TROUBLE" was blinking in our heads. We calmly retreated and lived to tell the story. Of all the lessons I may try to impart in this writing the most important of all is knowing how to identify and avoid a no-win situation.

As a group, the five of us had suddenly become incredibly hungry so the decision was made to find a sit down restaurant and chow down for a while and wait for the effects of the marijuana to wear off. After getting lost, or even more lost, we came across a little diner beside the road called "FOOD." Please don't ask me "what road?" Don't ask me what planet for that matter. The "Food diner" was not destined to become a nation wide franchise.

This somewhat less than earthly diner was completely out of context in California and looked like it belonged along the docks in Baltimore, or Newark, but certainly not in the suburbs Los Angeles. In New Jersey the chrome would be polished and all the neon lights would be working but this was SoCal and the place looked like a scene from an apocalypse movie. As we entered the old run down smelly dump a chill ran down my spine all the way down to my rapidly shrinking nut sack. If you have ever seen an old black and white episode of "The Twilight Zone," it was sort of like that. Imagine walking into a diner with a cast of fat zombies at the counter. We tried to act natural but everyone in the diner was staring at us with looks of disgust on their bloated, scarred, pock marked, faces. Mike suggested we make a run for it but we were starved and I said, optimistically "how bad can they fuck up a hamburger anyway." Mike looked at me and whispered "did you see those scary mother fuckers at the counter? They got that way by eating here, man."

We grabbed a booth and waited for Mario who had gone missing somewhere. The menu was predictable with hamburgers, meat loaf, liver and onions, and some kind of stew that smelled like it had been prepared with, "Out of town customer meat." I settled on the hamburger with a side of onion rings and a vanilla shake. Mario quietly slipped into the booth and started checking out the menu. Mario was toasted and seemed extremely distracted but fascinated by the choices before him. He finally went with the grilled cheeze. Mike ordered a chili dog. Frenchy had the tuna melt and Eric ever cautious, just ordered apple pie and black coffee. Our waitress was a stone cold nightmare. Judging from the name tag on her discolored waitress attire, her name was Marge. Marge had a half smoked Chesterfield hanging from her dry cracked lips. She treated us like five steaming piles goat shit but she took our order without a fuss. No smile no fuss.

We sat there waiting for our food and Mike decides to tell a new joke he had just heard. In a loud voice that you could hear out on the highway he says, "How do you get a dog to stop humping your leg?" We hadn't heard this one yet so we all asked in equally loud voices "I don't know Mike how do you get a dog to stop humping your leg?" After a well timed pause Mike exclaims "You just pick him up and give him a blow job." Another pause as the punch line sunk in and we all started laughing like lunatics including Mike and the cook, way back in the kitchen. This joke may not be funny by todays standards but it helped relieve the tension The other dinner guests glared at us like we were Satin's actual grand kids. At this point the comfort level was plunging rapidly but we wanted to eat so badly we would have stayed in our booth if a swat team had suddenly burst in the door launching tear gas canisters and blasting holes in all the ugly customers at the counter.

It seemed like it was going to take forever for our orders to arrive and Mike was freaking out so I had to assure him that the cook wasn't done jerking off on his chili dog. Mike chuckled and relaxed...because he thought I was kidding.....I wasn't. Just then the waitperson arrived with a giant dark brown tray with some of the stuff we had ordered but mostly things we hadn't. She said, "Who ordered the southern fried steak?" I shook my head and said it was mine because I couldn't stand to wait one more minute for some food, plus I didn't have the balls to send the order back to the kitchen in a place like this. We all settled for what ever wound up on the table and after a few trades we dug into the meal before us like it was our last. Mike enjoyed his corn dogs but Eric was pissed off that they had given him pecan pie instead of apple and hot chocolate not black coffee. I begged Eric to just relax and eat, and I would buy him anything he wanted when we got back to San Diego.

It was then that we heard a shrill voice loudly calling for someone, or something named "Buttercup." The voice was coming from a very large woman in a print dress and a red, gravy stained, apron with the word "FOOD" in white letters on the front. We guessed this her place and she was calling a pet of some sort. She started asking everyone in the place if we had seen her cat "Buttercup." I looked at my crew and everyone just shook their heads back and forth in a negative manner. Everyone that is except Mario who was looking around like he was reading a "Playboy" in church. I looked at him and shrugged my shoulders to gesture "hey man, what the hell did you do?" Mario rolled his eyes toward the front window and my big blue and white car parked right outside. This was when I saw the giant black furry animal on my dashboard staring back at us. "Shit" I thought to myself but I said it so loud inside my head I just knew someone had heard it. Mario did some weird stuff when he was stoned but he had crossed the weird line this time and he knew it.

I took one last bite of white sausage gravy covered deep fried mystery meat. I then grabbed the check and signaled the boys that we were getting ready to hit the road. We gathered up enough money to pay the check with a modest tip and hurried out the door to the car. Without being obvious I opened the drivers side door and the huge black feline disappeared into the dark night. We jumped into the monster mobile and made a speedy retreat without spraying to many rocks on the pickup trucks and choppers in the parking lot. Less than a minute later we were back on the freeway and cruising at a high rate of speed toward South America…or San Diego, which ever came first.

We were a band of very relieved travelers after the escape from the horror show of a diner and the possible "catnapping" charges. I was feeling confident that It would be clear sailing from here on. I had spent five dollars on a new tire and the spare was as good as any of the others we were riding on so we were all home free. Mike whipped out a couple of joints he had cleverly hidden in the ashtray and lit them up. We passed them around the car and soon everyone had a "smile on" in spite of the twisted turns our evening had taken up to that point.

The music was turned up, the windows rolled down and all I had to do now was stay awake and get us all back home alive. The air felt good as the mile markers flew past us at an alarming rate of speed. I wondered why with all this wind blowing around the car was there so much smoke. About then my question was answered when everyone started screaming "FIRE, FIRE, the fucking car is on Fire."

Yep, we were ablaze and the flames were coming from the back seat. Mike, Mario, and Frenchy were back there so I yelled "PUT IT OUT GOD DAMN IT."

Now. I must explain something. Mike was the 189 pound state wrestling champ in high school back in New Jersey. He was also pound for pound the strongest human being I had ever met. When he heard me yelling "put it out" without waiting to consider other options he kicked the door open ripped up the back seat and started to shove it out of the car. This strategy had a simple charm to it except for the part where there were still two screaming idiots on the seat at the time. I yelled for Mike to stop and put the fire out not the seat. The terror in the eyes of my passengers was making me very uncomfortable but I spotted a road side gas station up ahead and I guided the flaming beast over to a water hose in the back of the parking lot. We all jumped out and I got the hose going and the fire was out in less than a minute. There was still some smoke but no one had been burned, thank God or Frank or who ever was on duty that evening. Did I mention that I'm not a religious person? Besides I figure that if there is a god he probably has bigger fish to fry than a minor foam rubber fire in the back seat of a sixty-five dollar Buick, or who is going to win the next Texas, Oklahoma football game for that matter.

One of my guests had dropped a lit "Doobie" on the seat and had almost burned my car to the ground. No one would admit to the crime and I wasn't going to call the cops. After some cleanup and swabbing out the water with an old shirt we found in the trunk everyone got back in the poor beat to shit car and we headed on down the road. Someone started whining about the wet seats but I wheeled around and warned them to just shut the fuck up or they could damn well walk back to town. Frenchy, who was deathly afraid of coyotes, was extremely quiet all the way back to the apartment.

All I can say about the good part of our journey that night is that no one riding in my car was killed or seriously injured. I'm reasonably certain that we had the same number of passengers when we got back to San Diego as we did when we had set off to Los Angeles.

"And now, THE NEWS"

Mario and I went out one day and scored a cheap, second hand TV set at the used stuff store. With the help of some rabbit ears we found at the flea market, a couple of rolled up wads of tin foil and a "slinky" we were able to get a fairly decent signal. None of us were big on television at the time, however we did like to watch "Rowan & Martin's Laugh In" and I loved the "Smothers Brothers" before they crossed the line in some idiot TV executives head and did one to many skits about current events and were thrown off TV forever. Back then some things were considered out of bounds. Commenting against the war, or for marijuana use, or of course sex were what the younger audience was craving at the time. The bad news was when someone grew balls big enough to swim into forbidden water you would instantly be devoured by one of the sharks in your network's headquarters. Sort of like it is now except for the sex. Today the primetime shows are a lot sexier than in the sixties. Couples in sitcoms usually slept in separate beds back then.

I was really getting hooked on news about the war and I considered Walter Cronkite one hell of a news man. There were nightly updates on some of that days battles and the losses we were taking. We were loosing young people at a terrible rate and the Vietnamese were simply getting slaughtered. We were told the kill ratio was ten to one but by the end of the war our losses were around 56,000 as opposed to over 2 Million Vietnamese. (that's closer to 36 to one) The army we were fighting at the end of the war was huge compared to the tiny band of gorillas we started out trying to defeat back when Kennedy was president.

This of course was way before the complete corporate take over of the airwaves and you could get some fairly good reporting from the front lines back in the day. There were no Hooters girls from "Fox fake news" giving us the corporate spin on everything. I have nothing at all against Hooters girls. I'm very fond of the "big fish sandwich, hold the bun." They also have an outstanding food delivery system. I however am really not a fan of the stuff that passes for news on the Fox network, or any of the major news networks these days, really.

I was beginning to see what my friend Aileen was trying to tell me when she conveyed her deep sadness about the war and its terrible effect on our country, plus the effect it was having on the country of Viet Nam and it's population was just unimaginable. We were destroying unknown numbers of lives of people we had never met, not to mention the lives of the soldiers we were shipping over there for mostly political and economic reasons. This was before we learned of our bombing of Cambodia, and Kent State, and the Mi Lai massacre, when all holy hell broke loose. The pot was still just beginning to boil, so to speak. I knew I had to do something very soon to make a statement but I was still trying to decide just how, and when, and where that statement should be made.

Chris Peck

THE LETTER

Fate was about to make it's grand entrance, and something as innocent as a simple letter from the war zone would have a profound affect on my life forever. One warm evening I was walking back to the line shack after a launch when I saw my friend Bobby who seemed to be very upset over the letter he was reading. I asked if everything was OK and then I noticed there were tears in his eyes. I also noticed that his letter had no stamp on the envelope. He told me that the letter was from his brother who was serving in Viet Nam. His brother was a marine and was stationed at a small airbase near Saigon. He had smuggled the letter back to bobby by way of some sailor who was being rotated back to the states. The mail is a sacred trust here in the good old USA but you give up all of that shit when you join up. Letters were censored, and some mail just never showed up if the wrong sentiments were being expressed. This was one of those letters. At first Bobby was hesitant about telling me what was in his letter but I think he realized that if anyone would understand what he was feeling it would be me. By now the other sailors I worked with knew how I felt about the war and Bobby really needed to share this story with someone.

In this particular letter, Bobby's brother described a mission aboard a Chinook helicopter. His squad had been ordered to capture, detain and question some villagers from a hamlet that was suspected of hiding an unknown number of enemy soldiers. He was the new guy among a group of old hands and he was expected to go along with the program. He was told this was going to be a routine mission. The team flew into the village and promptly rounded everyone up without a fight. Men, women and children were lined up in a kneeling position on the ground and searched. These people were simple farmers and no enemy troops could be found.

Historical note: The Viet Cong played a dangerous game with the poor rice farmers and simple villagers of their own country. They would march into one of the thousands of small hamlets that dotted the landscape and set up shop for a few days while they rested and stocked up on rice and what other free supplies that they could appropriate from the helpless "village people" (No not them). "The home team" would leave after a short visit followed immediately by the uninvited guests from the magical kingdom far away where Levi's come from. Naturally the Americans would assume that the villagers were guilty of harboring the enemy and they would have to pay in some profound way for their crimes. Our Army would exact justice of one form or another and in at least some cases with war crimes of their own. Often the easy way was to whip out some "Zippo" Lighters and just torch the village. Sometimes someone with a medium amount of power would make a decision to do something to leave a more lasting impression on the people we were trying to protect from the "Red Menace." One such incident was the "My Lai Massacre," where Lt. Calley and his men murdered, raped, and tortured an entire village during the war. Calley was given a life sentence for premeditated murder but he only served three years of house arrest before being pardoned by president Richard Nixon. "Nice move Dick." What if two of the girls who were raped and machine gunned that day had been Julie and Trish? Would you have pardoned Calley then? Look at me, I'm getting all down on a dead president. That is just plain wrong on so many levels but that prick always pissed me off. I'm sorry.

After a careful decision making process, the American soldiers chose five villagers at random, sort of. There were three young teenaged boys, one old man, and an attractive, young girl, perhaps fifteen or sixteen years old. The soldiers tied their prisoners hands and shoved them into the helicopter, and then they lifted off. The pilot took them up to one thousand feet and hovered while the soldiers began to "question" the villagers. They asked the old man a few questions about the location of the Viet Cong enemy forces and so on but got no answers just a long winded speech in Vietnamese spoken out of fear and desperation that none of the Americans understood. The soldiers got really pissed off and grabbed the old man and threw him out the fucking door, screaming, still in Vietnamese. Bobby's brother freaked out and yelled at the others to stop, but it was way past late now. The other guys told him he'd better "Shut the fuck up and get up to speed." or he would be next. One by one they grabbed another poor villager, rattled off some bullshit questions and when they didn't get a proper answer in English. Fooom, another poor farmer in black PJ's went skydiving without a parachute. Finally, when they were down to the young girl, they didn't even go through the formality of interrogating her. They simply took turns holding her down and raping her. When they were done she was crying and screaming for her life but that didn't stop them from tossing her, mostly naked, out of the open chopper door. Her cries of terror faded as she vanished into the forest far below. Bobby's brother wanted to jump out after her but he didn't. He just flew back to base in silence and wrote his brother a letter.

Bobby's brother was truly damaged by the experience and getting the letter out to the real world was a form of penance. Poor Bobby was horrified and really didn't know what to do with the information. He looked up to his older sibling and this news was stuck half way into his brain and there just wasn't any room for the other half. After I read the letter we both had tears in our eyes. I felt so bad for him and tried to imagine what it would be like to find out someone who I was that close to had that kind of weight to bear for the rest of their lives. Since that day I've worked for many years in a Veterans hospital and have spoken to many veterans with similar tales and I've seen that look in their eyes as if a part of their life was lost over there. It's called the "thousand mile stare." These guys look off into the distance at nothing at all and that stare is like an open window to the pain in their heart and the incurable wound in their soul. It's like they are trying to reach out but most of them can never bring themselves to expose the horror of what they did or witnessed over there. "Over there" is all the same. Viet Nam, Panama, Somalia, Iraq, Afghanistan, it just doesn't matter. War is hell and the only thing that changes is the shade of brown of the people you are shooting.

This whole story came back on me and the horror of what we were doing to the Vietnamese people started to sink in. I recalled the gruesome stories that my crazy assed marine math instructor had told me back in "A" school. I thought to myself what if I had been born and raised in Viet Nam and that was my sister or daughter who was raped and murdered by those fucked up assholes on the helicopter. You could bet that the next time an American chopper or jet or truck or GI. came anywhere near me, if I had a weapon, I would be shooting it in their direction. I had a personal connection to the My Lai story. I had grown up in the same house with a Chinese family living down stairs. The mom was beautiful and very smart and we became close friends. I would watch her two sons when she went out and the boys were like my little brothers. They were both athletic and smart and would become successful in their lives to come. Because of this I had a real hard time when my fellow sailors would go off on a racist rant about "slants" and "slopes" and "gooks." After a while the people who used those words and other hurtful shit knew not to do it around me. Those people weren't all from Alabama, Mississippi, and Texas either. Many of the worst offenders were from the northeast states of New York, Pennsylvania, and of course New Jersey. Hate comes in all colors but once you realize that fact you can choose not to be an asshole.

In retrospect there is no mystery to the fact that the North Vietnamese army was a thousand times larger at the end of the war than it was when we first sent advisors over there in the late fifty's. President Eisenhower was the first to sound the alarm about the "Red menace" and the "Giant dominoes" fairy tail, as reasons to wage war in southeast Asia, but at least he was a cautious man and was also the first to warn the American people to the dangers of the "military industrial complex, and to beware of a world based on perpetual war." John F. Kennedy saw the war as a tool that he could use to show the world how dedicated we were to stopping communist aggression. However, Kennedy was a very smart guy and he came to realize that continuing to send more money and young troops to Viet Nam was a horrible misadventure. Personally I believe that is why, more than anything else, he was destined to become a "dead Kennedy."

Note: War should always be the option of last resort unless of course you are the CEO of a company that makes bombs or rockets or tanks or military warships, or killer laser beams mounted on 747 aircraft.

I spent the next few days letting the letter sink in. I'm sure I smoked a fair amount of pot that weekend, I really don't remember. Then of course if I could remember, than I didn't smoke nearly enough pot. Somehow I was able to come up with a plan. It was a two part plan. The first part of the plan was drive my big fat Buick over to "Mickey Dee's" and get me a couple of Big Mac's, and a big bag of salty fries at the drive up. Thinking back through the haze it's quite possible that I washed it down with a vanilla shake and a couple of greasy tacos from "Jack in the Box." I swear I can still remember a way to long conversation with that stupid clown head that sounded like it was three feet under water. This was my "last meal," like the one you get in prison before they walk you down the hall, because the second part of my plan took my breath away when I first considered it.

I was fully aware that some time soon I would be getting an order to report to some big assed floating airfield for my tour in Viet Nam. I also knew that I just wouldn't be able to obey that order. My mind kept flashing on the news footage of our F4's coming in low over some village and letting loose with the "napalm" canisters and watching as someone's sad little town went up in a giant ball of orange flames and black smoke. Children on fire running for their lives. I could not let myself be part of that insane picture. So here was my plan. I figured that you couldn't go to jail for disobeying an order you had never been given. I made the decision to protest the order before receiving it.

The following night I showed up for my late shift at about 15:30 or (3:30 in the afternoon) There was a short inspection that went badly for me, due to the "Peace Sign" I had artfully painted on my olive drab foul weather jacket. After failing inspection, I strolled into the sort of green sort of grey line shack and grabbed a request form from a plastic holder on the wall. The holder was above the molding so it was sort of green. An enlisted man only had access to one "form" no matter what it was that he needed or wanted. If you wished to take a vacation, or needed a new pair of "boon dockers," (feet killing low cut boots) or a request to be transferred to another duty station, you had to fill out the same 4" X 6" request form or "chit" as it was called.

I carefully filled out the "request chit" and walked it into my supervisors office. This person was an "old salt" who had been in the navy since they stopped using oars to power their ships. He was still a first class petty officer which meant that he probably had been a chief at least once or twice but had been busted back down to first class because of some drunken brawl or perhaps he got caught slapping skin with an officer's lonely spouse. At any rate he was nearing retirement and was simply trying to stay out of trouble long enough to keep a decent pension that he could collect while he was working for the post office.

I quietly handed the chit to my boss and took a step back as he read it. I was prepared to make a run for it if it looked like he was going to blow a vein in his neck or something, he was old but still quite deadly. He finished reading the form and he shook a little before throwing the thing to the floor. Then, quietly he said, "Now son, you pick that piece of shit up and walk it into the lieutenants office......I never saw it." He raised his

The Ranch

voice one precise octave and said, "Do you understand me?" I nodded and bent down picked up the paper and walked up to the wooden door with the frosted glass window and knocked on it three times, like a secret code knock. Very slow, very precise and deliberate, as if my life depended on the way I knocked on that door. The lieutenant's voice was calm and cool as he gave me his permission to enter his office. I stepped through the doorway and into the darkened room where the officer behind the desk started to size me up. From what I knew of him he was a good, fair, man and a boy scout who I believed could be trusted. He was a straight shooter and in a way I hated doing to him what I was about to do. I paused when I realized what was going down and how this would affect him, but it was something that had to be done. I handed him the request chit and he took it calmly and began to read the short but deadly words.

The request form had a place for your name and the date and line for your service number and a few lines for the actual request followed by a line for your signature followed by a line for the signature of your superior officer. The exact verbiage is a little fuzzy after all this time, but basically I had written that I was requesting a discharge from the Navy due to my personal beliefs and that I would not be available to help kill any more of the people of Viet Nam. My poor Lieutenant took a deep breath and sat back in his chair and just looked at me as if to say, "Do you realize what you are doing to me?" I nodded to acknowledge that I did. He shook his head and asked me to please leave his office. I did as I was told and turned and walked out into the warm California sun. He was bound buy the rules. He could have easily torn up the stupid little piece of paper and told me to fuck off and to go fuck myself in a hundred horrible ways as was tradition in the service but he was an honorable man and he chose to process my request. He knew all to well the implications that went with it. Because my brave lieutenant made the decision to process my request, he was transferred to sea duty in Viet Nam a week later. It could have been worse.

I really had no idea what would happen next. No one that I knew had ever done anything like this before and Portsmouth naval prison is full of people who had committed less severe crimes than refusing to fight the war. As it turns out, no one that anybody knew, knew somebody that had done something exactly like this in the history of, well..history. Sure Mormons, and Amish, and Black Muslims had been pulling the out the ever popular conscientious objector card for a long time, but my case was just something different. I didn't have any objection to defending the country from foreign invaders. I had no religious objections whatsoever. This had nothing to do with some deep belief in God or any of his close or distant relatives.

I did however have a problem with invading someone else's country on what turned out to be false pretenses. I still have a problem with that idea to this day." Ahem, Mr. Cheney, and your dopey little hand puppet George. What the hell were you guys thinking? Iraq? Seriously?"

The very next day I was transferred back to the day shift. No more sunny days at the beach observing the wonderful effect that the sun's rays have on the female body. The next day after that I was walking out to my big Buick for lunch with a couple of guys from the line. It was really hot as I remember and as we approached my car we noticed that there were two men in suits climbing all over the interior. There was this rather large ass pushed up against the rear window and we could see someone else upside down under the steering wheel. Instantly I decided that we walk to the chow hall and take an extra long lunch. Something was obviously going terribly wrong and I needed some time to figure out exactly what it was. Luckily I was with two of the best legal advisors in the navy. Dave was one of my most trusted allies in the war on reality and Tommy was a part time dope smuggler who knew many, if not all, of the angles. We all agreed that the suits rummaging around in my car were agents from CID. I never locked my car. There was nothing to steal including the car and I could always use the zero security feature as a defense against illegal search and seizure.

Note: When you are in the military ALL searches are legal. You don't have normal legal rights especially on base.

The Criminal Investigation Division (CID) is a little recognized and hardly ever heard of part of the military. The guys who bravely serve in the CID must ponder how they wound up where they were and not in the FBI. We took an extra long time eating and properly digesting our steak and lobster that day and returned to my car about two hours later. By that time the two guys who were "Rousting my Ride" were all spent and sweaty. The sun was high and hot. They had long since lost the grey jackets and their ties were all loose and pulled to one side like they had just helped

The Ranch

some fat lady give birth to twins in the back seat of a taxi. I told my friends to get back to work and I wandered up to the old car like I was completely surprised to see two grown men all tired and sweaty leaning on my Buick. They properly identified themselves as CID agents and said that they had found evidence in my car. That evidence was going to get me in "some kind of very bad trouble." The detectives held up this extra large evidence envelope that was about sixteen inches wide and twenty-four inches long and told me to get in their shitty, piece of crap, grey Ford Pinto. I had only paid sixty-five dollars for my Buick and I could have gotten four or five of those Pinto's for my car on a flat trade.

We all carefully climbed into that awful, tiny, cramped, grey, turd of a car and the two dorky detectives drove me to a small grey concrete building over by the front gate of the base. They had hand cuffed me because I was clearly a threat to the American way of life. I slowly emerged from the back seat. (not an easy chore when your hands are handcuffed behind you) I then followed one of them into this embarrassingly small office with the traditional two tone paint job only this one was dark grey on the bottom and light grey on the top. I was about to make some decorating suggestions when they cut me short and introduced me to a tall scary looking officer. He was wearing a commanders uniform and looked like he meant business. This process worried me for two reasons. First, these people, such as they were, had great power over me. Second, they were waving this giant envelope in my face as they began to question me.

My car was clean, I knew, because I cleaned it. I was extremely careful about that two ton piece of American steel and I was sure that I had cleansed the beast of all the roaches and stray joints after our last road trip. Of course there had been a fire, and sure Jerry the state wrestler from New Jersey had tried to throw the whole flaming back seat out of the car while we were doing eighty miles per hour on the freeway coming back from the "not a concert." Sure, there were two screaming friends of mine sitting on it at the time but after the madness I gave the monster a real good working over. I knew there wasn't any pot in the glove compartment because we had smoked it all on the way home.

The still sweaty suits made their case to the commander that they had found evidence and that they wanted to open a case against me. The commander asked them to produce their evidence and they proceeded to open the evidence envelope and turned it up side down over a large piece of paper on the desk. They shook it, they wiggled it, they tapped it on the side, they tapped it on the top, and so on for a few minutes. I looked at the commander and shrugged my shoulders and he looked at me and raised his up turned hands and shook his head like "who the fuck are these ass holes?" Just then we heard a faint but absolute sound. Something had finally fallen out of the envelope. It was very small and round and black. One glance and I recognized it as a pot seed. The black color meant it was probably involved in the seat fire and was likely imbedded in the melted foam rubber which explained why I had missed it when I did my house cleaning. I felt much better now that the mystery had been solved.

The commander hesitated and finally said "Are you people fucking serious? Do you really expect me to charge this man with drug possession over THAT?" and he glared at the tiny pitiful charred shred of toasted greenery on the desk. The detectives walked to his end of the room and whispered something to him so that I couldn't hear. I knew by now what was going on and they were pleading their case based on the fact that I was a dirty war resisting communist and had to be stopped before I brought down the entire democratic system as we know it. I was a public menace and I would have to be incarcerated, and shot, and then spend the rest of my life in the electric chair. All they could do for the time being however was reassign me to a non critical job while they built a case against me. As it turned out this was a huge stroke of luck and my Naval career was about to take a really sharp turn to the weird.

There was a process to all of this crazy bullshit and I was instructed to go to the legal department on base and have them assign a military lawyer to handle my defense. Clearly this situation was a serious one and it was going to call for something much more medicinal than ordinary pot. Thank goodness for those wonderful little native American mushrooms.

I was provided with government issue legal counsel. (Lawyer, 5'9", beige, one each) My legal counsel reminded me of a slightly taller version of Woody Allen. He was constantly uncomfortable and repeated himself so often I thought perhaps he was experiencing some kind of stroke. We had a short sit down meeting and he took some notes and told me I would have to be patient and that it may take a while for him to get my case together. I didn't see that dumb little douche bag again for two years. Rather than prolong the agony I'll tell you now that the government had zero evidence against me. The poor sad little seed was burned up so badly that there wasn't anything to run through the lab, either that or some clumsy military cop had accidentally dropped the seed down the drain. One way or another I was eventually going to be cleared of my terrible crime only I wouldn't know it for the next two years and this had absolutely nothing to do with my having a government lawyer.

For the remainder of my enlistment I would be under investigation that included some kind of surveillance. The government assigned a team of agents to try to find out who I was and why I didn't want to kill people for them. It is truly unbelievable…the crazy assed shit that the feds spent our money on, especially when you had a real live paranoid lunatic like Nixon in the White House. The FBI sent a couple of agents to my home town in New Jersey and they questioned everyone from my parents to my football coach. To this day there are people who don't communicate with me because of those agents and their dark suits and sunglasses. Thanks FBI, and thanks to the poor stupid taxpayers of who…I am one. See I told you I wasn't a writer. The worst part was and still is that the people we should be keeping an eye on are running the country. The sad truth is that the people who decide who has their phones tapped and who gets to have a guy follow him around all day are the very people we should be locking up behind really high walls.

Almost immediately after my interview with the lawyer I began to notice strangers in crappy suits who were just across the street or down the block, or following me two cars back as I drove to and from the base. Remember. "It isn't paranoia when they really are out to get you." One morning I was about to leave to work and I noticed this nasty white Chevy Nova with no hub caps parked just down the street from our apartment. There was someone in the in the car reading, or pretending to read a news paper. I didn't know for sure if he was my tail because they switched agents all the time. Just for fun I decided to confront him in the most unexpected way possible. I made some coffee and poured two cups and put in some cream and sugar, then I carried them both down the sidewalk. As I approached the car all I could see was the news paper. Up close I noticed a cigarette hole burned right in the middle. I walked over to the drivers side window and tapped on the glass. The driver set the paper aside and rolled down the window and I handed him one of the coffees. He just looked at me like I was from another planet. I simply said. " Have a good day pal." Then I turned walked to my car, got in, started up the big Buick, and with a couple of back fires and a cloud of smoke I was on my way to see what they had in store for me back at the base.

Overnight I had been transferred to a new department on base called "Special Services." Never to be confused with "Special Forces." I reported to an office, just off the lobby of the base movie theatre. There were no inspections in special services. There were no rules in special services or much of any organized structure at all for that matter. I soon found out that everyone assigned to special services had "royally screwed the pooch" in one form or another. The year was 1969 and most of the other guys in our group had been charged with pot possession. This meant that our strange little "band of busted brothers" had been pulled over with some amount of grass or another. In my case,....my case,....revolved loosely around a little black seed, but the guy who operated the base bowling alley got stopped trying to cross the border with thirty-two kilo's of "Mexican head lettuce."

People usually didn't get busted for LSD or THC or mescaline, mostly because they were the kind of thing you could swallow at the last second when you noticed the circus of cops chasing you down the freeway. However a bag of weed went down real slow, especially when you were trying to answer questions fired at you by the police or the shore patrol. I however was a special case because my status was considered political. That and the fact that my legal issue hadn't even gone to trial so I was still a third class petty officer. Third class PO is way down next to the bottom of the flag pole. Not the bottom of the pole but pretty damn close and yet I had rank over the other sailors in our unit. Ironic is just a word but this was "Dead clown ironic." I was in deeper shit than almost anyone else and yet I was more or less in charge. It was sort of like when the biggest crooks wind up running giant corporations and nations. This of course wasn't on that scale but the principal was the same. Looking back I realize how lucky I was to wind up in charge of other people and not walking around a military prison yard. Not that any of this was a good thing but somehow it was still kind of cool.

Because I was sort of the new kid on the block I had to depend on a few people who I could trust to show me the ropes. There was a tall skinny guy named Dave who was always smiling and laughing. Dave had the most devious grin I'd ever seen. Dave made you want to be in on what ever it was he was grinning about. I chose Dave to be my guide to the "special services" universe.

I was astounded by the scope of our responsibilities. We started each day at the movie theatre where we made sure that everything was ready for the afternoon matinee. We inspected the theatre to be sure the night crew had done a thorough job of cleaning up after the late showing of the movie of the week. Our crew also restocked the concession stand and ran a shop vacuum around the lobby. When we were done Dave and I got in a grey Chevy pickup truck and headed off to one of many locations in a very specific order depending on certain variables. For instance, if it had rained the night before the first place we went was the officers tennis courts and we took four foot wide squeegees and dried the courts so that, heaven forbid, some douche bag officer wouldn't get his "Converse tennis shoes" wet, or slip and fall and break his ass. The enlisted men had to play on wet courts if they wanted to play that bad. To be honest the enlisted men didn't play tennis when the courts were dry.

The next stop on our route was the bowling alley where we would pick up Dave's friend Terry and drive out to the car wash. The car wash was just a quancet hut with both ends knocked out so you could wash your personal vehicle in the shade. Here we would pull into the shelter and spark up a "doobie" and get our "smiles warmed up." Most of the time the next stop involved a trip off base to the closest "Taco Bell," "Jack in the box," or of course the ever popular "Mickey D's," for a "Big Mac" and fries. However the "Bell" had the best deal if you were really hungry. You could get four of anything for a dollar. Four taco's, four burrito's, four bell burgers, four tostado's or any combination. That place was very popular with sailors, hippies, and street people alike.

After our morning break we would drop Terry off before anyone noticed he was gone. Like that was ever going to happen. Then Dave and I would cruse over to the base car shop to hang out with our off duty "Hells Angel" who everyone called "dick finger." Not to his face and not because his first name was Richard, or that his last name was Finger. The true story was that when he was younger he had blown his right index finger off in an unfortunate M80 (giant firecracker) mishap. When the doctors tried to sew the thing back together it wound up looking just like a short stubby hard on. I'm sure it was not intentional and they didn't charge him any extra for it. I'm reasonably sure that his girl friend found his disability something she could live with.

Dick finger worked on our trucks and was a serious biker and a truly amazing mechanic. We would tear up our trucks something awful during one of our escapes from the shore patrol. After laying low for the appropriate interval we would sneak our bent and broken vehicle over to the car shop and after taking a large portion of cursing out (if you've never been verbally abused by a Hells Angel you have not lived a full life) We would watch in awe as Mr. finger would tear into the truck and have it back up and working like new in no time flat. It was like being back stage at a "NASCAR" event.

After the car shop it was time for lunch at the chow hall. The drug induced road trip for fast food was just a mid morning snack, but the chow hall was food heaven. You may think I'm joking but, seriously, the food on base was totally awesome. Our chow hall had won awards for having the best food in the entire US military. Even the chipped beef on toast was delicious. At Miramar we didn't refer to this traditional GI meal as "shit on a shingle" like they did every where else.

The only unpleasant part of the chow hall experience was the "apple watch." The Navy paid a sailor to get all dressed up in his white summer uniform, with a yellow lanyard over his shoulder and a night stick to protect our nations apples. It was the job of the apple watch to make sure no one took two or more pieces of fruit. Really? You could take all you wanted on lobster, or king crab day, but if you put two apples on your tray the apple watch was on you like…grey paint on…..well everything. We all hated the apple watch because he took his job way to seriously. His favorite line was "If you have a problem, meet me after work at "Judo school."As fate would have it, and quite by accident, I managed to do just that.

One particular afternoon I took a friend up on his invitation to try out the Judo school. This person knew I was a wrestler in high school and he reasoned that I might enjoy the experience. I had to put on a short white bath robe (gi) and white pajama pants. The instructors lined up the whole class and since I was the new guy I had to fight every one in order to find out where I would fit in. They started with the easiest and each opponent got progressively better. I defeated all but one of the students using my wrestling skills plus some totally made up shit. When the last guy stepped up I realized it was the apple watch. I hadn't recognized him out of his little white uniform and night stick.

Suddenly the fruit cop started screaming some crazy Japanese stuff and came running across the mat like he wanted to kill me. I waited until the very last second and when he was just close enough I used all his forward momentum and picked him up and slammed him to the floor. The screaming changed from Japanese to loud American cursing almost instantly and continued for what I considered "Way To Long." He had suffered a broken shoulder and the class got real ugly after that. They dragged the sobbing "fruit dispenser" off to the infirmary and the black belt instructor stepped onto the mat and tightened the belt on his robe and motioned me to the center of the mat. The teacher was a scary looking older "lifer." (someone who joins the military for ever) This hardened warrior looked like a bald Clint Eastwood. We circled each other until he made a move where he grabbed my robe by the collar and rolled backwards in an attempt to throw me out the front door. I didn't know that much about Judo but I had good balance and basic instinct told me to place a foot between his legs and drop on top of him. That part worked perfectly. If we were wrestling I could have pinned the guy but in Judo you have to hold your opponents shoulders down for like three days. I was doing my best to pin the master when he reached up and grabbed the collar on my robe with both hands and choked me with it. This technique turned me off like a light switch. Just so you know, your brain needs a constant flow of oxygenated blood to work properly, or at all for that matter.

I really have no idea how long I was asleep but when I woke up everyone was standing around me like I was a pile of money. I slowly got to my feet and tried to figure out where the fuck I was. What ever happened after that is a little fuzzy but I do remember not ever going back to Judo class…ever. I was however somewhat of a folk hero with the guys in the chow hall after that. The apple watch had his arm in a sling for quite some time and was rather timid from that point on. I, of course, stocked up on apples like they were gold doubloons at Mardi Gras.

After lunch Dave and I would drive out past the golf course and down a dirt road to our fish pond. The fish pond was a small lake stocked with trout that was a secret to almost every one, by that I mean no one was ever there. Perhaps the absence of anglers had something to do with the fact that, on base, there was absolutely nothing you could do with a fish once you caught one. We were on a friggin Navy base for Christ sakes. It's not like a sailor could take a trout back to the barracks and light a fire in the middle of the day room and have a fish fry. This was before the popularity of sushi in America. Consequently the fish pond was deserted most of the time.

Now and then we got to stock the pond with new fish from a hatchery somewhere far away. So far away that a good number of the fish were already dead or dying when we dumped them from the truck mounted container into the lake. We then tried to jump start as many "floaters" as we could by swishing them through the water by hand and forcing the water into their gills. Despite our best efforts we still wound up in a row boat skimming dead fish out of the pond with a net in one hand and a doobie in the other. This wasn't exactly what I had imagined when I joined the Navy but we were in a boat and this was better than helping to kill people who never did anything to me. Dave and I spent many hours smoking pot, telling stories and successfully staying out of everyones way. There is an art involved with staying out of the way and Dave and I were artists. Dave was Andy Warhol and I was Van Gogh. We disappeared in the morning like smoke on a breezy day, we covered or tracks, we touched all the bases, and we knew exactly when it was important to be somewhere.

One of the places that we knew we had to be was the warehouse detail. Our Commander ran an impromptu supply operation on base. He was a bit of a crook on some level and we were his trusted minions. He was well aware that Dave and I had our quirks and secrets and we knew that he knew. It all made for a finely tuned mixture of trust, mistrust, obedience, fear and loathing. While complicated the arrangement ran like a knock off of a Swiss watch.

A call would come in to the movie theatre at exactly 08.00 hours. The call involved some very expensive piano or billiards table or sometimes just a big crate that needed to be loaded onto a certain sized trailer from a ship that had just docked at the ship yard downtown.

The Ranch

Due to some very good fortune I had earned a license that allowed me to drive just about every kind of land vehicle that the Navy owned including dump trucks and tractors. I was the logical choice whenever a driver was needed and Dave was the logical shotgun. We were a team like in the buddy movies and no one ever even thought of us working alone on one of our "Projects." We would drive down to the San Diego Naval docks then out toward the dock. We then pulled onto the pier along side some big grey ship. All of a sudden, like magic, a crane would drop our cargo into the bed of our truck or trailer. There was no paper work, no questions, no names, just a load of stuff that we then drove over to the marine base at North Island, across the Coronado bridge past the place where Navy seals trained. Once there we would make our way to a warehousing area and hunt down our contact.

Our North Island guy was named Chief Manny and he looked like someone from an episode of McCales Navy. He had a large brimmed hat with fish hooks, football tickets, cigarettes and a World War II Zippo lighter with a bullet hole in it that still worked. There were also a couple of live 44 caliber cartridges. His fishing vest had dozens of little pockets that were all full of something but only a few had things that you could see, like the three Cuban cigars in the pocket over his heart. He wore a huge Bowie knife and had a Colt, 1911, 45 caliber semi automatic military issue pistol in a holster on his belt and I'm guessing a big heavy 44 caliber derringer in one of his boots. He was like a walking sports store. I would not have been surprised if he had unzipped his fly and an inflatable canoe popped out.

We would arrange for the chief's workers to unload the piano, or pool table, or pallet of pinocle cards, and then they would reload our truck with some other crazy assed traded cargo. We discovered that our commander was a master of the rules of supply and demand and that huge quantities of anything had inherent value. If you corner the market on some commodity like size 10 bowling shoes, well then, you are the "size 10 bowling shoe godfather." This may sound stupidly mundane but our commander had the market cornered on so much shit that he commanded some real power over anyone who wanted almost anything. We once drove back to the base with a marble statue of a hot naked Greek goddess and two tons of rubber bands. If you had all the rubber bands in the Navy you had real power over anyone who needed a rubber band. Please don't get me started on why any one would ever need ten thousand tubes of "Dr. Johnson's Joy Jelly." We didn't ask questions, we just carted all this crap back to the base and unloaded what ever the hell it was into our own giant warehouse back at the base. I'd be willing to bet that the naked marble statue was going to wind up in our commanders rose garden.

Dave and I hardly ever personally touched any of the stuff we hustled to and fro since there were always plenty of low ranking sailors, who I had some authority over. We could make them do pretty much what ever we wanted them to do. It was kind of like being a slave owner except for the whole whipping thing. We just told them to do it and they did it. Power is a drug and some people got off on bossing people around but I always felt guilty whenever I told someone to do something that I wasn't willing to do myself. This particular trait isn't exactly something you would want to put on a resume. I'm just making an observation based on personal experience.

Special services was a dumping ground for the human refuse that had screwed up so badly that the only evidence that they had once held any rank at all was the insignia shaped unfaded area on their shirt sleeves. You would think that the sailors hanging around the loading dock would cringe when Dave and I showed up with tons of rubber bands, or golf balls, or size 10 bowling shoes, but they jumped up the minute we pulled into the lot. I'm not sure if they were trying to redeem themselves for the crimes they had committed or perhaps they knew that as soon as they were done unloading our truck we would repay their efforts by sparking up a joint or two and hanging out with them until it was time to go back to the movie theatre. I have always believed that keeping the spirits of the young men and women who defend our shores at a "high" level, is a top priority. You would think the military would do more to improve morale among the troops. For the most part, the troops have always done just fine when left to their own devices, thank you very much.

All the while, we were doing our part to protect our country from the dreaded "commies." As taxpayers who read this story you may think that your money was just getting flushed down the toilet but I will have you know that this country didn't get "nuked" once and Russia didn't invade us even the least little bit while I was getting paid to defend it. Coincidence? Well…you be the judge.

CHAPTER 9

The Golf Course

When you are in the service you are provided with all the basics. Food and shelter are not a concern as long as you stay on the base. The small pay check you receive every two weeks is enough to cover your expenses. You can pay for bad hair cuts, cheap on base movies, Cokes and snacks, laundry expenses and of course cigarettes. Most of the money spent on base went for beer at the enlisted mens club. I didn't drink much beer and I didn't smoke so I was one rich sailor minus the ton of quarters I spent calling home on the pay phones. That is at least until I got that whiff of freedom from outside the fence.

If one chooses to move off base all the rules change and you need to come up with money to pay for a vehicle, gas, rent, food, and entertainment. This usually meant getting a shitty part time job like the one you had in high school. In 1968 part time pay was $2.50 an hour if you were lucky. There were plenty of jobs for those willing to work. If you didn't mind working like a coolie for junk wages you could scrounge up enough to make ends meet. Some guys, of course, took the easy road and sold or transported pot because it was, well...easy, and profitable. The war on drugs provided jobs that required a minimum amount of time and effort. I, on the other hand, was born with a fatal flaw. I grew up with the words, "If you work really, really, hard, you just might succeed in life. Just don't get your hopes up." Those words from my step dad were ringing in my ears and were words to live by and no one can fault my stepdad for screaming them at me every chance he got. Speaking as someone who, has since worked more man hours in my life than all the people who built the Empire State Building combined, (perhaps a slight exaggeration) I took those words to heart and started signing up for anything that offered a pay check.

When I was old enough I began working jobs that would make todays young people run away in terror. I found work in factory's that made perfume and hairspray. I ran deliveries for a pharmacy. I dug ditches, hauled cinder blocks and mixed cement for a brick mason. I nailed shingles, all hunched over like a monkey fucking a football, for a roofer. I've worked for landscapers, and I was a longshore worker. I've labored for plumbers, and I even put in some time in a pinball arcade. One of the most interesting jobs however was when I worked as a grounds keeper for the base golf course.

While in the Navy I was constantly short of money because I loved to party and go on dates with "Copper Tone" girls. I drove around in a car that only cost me $65.00. My car was a four door 1956 Buick Road Master and nearly a block long. This car used up more gas than a jet air liner and was constantly in need of parts and that meant I spent much of my time down at the local junk yard. One day a friend of mine told me of an opening that involved making short grass out of only slightly longer grass all day every day. I asked if there was any money involved and when he said, "Sure." I said, "I'm in."

I have always been a huge fan of power tools and the more power the better so when I first got a look at those magnificent lawn mowers with freshly sharpened blades and finely tuned gas engines, well that was all I needed. "Sign me up." I have to admit that the sound of a powerful gas powered engine gives me a hard on. Is that weird? No, it's not.

The following week I went to work with the weirdest group of guys I had ever known. That is saying something considering I was from New Jersey. The job was on the base but I was the only actual government employee who was also working as a greens keeper on the golf course and at first there was a certain level of suspicion among the menagerie of social misfits I was working with. Try to imagine a small group of people who couldn't get jobs with a traveling carnival who were also all as different as night and......frozen fish sticks.

"Glen" was a surfer who loved to get high and was a free spirit. Glen was also a woman magnet who was balling every "Cougar" in San Diego at the time. I met a few of these women and I was totally impressed. They were beautiful, smart and they just loved to fuck Glen. Glen was like a god to the rest of us and he made everything he did look way to easy. Glen and I became good friends and he showed me the ropes of our weird work place environment.

"Robbie" was a creepy, little, actual ex-carnival ride operator, who had gotten fired for letting one to many kids fall out of the "Tilt - a - Whirl" ride. I'm no expert but you would think it only takes one. Like most carnies Robbie was an ex-con who had more tattoos than the Easter Bunny has jelly beans. Robbie had swastikas tattooed on all ten of his fingers and wasn't much fun to be around. A comparison might be, Charles Manson wasn't much fun at parties, that is of course unless, you were the kind of person who wanted to go out and murder people after the party.

"Tommy" was the old pro and knew everything about the grass cutting business. He was kind of like the Bill Murray character in our little version of "Caddie Shack". Tommy taught me how to mow in perfectly straight lines and in a different direction every other day so that the grass didn't "lay down." He was a master greens keeper and I was in awe of his talent. We aerated the greens and spread sand to fill the holes and those greens responded like pool tables to the stupid little white balls that assholes insisted on hitting at them. Our greens were perfect, why couldn't people dressed in clown outfits just leave them the fuck alone?

Golf rant: I think that golf was invented to allow white guys to dress like black guys on the weekends but they never pulled it off. I'll admit that Tiger woods managed to add a high level of class to the golf dress code but when I was working as a greens keeper in the late 60's the outfits were to say the least…colorful.

I learned how to move the hole. They have this tool that cuts a perfect hole to a precise depth. We chose the perfect spot for the new hole and cut it out then we moved the plastic cup insert just far enough below the lip. The last part was to replace the cut out back into the old hole and make sure it came to the perfect level so that a golf ball passing over it didn't wobble or bounce. It was a science and Tommy was our mad scientist that kept it all running. If a good grounds keeper wants to make a particular hole nearly impossible to sink a putt into, there are a few tricks that are invisible to the eye, but absolutely deadly to a perfectly lined up putt, and it makes the best golfer look totally stupid. Don't tell anyone I told you this because some people take the "sport" of golf seriously.

Then there was Bernie who was a human golf ball magnet. When ever we heard a golfer yell "FORE" everyone suddenly looked to see where Bernie was and ran in the opposite direction because he was invariably going to be ground zero. I was told this by the other guys but assumed it was just bullshit until one day I was standing next to Bernie when out of nowhere a golf ball smacks him right on top of his head. He staggered a bit and then shook it off and shrugged as if this happened every day. Bernie must have really pissed off the ghost of Bobby Jones because his ability to attract those stupid little white balls was truly uncanny. The day I saw him get beaned I swear there weren't any golfers around anywhere. After making sure that Bernie was all right, I looked in every direction and we were all alone out there. It was then that I realized that there were powers at work here that were just plain spooky and from that day on I made it a point not to get within ten feet of poor Bernie unless we were indoors and no where near any windows.

The actual leader of our group was "Jack." Jack was a freakishly small red headed Irishman who looked like he had just jumped off a box of "Lucky Charms." Our little leprechaun over compensated for his stature by being as loud and annoying as was humanly possible. Some bosses teach by example and are protective of their subordinates. Jack wasn't one of those bosses. As assholes go Jack was in a class all by himself. He reveled in explaining the most simple, mundane, tasks over and over to people who already knew how to do whatever it was much better than he did, but he did it purely to hear himself talk in his thick Irish accent while we sat squirming, and wanting to stomp him out, like a little green cigarette.

Jack was afraid of some of us, especially Robbie, so he took out his vertically challenged wrath on Bernie who was the most sincerely sweet innocent and helpless worker on our crew. Poor Bernie would almost break into tears after some of Jack's pointless tirades. One such reaming lasted for fifteen minutes and revolved around the capital crime of forgetting to check the gas level in a mower that had just been serviced and sharpened in the shop. As a rule we didn't need to touch gas cans as that was the job of the mechanics who maintained the mowers. It wasn't Bernie's job to check the gas in his mower but that didn't protect him from the ass chewing he received from Jack, who managed to waste ten times the man hours it took to fill up all of our damn mowers. Jack was yelling and screaming as if Bernie was responsible for the sinking of the fucking Titanic. As we sat and watched Jack take Bernie apart, piece by piece, I made myself a promise to screw this nasty, cruel, munchkin, little prick, in some cruel and devious yet imaginative fashion.

I was inspired by the story of a previous employee who hated Jack much the same as we all did and when he had finally had enough of the constant flow of Jacks Irish bullshit, he came up with the perfect plan. Jack's birthday was approaching and our friend decided to retire from his course maintenance duties on that very day. His plan required rising at two o'clock in the morning, and after gaining access to the tool shed with a crow bar and borrowing a "Cushman" cart he visited all eighteen greens and removed the flag and cup from the first seventeen. He then used the hole cutter to plant all eighteen flags evenly around the edge of the eighteenth green. Indeed, it looked a little like a birthday cake when every one arrived the next morning. Naturally Jack had a meltdown and went off on everyone in sight, everyone that is except the actual party planner himself. He was long gone and we guessed he was off somewhere drinking some Irish whisky, and doing his own rendition of the "River dance." He was never seen again. I loved the story of the "eighteenth hole" and I aspired to do something equally as gratifying. The gauntlet had been laid down so to speak and I picked it up and kept it in my pocket.

One morning as we were about to go about our duties of giving haircuts to billions of blades of grass, Jack marched in and demanded to know if any one of us had any plumbing experience. I had worked with my stepdad and uncle one summer installing heating and cooling systems. I knew how to cut copper tubing and sweat joints. I was good with tools and figured I could do what ever Jack wanted and perhaps get some sort of raise. God knows $2.30 an hour wasn't very good money even by 1968 standards.

I raised my hand and took a half step forward. Jack dismissed the rest of the crew and said to me "get in the pickup, we need to talk." The deal went like this. They had gotten a shit load of cash to replace the old sprinkler system and Jack was going to do the job as cost effectively as was humanly possible. He would keep what ever was left over for himself. This explained why he wasn't going with a union plumber. He was hiring a crew of Mexican ditch diggers who he had helped sneak across the border from Tijuana. Ten Spanish speaking, sturdy looking guys who were being paid much less than the rest of us. That was ludicrous.

I assigned half of my crew to dig up the old sprinkler heads and the other half was filling in the holes and putting the grass patches back in place. My job was to cut out the old sprinkler heads, replace the plastic fittings and install the new "Rain Bird" sprinklers. Jack was going to give me a dollar for every installed head. I did the math and after an unsuccessful attempt to get a buck fifty each I agreed to the deal. Business negotiations was new to me and I didn't know enough to get our deal on paper.

The next day I put together a Cushman cart with all the tools and equipment I needed, I identified my translator among my crew of laborers. Jose was from TJ (Tijuana) and spoke decent English Jose was once the guy who stood outside the strip bar and talked the marines into spending their money on cheap drinks and young women. Jose could communicate everything to all of my workers except for the little Mayan guy. We named the Mayan "digger" because after handing him a shovel and pointing at the ground he went to work like a badger. Dirt flew out of the hole so fast we were afraid he was going to strike oil.

I became very good at replacing the sprinklers and with the crew working at full throttle we were doing about seventy heads a day. I would be making good money, "On paper." I worked full time starting at six in the morning and still had time to get out to the line and work my four to twelve shift for the Navy. You can pull shit like that when you are nineteen, and more or less bullet proof. After the first two weeks I had earned close to seven hundred dollars and for the first time in a long time I was looking forward to getting my paycheck. That Friday morning Jack, once again, let the crew go on ahead and asked me to stay behind. I thought that perhaps Jack was so impressed with my performance that I was in for a bonus. I was young and hadn't learned that the definition of the word bonus came from the Latin, "Bone Us."

Note: When your boss offers you a bonus it means he will insert a few extra dollars into your next pay check and cancel your medical benefits the week after.

Jack was acting strangely as he shuffled the papers around on his desk and he finally broke the silence. He said he had to leave in a few minutes so he could get downtown in time to appear on the local San Diego, TV morning show. Evidently Jack was some sort of hometown personality who dressed up in a green blazer and plaid vest and pleased the audience by telling marginally amusing golf course stories. Jack spiced up his tales by laying on his charming Irish Brogue like it was peanut butter.

I began to get an uneasy feeling in the pit of my stomach and somehow I knew the other shoe was about to drop. Jack looked up at me and told me with a fake sincere look that, "the board" had decided that the dollar for each sprinkler head was more than they could afford but they had agreed to give me a nickel an hour raise instead. I stood perfectly still, using all of my control to keep from grabbing a shovel and smashing the lying little dwarf square in his red cheeked face. I knew perfectly well that if "the board" had made some sort of decision Jack was behind it. He ran the place and he was the controlling factor in any thing that went on at the golf course.

I didn't say a word as I turned slowly and walked out the door and pondered my next move. I'm a firm believer in well conceived retribution, as opposed to physical violence. While secretly craving to go the violent route and pound jack into Irish pudding, I started up my cart and began the short drive to where my crew was working that day. I turned and looked back toward the yard and saw Jack begin his long climb into the cab of his giant pickup truck. I stopped and watched him adjust the cushion that allowed him to see over the dash board. He started up the big Dodge and drove out toward the freeway. I was seething mad when suddenly I realized Jack was going to be in town, all damned day. There was a big golf tournament starting the next day at our golf course and he was going to be hanging out with local celebrities promoting it at the Coronado hotel after his Television appearance. I smiled and headed over to the ninth hole where my guys were patiently waiting for my arrival.

I informed my Mexican foreman, Jose, that we would be doing something a little different that day and that instead of five guys digging up heads and five filling in the holes, I wanted all ten men to dig up as many heads as they could by three o'clock. Jose looked at me like I was a little loco but he obeyed my orders perfectly. I dropped off the cart and walked out to the parking lot, picked up my big blue Buick and headed for the beach. I spent the rest of the day trying to forget that I was going to need a new job. The day was perfect and there was a film crew doing some kind of suntan lotion commercial with more than a few beautiful young girls in bikini's. My mind was soon on something much more pleasing than some tiny Irish "Umpa Lumpa" with whisky breath.

Just a note to clarify. I myself am of Irish decent and I'm not trying to degrade an entire race of heavy drinkers because of one jerk off, who incidentally was to short to ride the rides at Disney Land.

When I returned to the base after an exceptionally pleasing day of fun in the sun I noticed that there was a sizable portion of the golf course with fairly large piles of dirt evenly dispersed in a pattern strangely similar to the layout of the sprinkler system. You could see the smile on my face from outer space. I never went back to pick up my last pay check to avoid the wrath of the "mad Munchkin." The story's of what happened when Jack returned that afternoon were the stuff of legend.

Jack had spent the afternoon drinking and glad handing with the San Diego elite and was quite drunk and happy when he drove up in his pickup that afternoon. At first he didn't notice the landscape. As he climbed down from the big truck he looked like a rock climber descending a cliff. He really needed to consider getting himself a smaller rig. Finally he made it down safely and after making a few adjustments old Jack turned around to inspect his beautiful course just to be sure everything was perfect for the tournament. It is said that Jack stood absolutely still for the next few minutes while his eyes darted feverishly, going from one pile of dirt to the next. Then he started to sputter and shake, suddenly he was yelling and screaming like a madman. He grabbed a shovel and ran like a monkey over to the closest pile of dirt and started to fill in the hole. He was still wearing his TV suit and was soon covered in dirt and grass stains. He was still trying to scream at no one in particular but was gradually loosing his voice until finally only sad little sounds like a kidnap victim in a trunk of a Cadillac were coming from his pissed off mouth.

Purely out of misplaced pity the rest of the workers picked up shovels and started filling in the two hundred or so holes. By morning the grounds crew had managed to get the place looking halfway respectable for the big event on Saturday, but Jack, I have to think, took his hatred for me to his grave. He wasn't a forgiving soul and probably never came to see the humor in the situation and the fact that being a perpetual douche bag has certain consequences. That and the part where he deserved everything he got.....Karma is a wonderful thing......as long as it's aimed in someone else's direction.

I found another job as a warehouse worker down on the docks at the port of San Diego. I drove a fork lift and shipped products for an Indonesian family, but I longed for the soft green rolling hills of the golf course. It was a private paradise to me and I missed the smell of the freshly mowed grass even though I was the one mowing it. I have to admit that to this day I still hate the sport of golf and the poorly dressed goofballs who play it. OK that's a lie. Since those days when I was ducking golf balls, I've hit a few long amazing drives and sunk a couple of impossible puts, which is all it takes to lock you in forever. You really can't explain why chasing that stupid little white ball all over acres of well groomed hills and dales is so addicting but I do get it. However I still cringe whenever some cock sucking pile of shit takes a huge divot out of that gorgeous green work of art. That includes Tiger Woods and Lefty. When I'm at the "tee" I always use "one." even on the short holes because I was once the guy who had to replace all those little pieces of grass after some silly turd in the plaid pants and white patten leather shoes made Swiss cheeze out of my perfect garden.

Golf note:

Say what you will about Tiger Woods but that guy did show the sport of golf how to dress. I mean I've seen pictures of Elin and like every other guy in the solar system and at least half the women, I say to my self "Tiger, dude? What were you thinking man?" In spite of his inability to control the brain in his pants,.....those are some really outstanding pants.

CHAPTER 10

The Fish Pond

Dave and I really had a stressful job, sort of, and we had to give ourselves some quality down time whenever possible. This occurred on a regular basis and usually involved finding a quiet spot to smoke some grass and stay out of sight until the redness in our eyes cleared up. We had plenty of choices on base because of the sheer immensity of our airstrip. Miramar was, after all, a pilot training facility and the bigger the base the better. When large, very expensive, flaming balls of metal come falling from the sky it is only prudent to have an extremely large fenced off parcel of range land for them to crash into. It was hard not to feel sorry for the young men who piloted their aircraft to a fiery date with eternity, although the irony of the fact that these people were training to drop napalm bombs on poor people in their own country wasn't lost on us either. In fact most pilots managed to eject safely and lived to crash another day. Usually the only people who paid for their errors were taxpayers. I tried to separate myself from the realities of the situation the best way I knew how. Most of the guys in my crew were there because of drugs and personally I think that the madness surrounding the war had brought us all together for similar yet varied reasons. The dynamics of the pro, and anti war movements were reaching a crescendo and none of us knew what would happen next, so we dealt with it each in our own way.

The Ranch

Training Day

One seemingly uneventful morning Dave and I were in the process of training a new member of our tightly woven group of misfits. There was a very cool aspect to being in charge of an (ABB) "already been busted" work force. These people had a lot in common with me, and,....they had a lot to lose. They also had a lot in common with each other and very little in common with our superiors. When we took the time to properly indoctrinate these people into the group the result could be quite stunning.

The "fresh meat" on the menu that day was a young kid who had been busted for going awol. (absent without leave) He had tried to go back to Tennessee to be with his girl friend but only got as far as the Greyhound bus terminal downtown. The cops found him asleep waiting for the ticket counter to open. It was 3:00 in the morning and when he couldn't present his leave papers they turned him over to the MP's. (military Police) The Navy gave him a court martial and busted him down to a pay grade that wasn't even legal in China. Fortunately what was bad for him was good for us. His crushed spirit was pitiful to behold but we were there for him and we all had our own baggage so it wouldn't take long to bring him over into our "special services fold." There was only the initiation portion of the indoctrination process remaining and the new guy could "legally" become a member of the coolest outfit in the whole damn US military. The new guy's name was John, "John Lennon." Dave and I decided that was just plain wrong. We renamed him "Ringo."

Our initiation generally revolved around a hair raising ride in our 1952 ford pickup truck at a stupidly high rate of speed and the more initiations we performed the better we got at making them seem like actual near death experiences. Dave and I persuaded Ringo to ride between us on the bench seat of the truck. We certainly didn't want him trying to jump out the fucking door in the middle of the desert at 70 or 80 miles an hour. In 1952 seat belts were severely optional.

There were several long dirt roads that traversed the base from end to end so we drove down the longest, scariest one of all. We had a huge cloud of dust following us down that road. "Who knew dust could travel at that speed?" The curves were coming at us so fast and we hit the bumps so hard that it was sort of like being on all the rides at Disneyland at once. Poor Ringo had nothing to hang onto and his head bounced off the roof of the cab of the truck several times with so much force that his eyes were starting to spin. I slowed down to a safe respectable speed somewhere around sixty so we could take a deep breath and get on with the initiation. We found our way down to the fish pond and parked in the shade at the far end of the lake. At this time Ringo was nearly in shock. There was only one road into the fish pond. From where we were situated we could see any one headed in our direction from about a half mile away.

Dave had already sparked up a joint by the time I shut down the engine and he passed it to Ringo who didn't hesitate to take a big long deep hit. Almost immediately he began coughing like he had swallowed a hair ball. Ringo, as it turned out had never smoked anything before,......ever,....not even a Newport. In no time he was smiling and telling us stories that had us crying with laughter.

Ringo, as it turns out, had worked for a funeral home back in Tennessee and it was his job to repossess the suit of the deceased during the hearse ride from the funeral parlor to the grave yard. Some people didn't have the money to buy a new suit for a dead relative so the discount funeral came with a rental. Also if the deceased did show up dead wearing a really nice suit the result was that he was destined to spend the rest of forever wearing nothing but a flattened out smile. Ringo was already in the back of the hearse when they loaded the casket and he had the drapes pulled. There was enough privacy to strip the body of its clothing,....as well as any rings and any other valuables he might find along the way. Just so you know, some people slip money into the pockets of dead friends and relatives when they give their last respects. This is probably a result of guilt for not spending more time with the horizontal one when he was, well, more...vertical. Dave and I were engrossed in the story that Ringo laid out before us.

The rental suit had a slit down the back to facilitate the speedy removal process. We were stunned and amazed at this revelation but somehow we couldn't stop laughing. Dave and I were roaring as Ringo told us the story of this really fat old gentleman who he had to wrestle the clothes off of, in the summer heat. The body started farting as the gases in the body

The Ranch

found their way out while poor Ringo fought to retrieve the suit before the hearse arrived at the cemetery. I'm guessing that not as much care is taken in the discount funeral to sew things up and replace all the body fluids with formaldehyde. The fat body was naked by the time Ringo was finished. Dead people don't wear underwear, and our poor goofy friend didn't even have time to pull the gold teeth from the corpse's mouth with his "leatherman" pliers.......WAIT, WHAT? HUH? Dave and I both went silent and looked at each other like we had just witnessed Pam Anderson making love to Larry King. Eeeyeeww. It was then that we decided Ringo should never be given a position of authority in our organization.

The timing of the gross punch line was strategic. As we sat in silence, slowly trying to absorb the twisted revelation, we heard the sound of a badly tuned six cylinder engine in the distance. I looked up toward the road and saw a beat to shit, grey, Chevy, pickup truck with two "turtle heads" (military police in very small, unflattering, grey helmets) bearing down on us in as big a hurry as they could manage. I started the big V8, revved it up and popped the clutch causing the tires to spin at first. Rocks and dirt flew as I worked the clutch to let the tires grab the hard dirt road. The truck popped a little wheely and we took off. It was similar being fired out of a cannon. (this is a guess as I my self have never been fired from a cannon) I told my faithful, if slightly petrified crew to hold on tight as this was indeed going to be a very bumpy ride.

We were charging headlong at the grey truck at full speed. I could see that the driver of the other vehicle was beginning to question his core beliefs in just how important it was to break up a three person pot party and was this really worth dying for. His truck wobbled from side to side and he was about ready to drive it into the lake. I waited until we were perhaps fifty feet from the his bumper and certain death before hanging a hard hairy left turn into the slope. I geared down and spun the rear wheels just enough to get us pointed up the hill and this move also kept us from rolling over. We caught quite a bit of dirt and rock at first and the truck shuddered as it began to climb the hillside. Our tires were launching a great deal of crushed rock in the direction of the grey shore patrol truck. Remarkably we gained momentum and soon were heading up the hillside at an ever increasing rate of speed.

Dick finger must have souped the shit out of the drive train and that suspension. The engine seemed to get stronger as we headed for the crest of the hill. When we topped out the truck went air born. I mean we just kept going up for a while after our wheels left the boundaries of the earth. For a few seconds the three of us were staring at nothing but blue sky. Then the nose of the truck rolled forward and came down extremely hard on a road we didn't even know was there. We crossed the road and spun out into the desert and dust and smoke were everywhere but we were safe....for a brief time at least. The engine seemed fine and the tires were still intact as I got the truck straightened out and we headed for more familiar territory.

There was a series of winding dirt roads that meandered and intersected all over the west end of the base and we just needed to head east with the afternoon sun at our back and we would be able to find our way back to the movie theater in no time.

Dave and I were damn proud of our escape from the turtle heads but we let Ringo believe that shit like this happened to us every day. Dave had a huge shit eating grin on his face and I was laughing so hard I almost lost control of the truck. There are times that are just so special and this was, by god, one of those times. The windows were rolled down and the wind was in our hair. "White room" by "Cream" was playing on the AM radio and I turned it all the way up. Ringo was in a state of shock, his eyes were rolling around in his head like a dolls eyes and he was moving his lips but no words were coming out. He probably could have used some sort of medication but this was not the time and I wasn't driving an ambulance.

We started winding our way back to a real road when we spotted the car wash up ahead. I smiled at Dave and yelled over the music "Now that was special!" Dave began to crack up. Just as we were approaching the quancet hut I noticed a grey beat to crap, Chevy pickup, come blasting out of the East end of the building and it was clearly going to get to road ahead of us, and cut us off. I cranked on the steering wheel and began to circle back to avoid the impending roadblock when I saw that a second truck had just emerged from the same building from the West end and was getting into position to block my retreat. I also noticed one other thing at that precise moment. The harder I pressed on the gas pedal the larger the cloud of powdery sand behind the truck grew. I made a snap decision that our only chance was that growing dust cloud and I accelerated to a speed that started churning out dust like a volcano. I kept on the steering wheel hard left and felt the tires slip smoothy like those Nascar drivers do after winning a race. The pursuing trucks disappeared as did every thing else. We were completely enveloped in the light brown dust cloud as we spun doughnuts for what seemed like a ridiculously long amount of time. We had to roll the windows up just to breathe and it was then that I noticed the unmistakable aroma of soiled pants. It wasn't me and judging from the giant Cheshire cat grin on Dave's face, it damn sure wasn't him. The only logical choice was Ringo who was trying to climb over Dave so he could jump out of the window.

This was more fun than I had had in a long time but all good things must end. I straightened out the wheel and crossed my fingers. There was a very good chance, after all, that we would slam head on into a truck full of really pissed off sailors with "Billy clubs" at any moment. Somehow, magically, we emerged from the giant dust bubble without ever seeing either of them. We quickly rolled down the windows and slowed to a crawl and we could hear the groaning "six bangers" (underpowered six cylinder grey piece of shit pickup trucks) tearing away at the desert. Suddenly we heard a loud extended series of crashing noises and metallic thuds emanating from the dust storm followed by the unmistakable sound of angry overweight white sailors, wearing tiny grey helmets, swearing at each other at the top of their lungs. We took off like a class full of eighth graders on the last day of school, who nearly got caught stealing cigarettes from "Newberry's department store." Oops, sorry, totally different story.

When we got back to the theater we made Ringo clean himself up, and then we made him detail the truck, really well, inside and out. Then we made him clean himself up again. He also had to promise not tell a soul about our little adventure or Dave and I would swear he was driving. The next day we drove the old trusty pickup over to the shop where we received an awful reaming from Dick Finger. No wait...Sorry, that sounds terribly wrong. What I meant was, he called us every name in the big book of words no one wants to be called....ever. Apparently we had blown out all four shocks and broken one of the leaf springs. Dick really wanted to know what the hell had happened to his prized machine and we told him that it was better that he didn't know anything, just in case the CID guys came to call.

Dick smiled knowingly because there were already rumors flying around the base about some crazy civilians who had snuck onto the base and somehow evaded capture after an amazing chase and getaway. As it was, none of the shore cops who had tried to set us up that day had gotten a good look at the plates on the truck and even though we had the only tan 1952 ford pickup on the whole goddamn base. No one ever figured out who the hell we were. I think the whole thing was so embarrassing to the shore patrol that they just decided to try to make believe it never happened. Mr. Finger had that old truck back up and running like a Ferrari in no time. He made a hell of a noise but he loved working on that truck. Dick knew we knew his love for his job and how much we appreciated his abilities. I think secretly Dick was creaming in his jeans every time we pulled off one of our escapades without getting caught. He was a Hells Angel after all and like it or not he was an important part of our operation. He once told me "If you ever get caught it better be because you ran out of gas"

There was more going on here than we knew, and I'm sure there was a reason that we seemed invincible at times. It was like either the authorities were, dumber than a bag of ball peen hammers, or we didn't get hauled off to the brig due to some higher purpose. Dave and I knew something was up and I was reasonably certain it had something to do with my pending investigation. The FBI was involved and all sorts of crazy shit can happen that just don't make any sense when the "Men in grey" are involved.

One day I decided to visit the legal aid office in down town San Diego. I had decided that the legal counsel assigned to me by the Navy might not have my best interests on his agenda so getting a second opinion just seemed to make sense. I had been handed a news letter after donating a couple of bucks to the "Black Panthers" downtown one day. There were numbers to free clinics, places to get free food, and the local legal aid office. There were also the locations of several events that were taking place around the city. San Diego had a very well established underground network at the time and there was always something cool going down that didn't appear in the local paper.

That evening I found my way to an old red brick, three story building with a steel stair way in the back. It was chilly and raining that night and I remember wondering if I had picked the wrong time and place to go looking for free legal assistance. The office was on the third floor and the lights were on. There was also a street light and a couple of porch lights in the alley that made the stairway visible. There was no moon that evening. As I climbed to the top of the stairs I noticed the door to the law office was partly open and I walked right in to the smallest shitiest office I had ever seen. There was a teenaged girl sitting in front of a small wooden desk that had one leg missing and there was a cinder block in its place. Behind the desk was a skinny young man with a pair of thick glasses that were way to big for his little head. I thought that perhaps the ghost of Buddy Holly was working the night shift for legal aid. He was sort of surprised to see me and asked me if I could please wait out side for a couple of minutes. I had made an appointment and I was right on time but I'm guessing that most of his clients showed up late or not at all. I stepped out onto the landing and waited while the young girl finished getting her free legal advice. Her problem revolved around a recent pot bust, and what was she going to with her baby if she had to spend some time in the can. I didn't mean to listen in but I was only five feet away on the tiny landing. They finished up and the girl looked really scared as she made her way down the metal stairs, I think she was crying.

I went into the tiny cluttered office and sat down. As I looked around I began to wonder what the hell I was doing there. The goofy little lawyer had all kinds of junk scattered about. It appeared that his decorator was a blind acid freak. I guessed that most of the junk were payments from destitute clients with no money to pay for his services. There was a replica of a British double decker bus on his desk along with a Malibu Barbie doll driving a pink dune buggy, a stuffed owl mounted on a branch and what appeared to be some kind of shrine with some beads a dried up bird foot and a stick of burning incense. At last I noticed a picture of Mickey Mantle with what appeared to be a genuine autograph. I was finally impressed. I was a huge Yankee fan and "The Mick" was and will always be my favorite sports idol. If he had also possessed a football signed by "Joe Namath," there was a slight possibility that the sad little lawyer was way cooler than he looked.

The legal aid Lawyer was named Quincy Beaumont. He told me he had grown up in Brooklyn but his momma and daddy were originally from New Orleans. This explained what I now realized was a Voo Doo shrine.

Quincy was a "Mr. do good" kind of person who was trying to heal the wounds of a troubled world. He obviously wasn't making a ton of money at his chosen profession and his clothes reminded me of a door to door vacuum cleaner salesperson. We made small talk as he moved some papers around and emptied the ashtray.

After puttering around for a few minutes Quincy sat down behind his desk, looked at me, and asked how he could help. I began telling him my story and he began to fidget nervously. The more I mentioned the fact that I had a crew of shady government issue suits following me around, the more he looked like he was going to pee in his pants. Quincy was literally turning colors and looked around his tiny office as if he expected the entire FBI to descend upon us like a pack of hungry dingoes, who had just run out of babies to eat. Finally he couldn't take it any longer and suddenly he said "Stop, please stop, I can't help you. No one can help you, least of all me. You are in shit so deep, they are going to need a special kind of shit submarine to get your ass out of prison or off a deserted island some place no one has ever heard of. You have managed to get your self so screwed that it's going to take a screw driver the size of the fucking Eiffel Tower to get your self unscrewed".

"OK-OK" I said " now you're just making shit up."

"No man, I'm serious. You are totally fucked and I don't have the power to UN-fuck you. You really need to go now. Your problem is way out of my league and I don't want the feds to come in here and close my office down. My regular clients need me right here. Have you thought about relocating?........To another country...... I hear Canada is really quite pleasant at this time of year."

"Are you fucking nuts?" I exclaimed. "It's December.....In San Diego..... the only way to tell It's Christmas out here is all the kids at the beach are riding on new surf boards. Canada is white and cold this time of year. I'm not talking the kind of cold that makes your nipples hard, I'm talking about the kind of cold that makes them fall off." I almost lost it, and went off on the poor guy but I could see in his eyes that he was really afraid and dead serious about the gravity of my situation and I appreciated his honesty.

I was scared and dejected but at the same time I understood his reluctance. Lawyers don't become lawyers so they can get their asses fired for defending a lost cause like me. The FBI can be very intimidating to some people, but being a "Jersey Boy," I never took cops all that seriously, even when the cops in question were wearing dark suits, had bad haircuts, and dark sunglasses. I was sure this lawyer was indeed out of his league and so I respected his wish for me to move along. I felt like a dangerous poison that had the power to hurt the people who got to close to me. This is not a positive emotion to have and since that time I've tried to develop my sense of humor to fend off the loneliness gene in my personality that makes me do crazy ass shit sometimes.

Note: Prisons are full of people who couldn't afford a good lawyer. Country clubs are full of crooks who can bend laws and steal money and their law teams handle the paper work.

CHAPTER 11

The Party

One beautiful Saturday morning something so strange and so bizarre happened that I started to finally grasp the weight and scope of what I had done to myself. Up to this point I had this imaginary image of me being in control of my own destiny and by using a little trickery and guile I could prevail and emerge relatively unharmed by this latest tangle with the United States government.

My roommates and I had just returned from a trip to Tijuana where we had danced at the "Blue Note" bar all Friday night and well into the morning. We danced so good that night I was sure we would be on Mexican television the next day. Before leaving "TJ" we had an enjoyable meal and plenty of strong coffee we headed home to San Diego in the big Buick. Once back across the border I had to drop off another long haired civilian friend whom we had smuggled into Mexico in the trunk of my car. He was white so we smuggled him back into the United States in the front seat. The border guards mainly concerned themselves with keeping brown people from coming to America. Things haven't changed much since then.

It was about eleven o'clock Saturday morning when we arrived home and Sunny and Mario opted to take a shower together so I hit the living room couch and closed my eyes for a long awaited siesta. I was fast asleep in about forty-seconds and was dreaming about me and Joey Heatherton (beautiful movie star of the day) on the beach at La Jolla doing absolutely amazingly illegal things to each other when suddenly the front screen door burst open with a crash. I was asleep but I was always ready for unexpected visitors and this was totally unexpected. At first I didn't move a muscle, but I opened one eye just the slightest bit. I heard the back door to our first floor apartment slam. As I slowly looked up there was a large balding man in a bad suit standing almost on top of me. As I peeked up at him my first question was, "Who the hell do I know with bullets on his belt?" This gentleman had two 38 caliber speed loaders on his left hip and what appeared to be a shoulder holster up under his cheap grey sport coat. What the hell is it with grey? It's not even a color. There was also a gold badge and a giant radio clipped to his belt. The radio made his coat bulge out as if he had just shop lifted a toaster. The holster was empty and as he turned toward me I saw the short barreled 38 caliber revolver in his right hand. He awkwardly pivoted around while sizing up the situation.

I started to evaluate the situation. We clearly had a cop in our living room and incriminating evidence was lying around everywhere. There was a four foot tall water pipe on the coffee table and the huge bowl was almost full with at least an ounce of partly smoked Mexican weed. There were the only three copies of "Horse Shit" magazine ever printed at the time next to the pipe and a very large Mexican plaster Buddha with a pile of flash powder in his lap In the corner. The flash powder came from a military battle flare that had somehow found it's way from the base to our home and the associated parachute was hanging from our ceiling. No one knows how it got there. We would light a conical shaped piece of incense during a party and set it carefully on top of the pile of the flash powder and the effect was really quite astounding when the giant ball of white fire erupted spontaneously in the middle of a "Moody Blues" song. Just when everyone was about to nod off, FOOM, the whole place looked like the surface of the Sun for a second or two and of course the only ones wearing sunglasses were my roommates and I, oh, and of course Smacks. Smacks was also the only one of our guests who didn't react with screams and panic. Smacks simply smiled as he enjoyed the fear and chaos all around him. He was either totally wasted or the coolest person on the face of the earth.....or quite possibly both.

The detective slowly took a look around and just as slowly backed out of the room and onto the front porch. He then whipped out this monster radio that was the size of a mailbox and called his station. I naturally assumed he was calling for backup on the scale of the Waco incident. (No, Waco hadn't happened yet, please try to stay focussed) I considered making a break for the back door but I knew that police detectives, like ice dancers, and Siamese twins usually travel in pairs and there was possibly someone waiting in the alley out back with his weapon drawn. I waited for the sound of sirens and helicopters while I alerted Mario, and Erik that the cops were on the way. Sunny was already good and gone. I figured that it was her that I'd heard leaving the very second the detective first entered our apartment.

As it turned out Sunny had lent her Pontiac to a friend who went by the name of "Son of Moon Dog." I'm making the assumption that his parents didn't name him "Son of Moon Dog" but this was California in the late sixties so naming kids while stoned was a popular sport. Besides being a severely flaked out street person, Son of Moon Dog was also quite fond of snorting heroine and should never have even been allowed to borrow a skate board, no less a giant purple Bonniville convertible. Sunny certainly had some seriously bent out of shape friends but Son of Moon Dog was in a category all his own. We later discovered that he had driven the giant car down an alley near our apartment and totally ruined it. The alley I mean, the car didn't look to bad but the alley was trashed. Son of Moon Dog must have run into six or seven back walls and a telephone pole but the giant chrome steel bumper had done exactly what it was designed for. The pole stopped the car, but it paid a terrible price and was leaning at an angle somewhat less than ninety degrees. The heroine induced driver became a missing person at that very instant in time.

By the time the dust had cleared everyone in the immediate area had called the police. The accident helped explain the sudden visit from one San Diego's finest but it didn't begin to answer the question we all had from that day on. Why the hell didn't they come back? We were all waiting in breathless anticipation for a full scale siege. California police departments live for shit like this. Drugs, crashed cars, native Americans, Navy guys with long hair who were probably AWOL. The cops must have been close to a giant gang orgasm at the very thought of getting to beat a band of twisted malcontents and war resistors to death with night sticks. However and alas, something had gone terribly wrong somewhere along the way and they were pulled off the raid at the very last second. The three of us were all looking out the windows waiting for one of those "urban assault vehicles" that were rumored to be part of the arsenal that the boys in blue had at their disposal. The point is…....They never came back.

We all came to realize that what ever was going on was huge, immense, scary, and definitely had something to do with the Chevy Nova parked down the block. Indeed, the FBI trumps local law enforcement every single time, in spite of what you see in the "Die Hard" movies. Finally we all decided to just go with it. We had just been given a "get out of jail free card" and something like that didn't come along often and should not be wasted or treated lightly. Eric was freaking out but Sunny and Mario were really starting to get in to the whole thing.

I suggested we throw a party and see who shows up. I reasoned that if the feds were watching our every move, then one or more of them would be In attendance. At least we might be able to figure out who our friends were. Even though we were all very tired and perhaps a little high, the decision was made to push the envelope and we started to plan a truly epic event that would either get us all busted or at the very least, drive the guy in the piece of shit Nova and his superiors fucking crazy.

Note: I chose to bad mouth some truly bad choices in American automobile history in this book. The Ford Pinto, the Chevy Nova, along with some very average low powered pickup trucks among others but make no mistake, I love American steel and muscle cars in a way I can't describe. It seems like the best cars we ever made in this country were built in the late 1950's all the way thru the 1960's. The early Corvettes and Thunderbirds, and Mustangs were legend. The GTO, the Olds 442, the Dodge Challenger and Charger, not to mention the Barracuda and Cobra. The list goes on and on before you come to any cars from somewhere else. I want to see Detroit come roaring back with the baddest fastest yet fuel efficient cars ever built.

Wouldn't that be cool?

As far as finding people to attend the party, that was not going to be a problem. As a group, my roommates and I knew a shit load of people and those people knew a much larger and way more diverse load of people. Sunny's friends were crazy and belonged to some kind of native American organization who I think wanted to take the country back from the "white man" but they were mostly cool with us. Barbara was Eric's girl friend at the time and she worked for a famous artist at his greeting card factory that employed nothing but beautiful women. One of these amazing young women was scheduled to be a "Playboy" playmate of the month for Mr. Hefner's Magazine" and she was beautiful and smart. I was inviting a few of the girls that I knew from the beach and some of the guys from the base including our old friend Smacks.

The food was being supplied by the girls. (this was before a phrase like that was considered sexist) Airline stewardesses were all female back then. (My stupid computer just informed me that the word "stewardesses" is a sexist gender specific term. My computer can be a real asshole sometimes) Our female roommates cooked a mixture of Mexican, German, Italian, and Sunny stew. You never did know what Sunny was going to put in that stew of hers but it was always good and it always got us high. There would be plenty of tortilla chips, popcorn with parmesan cheese, pretzels and other salty snacks. Because this was southern California a giant bowl of guacamole would be centered on the table. The bananas were in the freezer, dipped in chocolate. "Frozen Chocolate Bananas" were considered a fancy treat back then.

I was chosen to be in charge of "special effects" mostly because of my emerging talent as an artist....of sorts. Oh yeah, and because I had more jobs than a Jamaican, I always had some extra money to go shopping. The very first thing I bought was a four foot long "black light." We had recently purchased some velvet paintings during one of our many trips to Mexico and I was dying to see them in living ultraviolet light. There was this particular piece with a beautiful nude black girl with a big afro that lit up quite well indeed. Next I hit the flea market and found an old but usable tubular vacuum cleaner, an old pot belly stove and a big round fish bowl, like in the cartoons. On the way home I stopped at a Woolworth's and picked up some jars of glow in the dark paint and a big bag of ping pong balls. "I didn't go shopping for this stuff, but rather I just let the stuff go shopping for me."

When I got back to the apartment everyone else was gone so I went to work painting the balls with flowers and peace signs and some stuff I just made up. Then I hung the vacuum out the window in the hedges and plugged the hose into the exhaust end, and ran it through the window and into the stove via the stove pipe hole in back. Next I filled the fish

The Ranch

bowl with the brightly colored ping pong balls and taped a round piece of card board to the top of the bowl and I cut a hole just large enough for the air hose. Then I taped the hose in place and flipped the bowl upside down, removed the cast iron plate on top of the stove, and gently set the bowl over the hole. When I was done It looked a little like someone was cooking little round Easter eggs in a space helmet. If Martha Stewart had seen my creation she would have given me a big gold ribbon. It was dark out by the time I finished my project so I set up the black light on the coffee table and lit up the vacuum cleaner. The balls began spinning around the bowl and the light made them glow. It was almost perfect except for the part where I could still hear the vacuum running in the bushes out side the mostly closed window. I went over to the stereo and spun up some "Canned Heat" and "Frank Zappa." I cranked it up and lit a joint and now It was perfect. Clearly the missing key to my invention was "volume." We were ready to rock!

Note: To my readers, If my invention winds up on "The shark Tank" I will hunt you down and break your eyeballs.

The party began as most parties do, where the people who you were kind of hoping had lost their invitation are always the ones who show up an hour early. In this case that meant Cousin Brucie. (the real cousin Brucie was a famous New York, radio, DJ) Our cousin Brucie was a local neighborhood sneak thief and he didn't have an invitation. No one knew how he knew us. He just started turning up. I thought Sunny knew him. Sunny and Mario thought I knew him and Eric didn't give a shit who knew him, he just wanted him to go away. None of us trusted our new friend and he was constantly trying to sell or give us stuff that he had recently ripped off. Once he tried to sell me my own skin diver watch after he had broken into my car. We asked him to please stop coming around and he agreed. Then he apologized profusely and gave us a box of stuff to show us how sorry he was. In the box was a dice tumbler like the kind they use in Las Vegas, a radio alarm clock, a giant brandy snifter, an "unopened" box of a dozen relatively unused golf balls, and my skin diver watch. A week later there he was at our party. None of us had invited him but there he was. I have no idea how he knew we were even having a party. As I look back, it was possible that our unwelcome stranger was some form of deep cover informant. However, that would be paranoid, right? The plan was to enjoy the party but keep a close eye on Brucie and if you had any valuables,... put them in your pocket.

The next guests to show up were Ron, the artist, and five of his girls. We were all curious as to the relationships Ron enjoyed with these women. We suspected that he was giving horizontal dance lessons to several of them. No one could really figure it out because Ron was anything but a hunk. Ron was dark, swarthy, (way too much hair where it didn't belong) short, and he reminded me of the Gypsy con man who sells you stuff that doesn't work the day after you buy it. Ron was smart and wealthy and seemed to have some kind of power over his women. Ron was sort of like Charlie Manson with a new Cadillac and a much better wardrobe. Ron and I never got along all that well. I was a hippie peace freak and Ron said he was an ex-marine who still thought we were going to win the Viet Nam war. Ron was not your typical ex-marine. When he told me he was, I had to bite my tongue. If he was indeed a marine he looked like the guy who cleaned up after the 4th of July parade. I really didn't really care since anyone who brought five gorgeous young girls to our party was an asset.

Smacks showed up with two young girls of his own. The problem was that these girls looked really young. Like "high school freshman" young. Like "isn't there a law against that?" young. Like "we are all going to die in prison" young. Hey, we had a get out of jail free card, right? I kept thinking how in the hell did a "Jimmy Hendrix" looking black man not get pulled over in a Purple "Monte Carlo" smoking a giant blunt, with two fifteen year old girls, lap dancing him, as he drove down Adams Avenue at ten miles an hour. Smacks was "styling" in his black skintight leather pants and "Beatle boots." His huge "Afro" was wrapped in a tied died scarf. He had a gold peace sign necklace the size of a hubcap, and of course he was sporting his ever present super dark "Foster Grant" shades. We all assumed that Smacks was also sporting eye balls but no one could swear to it because no one, that we knew, had ever seen them.

The college girls from upstairs came to see what the "hippies" were up to. They were from somewhere in the Midwest, Kansas maybe, and they thought we were cool. The girls were always hanging around asking questions about marijuana and our life style choices and we would put them on a little and tell them they could come in and see our apartment but they would have to get naked first. Personally I think they were a little

The Ranch

surprised when they showed up at the party and everyone was wearing clothes.

We gradually turned up the volume on the turntable and played all our favorite "LP's"(long playing 33 and a 1/3 rpm. records). "Santana, Tommy by The Who, Buffalo Springfield, Jefferson Airplane, Poco, Sly and the family stone, Ike and Tina, the Iron Butterfly, Janice, Beautiful Day and Cream." The music of the late sixties was influenced by so many things it was simply perfect. The war, the civil rights movement, the poets in the Village, the hippies in Haight Ashbury, the youth of America finding their place in history, and of course the blossoming drug movement. Everything came together in a wonderful crescendo of voice, strings, horns, and a drum beat you could dance, or march,.....or make love to.

The dancers hit the floor and Smacks led the way. Say what you will about drug abusers but some of them can rock. I have no idea what he was using to enhance his personality that night but Smacks wore out the two teeny bobbers he came with and was free styling with every girl at the party all night long. If we had been in Alabama, South Carolina, or Mississippi, there would have been a cross burning on the front lawn by the end of our party.

At this point many of you reading this are thinking, "What the fuck is a record?" Well you can just blow me. It was the best technology we had, and the sound was so damn good and you could separate the tracks on a good sound system and just listen to the drummer if you wanted to. This is back in the day when all the bands had actual musicians playing real music on real musical instruments and not just some piece of shit, made in China, synthesizer, doinking out random sounds like a wind chime in a hurricane. (Sorry China)

I turned on the ping pong ball machine about half way through the party. Several people sat around my invention, shared a joint, and said, "WOW." and far out.....way to often. I went out side to get some fresh air and the whole street was awash with our music. The neighbors had their windows open and many of them were at those windows waiting to see what was going to happen next. I'm guessing that their interest perked up a little when the young, female, naked, flower child showed up. There was a considerable amount of marijuana smoke coming from the front door, which was open most of the evening and I'm sure I saw at least one bat fly right into the telephone pole near our apartment as it circled the street light in search of flying insects. He was smiling when he hit the ground, but then bats are always smiling. They are born that way.

Amazingly nothing really went south. I was expecting someone to call the "boys in blue" but the cops never came. I was sure someone would take exception to something and a huge fight would break out but no one lost control and not one drop of blood was spilled in anger all night long. One young girl puked up some wine and parmesan cheeze popcorn but she was fine. By that I mean she was fine, even while she was getting sick she looked really damned good. How many people can say that?

Toward the end of the evening we set off the Buddha flash powder trick with a truly crazy amount of powder that nearly set everyone on fire. It sure as hell woke their asses up. The plaster buddha cracked down the middle and fell in half but once the screaming subsided we found that everyone had survived with most of their body hair and clothing intact. I don't think cousin Brucie stole anything although our huge supply of grass did seem to dwindle at an unprecedented rate but considering the water pipe was going all night long we weren't all that surprised.

Our detective sat in his shitty little car up the street all night, and if there was a government "plant" at the party we never figured out who it was. Everyone had an awesome time and if one of them was a spy they sure as hell didn't pass the drug test when they got back to the "bat cave." I like to think that we turned someone away from the dark side that night. There is this picture in my mind of a somewhat "less than gruntled" guy in a rumpled dark suit with one shirt tail hanging out, walking slowly into his supervisors office, throwing his gun, his badge, his other gun, his Captain America ID card and of course his super dark sunglasses, onto the desk. After saluting to the Nixon picture on the wall he pulls a doobie from behind one ear, sparks it up, spins on one heel, and walks off into the California sunset. Nice. Oh except for the part where eleven other guys in dark suits and sunglasses tackle the him in the parking lot, beat the piss out of him and drag him off and "lock him in a room and throw away the room." (I just love that line, I borrowed it from a movie I saw about some kid who hacks into a government computer and almost starts a war, I don't want to be accused of plagiarism.)

The following morning there were still several guests sleeping on the floor and the couch. I was up early and the first thing I had to do was to cover up a young naked girl who I believe came with Ron but didn't leave with him. There is a problem with showing up with to many dates. You should always be prepared to take some sort of inventory, before your departure. I'm not complaining by any means. Waking up to find a simply lovely young woman asleep on your carpet, missing all of her clothing is right up there with hot bacon, eggs, toast and mango jam.

Everyone was welcome to spend the night after one of our parties and sometimes someone would hang out for a few days or a few weeks if they were in between deployments and had no where else to go. This did not include the base of course. Our little apartment was crowded at times but still better than barracks life, which was really closer to prison than anything else. From time to time we would discover some complete stranger, all crashed out on the floor and we would try as we might to solve the mystery of the "uninvited tourist." I came home from work one morning and there was some young guy sporting a spiked Mohawk, zoned out on our sofa. I poked him rather hard with my baseball bat to wake him up. I didn't know him but if he woke up angry, I had a baseball bat. He didn't wake up but when he slowly rolled over there was a dark colored sock glued to his nose. We didn't really condone glue sniffing but I wasn't going to throw him out on the street or call the cops with a black tube sock hanging off his face. If we had film in the instamatic camera we would have stripped him naked and put him out in the yard propped up against one of our palm trees and done a portfolio for his new modeling career in the mens hosiery section of "High Times magazine."

All things considered I feel our party was a huge success and people were still talking about it for months afterwards. Some folks who we didn't even know had attended the affair. If People magazine had been around back then I feel confident that there would have been a spread devoted to our shindig. Sure there were some people who had fallen asleep around the house but the important thing is that they all eventually woke up. With the number of parties that we had in our little apartment, we never once had to take anyone to the hospital or the free clinic to be revived or pumped or sewed back together…ever. That's what the dumpster down the alley was for. No, no…I'm kidding….really. No body knows how that guy got into the dumpster. Personally I think he lived in there and somehow slept through the part where the truck came along and carted his ass away. That was his problem not ours. We didn't serve alcohol at our parties, and that explains the lack of bodies and chalk outlines following our get togethers. A few people would bring a bottle of wine but once we passed it around no one really got very much and one way or another, everyone got home safely.

CHAPTER 12

The Horse Ranch

When most people think of the United States Navy there are usually very large, grey, steel, floaty things involved. The very last thing you picture is a sailor riding a horse across a desert range in southern California but this book never claimed to be anything close to the normal every day Popeye the sailor man story. If this comes as a disappointment to any of you, well you can go out and buy yourself a comic book, or better yet you can just kiss my Navy blue saddle worn butt. Just kidding, I need you all to hang in there and finish this book and then run out and tell all your friends to buy it and read it so I can retire and move to Jamaica.

The whole horse ranch thing was a plot to screw me over in the worst way imaginable. Someone on base knew all about my "situation" and was distressed that due to the pending nature of my drug case, and the ongoing, FBI investigation, there was virtually nothing being done to me as far as incarceration and or torture were concerned. A certain unknown person with a reasonable level power came up with a plan to pile the shit up so high around me that it would take me a lifetime to dig my way out. The grand plan revolved around the fact that there were miles of desert east of the base that the Navy owned and used as a secondary landing strip for pilots who couldn't find their way back to the main base runway.

Occasionally we would be startled by the sound of a loud explosion coming from the direction of the low hills across highway 395. We would run outside to see a plume of smoke and flames raising from a blackened hole in the ground surrounded by large and small pieces of very expensive taxpayer funded aircraft and hopefully a live pilot landing somewhere after a brief parachute ride to earth. One of our young pilots came in way to low on a dark evening and clipped a hill top and in his moment of disoriented panic he pulled the ejection seat handle. Normally he would have been launched clear of the plane and provided his chute opened he would have had a thrilling story to tell his buddies at the officers club. In this case however he failed to notice that the initial impact had inverted his aircraft and he was up side down when he ejected and the rocket seat buried him in the sand so that only his boots were visible when the rescue team arrived. Ironically the plane itself was still in one slightly beat up piece and the pilot might have survived if he had stayed in it.

The vast stretch of undeveloped land was begging to be used for something besides being a handy crash site and that's when some old chief petty officer from a tiny spot on the map of Texas, came up with the idea to build a horse ranch out there. It would be cheap because they had some old portable buildings and plenty of free labor, and of course me. The plan was perfect as far as they were concerned. The officers would have a convenient place to dump their kids while they spent some quality time in the strip clubs that were scattered all over downtown San Diego. There would be a constant source of quality fertilizer for the golf course and the best part was that I would be spending my days shoveling horse shit from dusk till dawn and back to dusk again.

Alas, some of the best laid plans sometimes contain one fatal flaw that turns the whole "plan thing" on it's axis and the desired results are twisted into something entirely unexpected. The fly in the this particular ointment was my Navy drivers license. Along my long strange and winding road, I had taken the time to get certified on every piece of wheeled machinery that the Navy owned. My license had been stamped so many times that I was allowed to drive just about everything short of a tank. When I was transferred to the still to be built horse ranch, the first thing I did was to use my vehicle passport to sign out some needed equipment from the motor pool.

I was quite fortunate in that I had friends in moderately high places who pulled on the strings that granted me access to a very well rounded

The Ranch

stash of government vehicles. I checked out three pickup trucks, two standard grey Chevy pickups, and the choice little souped up 52 ford that came with a mechanic named "Dick Finger." I also acquired a two and a half ton dump truck and a cool Ford tractor equipped with a PTO, (power take off) that connected to a detachable post hole digger and a back hoe. The tractor also came with a drag rake that made short work of cleaning up after a herd of horses that only knew how eat and shit all day long. There was only one draw back and that was that I would now be forced to learn how to operate a dump truck and a tractor. I was certified, but not trained on all of these vehicles so there was much to learn in a short amount of time. The tractor took a little practice and some paint for the stuff I crashed into but mostly I was ready to rock in no time. Me and motorized machinery have always had great working relationship. The good news was that now I was able to complete my appointed rounds at the ranch in an hour or two and not endless days as my unknown superiors had planned.

We soon built a corral using railroad ties for fence posts and thick nylon straps that were once used to capture run away aircraft on the flight line. The post hole digger came in real handy for planting the railroad ties, and we nailed three rows of straps to the ties to form the corral. The "base" welding shop built us a wide swing gate and our very own base special service commander came up with saddles, harnesses and a whole "tack shed" full of other horse related leather items that reminded me of some of the stuff you see hanging up on the back wall of a full service strip club. It wasn't long before our little ranch began to take shape. Soon the only things missing were the long legged creatures with those gigantic faces, and hooves that could kick you into an alternate universe if you weren't careful.

Our chief had the horse issue covered. The Navy had given us five hundred dollars per horse and the chief knew some guys in Mexico who had "caballos" for fifty bucks each. For an extra five bucks you could even get a "pink slip." That's Four hundred forty-five dollars profit per animal. There was an issue with the actual transaction that involved a freeway underpass, an illegal border crossing and the dark of night. On one trip our Texas horse trader bought this poor, beat up, Picasso looking horse that was missing a right front knee cap. I'm not a vet but I'd guess it was going to take much more than five hundred bucks to repair the damage. I asked the chief what the hell he was thinking and he just said. "Cost of doing business in the dark, under a bridge son." It must have been real god damn dark under that fucking bridge. The chief knew he would get his fifty bucks back because people and dogs still ate horse meat and you can't build furniture without glue. Life can be cruel, and if you happen to be an animal of any kind sometimes it can get real cruel in a hurry.

When all was said and done we had over fifty head of horses to feed and care for, oh yeah, and one little pissed off pony named "Sarge," Ponies were bred to haul mine carts out of holes in the ground that were way to small for normal sized horses. Ponies were just as strong as normal sized horses, only mini size. Sarge was a little prick of a pony who drove all the other "real" horses nuts. Sarge would break out of his stall on a regular basis and run circles around the big corral causing a horse riot until one of us chased him down and roped him. You couldn't chase the little stallion pony from "horse back" because the horse you were riding would be going crazy the whole time. You didn't even think about chasing Sarge while riding a mare because Sarge would try to fuck her, whether you were on it or not. Sarge had a huge dick for such a small animal and he was in a constant state of "horn." Sometimes we would let Sarge try to have his way with one of the mares just because it was so god damned fun to watch. These horses were twice as tall as Sarge and he would try to mount them from behind with his big dick sticking straight up but at least a foot short of the horse pussy he was craving. Sarge often got kicked for his efforts but he never stopped trying. You have to honor and respect that level of dedication.

Our chief purchased a goat one day and we all wondered, "a goat? What the hell are you thinking chief?" Not being ranchers ourselves we couldn't make the connection. It turns out that a goat is like a Zen Bhudist monk to a herd of horses. If we didn't have that stupid little goat our small gang of Mr. Ed wannabes would have been all trying to kill each other. The goat worked like marijuana and the vast majority of our four legged corral dwellers became totally mellow and subdued,…most of the time, except when that damn pony got loose.

There however was one holdout that nearly kept me from attending my next birthday party, and all the rest of them for that matter. One particular horse was huge and white with little black speckles that made him look dirty even after we had hosed him down. His eyes were like snakes eyes.

The Ranch

They were yellow and had little black slits. He looked like pure evil. We eventually tried to hang a sign around his neck that said DANGER and that became his name. "Danger" didn't put up with the sign for long and no one had the guts to put the sign back on after he ripped it off with his teeth and stomped the ever loving shit out of it.

One strangely cloudy day Sarge broke out….again and it was my "turn in the barrel" to chase him down. I walked over to the fence post where we kept the coiled throwing rope and took the loop in my right hand and after uncoiling a few feet I climbed through the nylon straps, took a deep breath and began the pony hunt. For those of you who have never hunted ponies, you have to start slowly with stealth and cunning. Of course stepping into a fenced area packed full of large animals, with a rope is as about as inconspicuous as a cop car with the lights on his "crown vic" flashing and his siren blaring in Watts on a Saturday night. I began my pursuit by trying to triangulate the corral and I attempted to get the pony to move toward a corner and then slowly move in until I was close enough to launch my rope at his face. This practice almost, always ended with me running around like a lunatic, chasing a crazy short horse with a hard on until I was totally out of breath and patience. Hey, give me a break. I was from New Jersey, not New Mexico.

Phase two of the hunt had begun and there I was running my ass off waving the silly rope at the stupid pony when out of the corner of my eye I happened to notice something as I approached one of the horse feeders in the middle of the corral. The feeders were wooden and slatted and stood about seven feet tall. You could see through the part of the feeder that wasn't full of hay. At first I saw a tail flick at the far end of the feeder. Upon further inspection I happened to catch a glimpse of a yellow eye gleaming at me through the slats. The stare was cold and threatening and sent a chill down my spine. I was running directly toward the far corner of the feeder at full speed and couldn't stop in time. Instinctively I dropped as if I was sliding into third base. At the same time both of Danger's steel lined rear hooves flew past my face at a thousand miles an hour. I sprang back up just as Danger spun around and rose up on his hind legs and tried to finish me off with his front feet. I was just fast enough to avoid certain death or at least having all my bones crushed to powder by a ton of raging equine monster with a Hitler complex. I bolted for the fence and dove through the straps with Danger hot on my heels. He pulled up at the fence and just looked at me as if to say, "I'll get you next time asshole."

There was another very dangerous yet beautiful contestant in the "worlds most badass horse contest." We had this magnificent Indian palomino named "Moncho." Moncho looked very similar to the palomino "little Joe Cartwright" rode around the Ponderosa on the show Bonanza. Moncho however was bigger and stronger and had huge hind quarters and thigh muscles. He looked like he could jump over the tack shed without benefit of a running start. There was only one person on the ranch who could go near Mancho and her name was Natasha. Natasha was like a female version of Mancho. She was big, beautiful and extremely dangerous. All the men on the ranch knew not to screw around with either one of them. All of us that is except sergeant Merf. Merf was assigned to the small marine station at the North end of our corral. The marines patrolled the base perimeter on horse back and most had all seen action in Viet Nam. Merf was a tall, slender, country boy and only a little bit smarter than a coat rack but not nearly as useful. One afternoon horny old sergeant Merf decided to put the feelings of his constantly erect, yet still inordinately small penis ahead of his better judgment and asked Natasha out on a date. No one knows exactly what happened that night, but speculation had Merf saying and or doing something really stupid that resulted in Natasha getting all medieval on him. When he got out of the VA trauma unit his arm was in a sling, his left eye was swollen shut, and he had a mild concussion. Wisely Merf claimed to have fallen down a flight of stairs. Natasha was back at work the next day as if nothing had ever happened.

The Cowboy

We were running a riding stable and most of our riders were young teens who got a couple of hours of guided quality time aboard a slightly over used but basically well treated Navy issue horse. Every now and then however we would get a special request from a much more experienced equestrian and we did all we could to accommodate these "special needs riders." By far our most memorable customer was the "Texas Cowboy." Being from New Jersey I always thought of cowboys as being the guys that hang out in Times Square wearing big hats and leather jackets who make a few extra bucks selling blow jobs to tourists in the subway restrooms. Out west it seems they have relatively real "cowboys" who apparently know absolutely everything you always wanted to know about all the magical things boys can do to cows. Without cowboys there would be no Big Mac's.

Our particular cowboy was an unnecessarily loud Texan douche bag who, like all to many Texans, thought that the more noise you make while expressing your self, the more people will want to listen to what ever it is you have to say. We could all hear his dumb ass coming way before he showed up. First, this noisy, smelly, diesel, entirely too large, black pickup truck came racing down the road stirring up all of our horses. The truck skidded to a stop causing a big brown cloud of dust that pissed all of us off. Next, after striding down from the truck like he had just conquered Europe, the super boisterous cow person was bragging and yelling orders at a crew of people he didn't even know. He was acting like he had the lease to the ranch. The cowboy was wearing a Green leather cowboy hat with a big silver badge that he loudly told us he had won at the rodeo, in some Texas town with a name like "Cow Pie" or "Turd City" or "Cowturdyville." He also had a belt buckle the size of a goddamned frying pan, also supposedly won at the rodeo in some god forsaken Texas burg whose only claim to fame was it's best in the west Dairy Queen. I thought to myself "Do they have a worlds biggest fucking asshole contest at these Texas rodeo's?"

The "Cowboy" said he didn't want to ride no sorry beat to shit stable pony. He wanted the toughest, meanest, badass horse on the ranch. I squeezed out a little smile as I realized that this country nut bag had no idea where he was and who he was screwing with. Initially I considered putting him on "Danger" but there were two serious issues involved with that option. The most important drawback was that by attempting to put a human being on Danger the result would be quite similar to the crime of murder. I was already in a reasonable amount of trouble with the government and homicide would make my case a lot harder to defend. Second, and this was the show stopper, no one had ever successfully put a saddle on "Danger." Not that a few brave souls hadn't tried and those who did had paid the price. Suddenly the lights came on and I arrived at the perfect solution. I looked over at Natasha and gently nodded my head toward Mancho. At first she looked at me like I was bug nuts crazy but after a few low rent comments from Tex about her "big old Texas size titties" Natasha nodded back at me and I detected a dark evil smile that I had never seen on her stunning face before. I asked Natasha if she would be so kind as to saddle up Mancho. She gave me a brief salute to the brim of her cowgirl hat as she turned and walked off toward the tack shed with a sly shit eating grin as she whistled the theme song from "The Good the bad and the ugly." Go see the movie......(Get high first)

A few minutes passed and Natasha brought Mancho out, all saddled up and ready to go.....sort of. "Bronco Billy" was impressed and he exclaimed loudly enough to be heard on Mars "Wooeee,That there is what I'm talking about boys and girls now stand back, watch, and learn." He did his best "John Wayne" walk as he sauntered over to the amazing animal and grabbed the saddle horn and effortlessly rose into the saddle. The great horse stood motionless, his steely blue eyes straight ahead, like a beautiful statue. At this point we all were holding our breath in anticipation of what was certain to be a memorable event in horse history. Have you ever been to a carnival were a daredevil gets into a box with a large amount of dynamite and everyone is on the edge of their seat waiting for the explosion, and possible death or dismemberment of the misguided soul in the box? This was our carnival and we quietly awaited the explosion.

Our noisy Texan gathered the reins in his left hand and took off his big green leather "Texas douche bag hat" and he used it to whip Moncho's muscled hindquarters. The horse didn't move an inch and the cow person looked a little perplexed as he made this silly clicking sound with his tongue and cheek. He had wanted to wear his spurs which looked like big sharp fancy earrings for his feet but we made him take them off. If he was going to ride this horse, he certainly wasn't going to be wearing sharp metal things on his brightly colored cowboy shoes. He gently kicked Moncho's ribs with the heels of his shiny painted boots but nothing happened so he kicked harder and the horses ears began to ever so slowly lay back on the sides of his head. I looked at Natasha and she at me and we both had goose bumps as we realized that all holy hell was about to break loose.

What happened next is burned into my memory like a first kiss. Just a helpful note to anyone who has ever wondered what to do when their horse doesn't start. I obviously didn't know this before that day, but the one thing you do NOT EVER want to do is hit your horse in the side of his giant horse face with your big green leather douche bag hat. No one had told Tex this, so when he did it the result was spectacular. Moncho turned his giant head and in an instant grabbed the hat in his teeth and ripped it out of the cowboy's hand and dropped it on the ground. The magnificent animal began to stomp it violently with his front hooves while his helpless rider did all he could to hang on to the giant beast writhing between his legs. When Moncho was absolutely positive that the hat was good and fucking dead he reared up on his immense hind legs and did a complete turn before dropping back down where he crouched down like a cat charging his muscles and took off so fast we all did a "Scooby Doo" double take. Vwoooof?

There was nothing but a cloud of dust and the corpse of the dead douche bag hat lying on the ground. We were jolted back to reality by the cries of a desperate man hanging on to the powerful neck of an animal who was approaching the speed of light. The road east of the ranch was long straight and flat so we got to watch the whole damn show. To this day I've never seen anything quite like it. A grown rodeo star screaming at the top of his lungs like a little child who had just had a lollypop slapped out of his or her mouth, and she (he) was growing smaller and smaller by the second.

There was a dry river bed about a quarter mile out. The road took an abrupt hard left at that point. When they got there Moncho didn't turn left, he simply dropped his head and stopped. He didn't slow to a stop or skid to a stop he just fucking stopped. He was so strong that this maneuver would have blown out the legs of a lesser creature but not Moncho. The physics of the abrupt halt launched the stupid farm boy like an Apollo missile. The screaming cowboy flew half way across the rocky dry river bed.

From our vantage point all we could see was a tiny human shaped object flying spread eagled into the unknown. His faint screams faded as he went out of sight. I instantly jumped into the ford pickup with Natasha right next to me, riding shotgun. She was worried that Moncho had hurt himself, and I was worried that we had just helped kill someone. Perhaps a someone, who the world would be better off without, but still being party to the death of a douche bag would be a scar on my anti war credentials. I certainly didn't need accessory to murder charges on my paper work. In a very short time, (I was driving the 52 ford pickup) we arrived at the edge of the abyss in time to hear a special brand of Texas cursing. We couldn't see the source of the profanity but every other word was "sheeeit." (not really a word but you have to consider the source)

When we inspected the arroyo we found one very damaged but still loud and annoying rodeo clown. We had demoted him from bronco buster right about the time he started screaming like a scared little school child. No offense to rodeo clowns by the way. Those guys are super brave. In retrospect lets just rank rodeo boy down to third grader in a funny hat and leave it at that. Oh except for the hat. The hat was dead. Natasha found Moncho in good spirits and in excellent health, all things considered. I think he was smiling, if that is even possible. The same could not be said for our new friend from the ego enhanced second largest state in the union. Tex had a broken arm and was so beat up we really didn't want to let him bleed all over the seats in our truck so we split open a bale of hay into flakes for him to lay on. I drove slowly, mostly to keep the yelling and screaming to a minimum and we got him over to the base sick bay where we dropped him off after a brief explanation of a terrible accidental fall down a hill side while he was taking a leak. Tex didn't want the truth to get out and neither did we. This was the last time we saw the Texas cowboy, and that was good.

I was beginning to get a feel for this whole horse ranch thing and I even jumped aboard one of the less lethal animals from time to time and learned some cool horse stuff along the way. Did you know that there is a correct side of a horse to climb up on one......on? It's the left side for those of you who didn't know. If you grew up in the country, your daddy taught you all this horse stuff at a really early age, however the only stuff my step dad taught me about horses was how to guess which one was going to win the third race at Monmouth. Now that I think back, he didn't even teach me that or he wouldn't have come home from the track all broke.....every damn time.

At the ranch I learned how to persuade a charging herd of stampeding horses to turn suddenly at the last second into the corral by standing firmly in their path and waving my arms in a convincing manner. I was (told) how to do this circus trick (not shown) by Natasha who I think was just as amazed as I was that it worked. I like to think she would have felt terrible if I had been trampled into a bloody pile of sailor paste.

The ranch was the perfect duty station for a person like me. I liked animals, I enjoyed the pace of the job and I was becoming rather fond of the cute girls who our dirty old chief kept hiring to help run the place. These young women, were competent ranch hands, and they all knew what they were doing. That's more than could be said for Navy washouts they kept sending me. Most of our girls had been recruited from ranches and 4H clubs in the area. Evidently the chief was an advocate of the women's rights movement because, not some, but all the civilian ranch help he hired were attractive, young girls. There was the element of distraction to deal with at times. That fact helped hone my concentration skills to a razors edge.

One afternoon after I had spent the morning gathering a couple of tons of fresh grade "A" horse shit into a neat pile using the rake on the back of our tractor. I was in the process of loading the fragrant quality fertilizer into the bed of the dump truck. I had just plowed into the steaming pile with the scoop and I was raising the load to the proper height when a shiny red pickup pulled up and parked next to the corral. At this point a simply gorgeous, young cowgirl jumped out of the cab. She was wearing the tightest pair of Levi's I had ever seen. Her white long sleeved shirt was tied at the waist and she had a cute cowgirl hat tilted back on her long wavy dark brown cowgirl hair. Of course while I was making these observations my right hand was still on the lever that was raising the scoop. As luck would have it, I waved my left hand and caught the cowgirls eye and she smiled and waved back just as the load of range dumplings came to a very sudden stop as the pneumatic arms of the tractors scoop couldn't go any higher. The bad news was that almost the entire payload emptied out on my stupidly smiling face. In way less than a second I was sitting in a giant pile of ripe road apples and spitting out partially digested hay and dirt.

Laughter is a wonderful gift from god or gods as the case may be, however when the laughter is loud, and continuous, and directed in your general direction, it's more painful than wonderful. There was literally no place to hide and the crowd of people who were gathering at the corral fence seemed to grow to the proportions of a New York City, street scene. I bowed my head, as my mind, slowly, but surely, began to see the humor in my predicament. I smiled weakly and began laughing along with every one else. I realized it would be a long time before I lived this one down. It would also be a long time before I smelled right to my human friends. The horses didn't seem to notice. If my mishap had occurred today I would have been the lead story on "Face book" for a week. Now I knew why cowboys wear those big old hats.

There was one part of working the ranch that everyone disliked. Once every six weeks or so one of our crew had to pull "night duty" and we spent the week putting the herd down for the evening. We got our days off but we came into work while everyone else was leaving. We slept in the bunk house and got up early each morning for a week to feed all of our horses their breakfast. This was a real chore "horse breakfast" is very much the same hay as horse lunch and horse dinner but it had better be on the table at the same time each morning or the crazy long faced bastards would find a way to break out of our makeshift corral in search of greener pastures. Literally!

Whenever the horses escaped we would have to round them up with our pick up trucks, because,......well,......all the damn horses had escaped. We would drive all over miles of California desert chasing down a whole herd of very large, very dumb, very swift, animals with a bad case of "I don't want to live in a corral anymore." I would jump out of the truck once we had herded up all the escapees into one large group. Then I would swing the gate to the corral wide open and position myself between the gate and the bunk house and then the cowards in the other trucks would drive the herd directly at me and I would attempt the " stand in front of the stampede, waiving the arms thing." I was starting to lose my confidence in this procedure because the last time I had tried it I saw this look in

Danger's eyes as he came way to close to me on his way through the gate. It was like he was telling me "hey fuck head, next time I'm not turning at the last second, I'm going to run your stupid ass over and turn you into a bloody pile of dead, government issue, finely ground sailor meat."

Most of the horses on the ranch were stupid, docile and easily manipulated, however a few of our four legged friends were cunning and deadly. "Danger" was certainly in the second category. I was constantly on my guard whenever Danger and I were on the same side of the fence and he always seemed keenly aware of my every move as well. We developed a relationship based on fear, respect, and hate. My fear and respect, and "Danger's" hate. Danger made me understand that he wasn't born to be confined in a corral, and we were really kindred spirits in that respect. Some animals and people for that matter are perfectly content surrounded by boundaries and rules but Danger and I were not woven from that thin fabric. I respected danger and even liked him in a strange way but he was a big wild animal and not to be taken lightly. Some such relationships just are what they are. I wasn't going to change Danger and he sure as hell wasn't going to change me.

One particularly beautiful moon lit evening as I was getting ready to turn in for the evening I heard this blood chilling screaming sound coming from out side the bunk house. I was all alone, except for "Major," our super nasty smelling, beat to shit, boxer dog and I knew it wasn't him because Major couldn't make a sound. Major was like most of the other animals that our crazy chief brought back to the ranch. Major was a defective dog, he couldn't bark. Major was a watch dog,......that couldn't bark. Either Major had been born without vocal cords or he had eaten one to many of his own rotten assed turds and had gotten some kind of horrible throat infection. Whatever had caused the sad creature to become bark-less, the result was the same. He was useless when it came to warning us of danger.

I left Major in the bunk house because dogs tend to overreact and I didn't want to put him in a situation where he could be killed and eaten. Slowly I ventured out into the moonlight and tried to focus in on the origin of the screeching noises that had grown much louder once I had moved outdoors. There was a giant stack of hay bales piled up into a wall eight bales high, four bales wide and about twenty bales in length. We had pulled several bales from the stack to provide ventilation leaving void spaces variously spaced along the sides of the pile. As I approached our hay depot the ear splitting screeches seemed to be coming from one of those holes. Just as I was about to peek into the noisiest of the dark spaces, this giant "Rodan" looking monster of a bat flew at my face. I leapt backwards and the huge bat narrowly avoided me as he flip flopped his way up into the night sky, silhouetting himself against the full moon before he disappeared like a big black ghost. I'm reasonably certain that I may have peed myself, just a little bit.

After the live nature exhibition I returned to the bunk house and made a fateful but fortunate decision. It was getting cold so I decided to let "Major" stay in the building for the night. Normally Major slept on a small pile of straw just outside the bunk house where he could silently defend us from any intruders He was like a Ninja guard dog, but just this once because of the cold night air I was granting Major temporary amnesty. I was hoping that his horrible smell would't keep me awake all night. I had no idea that this simple choice would prove to be a life and death decision.

Inside the bunk house we had this ancient World War Two era oil heater that had a reservoir of fuel oil and I wrongly decided it would be a great idea to light that sucker up. After twenty minutes or so I finally managed to get the beast of a heater lit and adjusted. Slowly the old wooden building began to get all warm and toasty. I was really tired by now so I climbed into my bunk and soon I was dreaming of Catholic school girls in plaid skirts riding surf boards. This dream wasn't nearly as weird and twisted as it sounds because the school girls were all wearing plaid berets.

Exactly what happened next I can only speculate, my guess is that a strong gust of wind had sucked the flue in the heater's chimney closed causing the old oil burner to start belching out smoke. I don't mean a little smoke like when some guys play poker all night puffing on "cigars and Lucky Strikes." I'm talking about thick greasy black as coal oxygen free smoke, like when a pile of tires catch on fire in a closet. Within minutes I was in mortal danger and was completely unaware of my impending demise. Luckily Major was on the case and jumped into action. When the building began filling with noxious fumes he initially tried waking me by licking my face with the same god awful tongue he used to wash his dog nuts. I only stirred long enough to slap him away and went back to sleep. Major was desperate and he opted to use the most potent weapon in his arsenal. He turned around and backed his rotten ass as close to my face as he could and let loose with the most atrocious dog fart of all time. The sound alone was enough to wake up dead people but the smell was something that could peel the paint off of a battleship. I woke up instantly and thought I must be inside a giant fried goat turd. "OH MY GOD what the fuck is that?" I began choking and I was blind.

When I went to sleep the moon was coming in through the blankets that we used for curtains, but now I couldn't see a thing. I lost my bearings and tried to feel my way toward the door and then the old nasty dog came to the rescue again by clawing loudly at the front door. I worked my way in the direction of the sound while trying not to breath. I was aware of the danger now and realized how much trouble we were in. I was dizzy and close to passing out when I found Major, the door, and the door nob all at the same time. I blasted the door open, grabbed the dog, and staggered out into the bright moonlight. I fell to my knees and started choking up this thick black gooey crap and I kept on gagging for several minutes. Finally I was able to stand up and take a big deep breath of fresh clean air and try to figure out what the hell had just happened. I looked back at the building and the filthy black cloud was still pouring out of the door as if the gates of hell were in the basement.

I pieced the story together in my head including the "stuck flue and the flue suck" theory and realized that the only reason I was standing outside the building and not fast asleep, forever, inside it, was that nasty, smelly, silent, boxer dog who at the moment was happily bathing his rotten ass hole with his sloppy foot long tongue. Again I dropped to my knees but this time it was to grab Major around the neck and hug him. He licked my face and I didn't even cringe or throw up, only looking back that was really gross. I had tears in my eyes but that was because Major had farted again and I almost lost consciousness. From that day forward I became Major's benefactor. I defended him whenever someone tried to give him any shit. I also made sure he got regular rations of prime beef, even though I had to trade a few pairs of size ten bowling shoes and other items to the guys working over at the chow hall. What the hell, our commander would never miss them. That poor smelly old dog was not a heroic figure in the traditional sense but he was and always will be a hero to me.

RANT ALERT! I'm an animal lover and always have been. Some of my fondest memory's revolved around the dogs and cats...and squirrels in my life. I'll never understand the goofy morons who think we need to put an end to scientific experiments involving embryonic stem cells, but these very same misguided, uninformed, missing links, (this statement by no means is meant as a slur against actual missing links) think it's fine to do truly terrible things to beagle dogs that are bread only to get injected with bugs that all the other bugs are terrified of. Then when all their hair falls out they get injected with stuff that will either cure them or kill them or make them grow flippers. If they die somebody puts them in a red plastic bio hazard bag and they throw what was once a cute little brown and white puppy in the bio hazard dumpster. I'm sorry but there is just something very wrong with this picture. "Dogs are people too. They put "Michael Vick" in prison and his dogs at least had a chance to fight for their life. The poor dogs in medical labs don't have a chance. I suppose the fact that they don't use human minorities to test scary stuff on was a step in the right direction. Hey Alabama! You did stop experimenting on African Americans in Tuskegee, right?

For those of you who think a tiny cell on a petri dish is more viable than a cute little puppy. Why don't you simply adopt the cells and raise them as your own? Perhaps you can convince the pet food company to come out with "Purina stem cell chow." Good luck with that by the way. I can see you now taking your petri dish for a walk in the park with the tiny red plastic dish in a stroller as normal people point at you and chuckle. Then you could sign your cell up for soccer, or god forbid football. How would you even know if your cell had a "hammy?" Maybe you could take George Bush or Rush Limbaugh, or Glen Beck, with you when you take your super smart stem cell to get him enrolled at Dartmouth or MIT. Although I'm willing to bet that your stem cell would probably be smarter than those other three guys combined.

It's all about priorities and actual humanity. When people are starving in Newark, or drowning in New Orleans, or raising a family in the back of a Dodge station wagon just about anywhere, and the tiny brained folks are more concerned about a stem cell then they are about caring for the less unfortunate among us? Come on people, you have got to stop living your lives based on the absurd talking points you hear on "Fox fake

News" and right wing talk radio. You were born with common sense and misplaced it somewhere. Go back in your head and look for it,....now.... and don't go outside until you find it. Oh, and please don't send me any more stupid E-mails about President Obama being a communist, born in Africa, Muslim terrorist, Nazi, with an expired library book on his record. Really, please, I'm serious. You dick heads are driving me fucking crazy.

CHAPTER 13

This is the end my friend

My Navy days were nearly numbered. My enlistment was due to end in a few months but there were several loose ends that still had not been determined. I was still on legal hold, pending prosecution for possession of a large amount of illegal something or other. The seed I was accused of transporting was sort of chubby as seeds go I suppose. No one had contacted me since the giant drug bust in the parking lot and the subsequent assignment of free legal counsel. I was curious but for the last year I was trying to forget that this legal matter was hanging over me like a big black go directly to jail cloud. I imagined that I could be shipped off to Portsmouth Naval prison for a very long time. One of our sailors at Miramar had written a document explaining his feelings concerning the war and the military in particular. He turned it in to his superiors and was never heard from again.

Besides the legal issues I had to deal with, there was also the issue of finding a suitable replacement to take over for me. I was either going to be discharged or chained up and hauled off to room somewhere that doesn't have a doorknob on the inside. This was a heady decision because my job in the Navy didn't exist. The Navy has patches that defines your job description. You Iron it on your denim work shirt or sew it on your dress uniform. There was no such patch to describe a Navy sailor who works on a horse ranch. They have a patch for people who work on aircraft, a propeller

The Ranch

with wings. They have a patch for people who dispose of explosive stuff. A mine with crossed torpedoes. Try as I might I could snatch no such patch with a horse of any sort. (sorry Dr. Seuss)

At the ranch my second in command was an Italian kid named Vinnie Badetto but everyone knew him as Bandit. He was a city kid from New York but he caught on to the ranch routine in no time. The initiation we put him through didn't seem to bother him a bit. He was smiling the whole time as we drove him all over the base at break neck speed. I nearly rolled the truck trying to get him to break a sweat but he was like a kid on the Magic Mountain ride at Disneyland. Bandit was soon to be discharged for the crime of setting up a nice little gambling operation on base. He would have been the perfect choice to run the ranch when I was gone. The place ran like a Swiss watch and he knew all the tricks to keep our little piece of horse infested heaven Tip Top.

Another candidate to run the ranch operations was almost too scary to take seriously but was very cool and quite funny, for an alcohol abuser. This persons name was Pat and he was usually wearing a cast or bandage or using a crutch, from a recent accident. Pat was always in the wrong place at the wrong time. I met Pat when he showed up for duty on his first day at the ranch. He had been busted for selling small amounts of pot around the base. He was wearing a short sleeve denim work shirt with the tell tale unfaded area on the shoulder where his rank patch had once lived. He also had a large bandage covering the top of his head and under his chin. We were all curious about the gauze so we asked Pat to explain his injuries. It seems Pat was at a party, got drunk, and walked thru a glass patio door. Twenty-two stitches and a series of little haircuts about his head and he was just fine.

A week later Pat showed up for work with an abbreviated version of his original bandages plus a cast on his left arm. We asked Pat to tell us how he had broken his arm. Pat explained how he was at a party at the same home where he had injured himself a week earlier. This time he got drunk and performed a perfect jack knife from the diving board of the swimming pool but didn't notice that the pool had been drained so that kids who lived there could shred the pool with their skate boards. I told Pat he might want to consider smoking pot.

The third week Pat had lost the bandages on his head, he still had a cast on his arm and was walking with a severe limp. I said. "Hey man, what the hell did you do to yourself this time, for Christ sakes?" Pat sheepishly told me that he had gotten drunk, yet again, and he was riding his 650 Triumph motorcycle back from another party at the same home that had been so cruel to him in the past. Half way to the base he blasted through a stop sign and got run over buy a car. When I say he got run over I don't mean that in a figurative way. There was a cop parked close to the intersection who saw the whole event. The patrol officer jumped out of his cruiser and ran over to Pat expecting to find a crushed and bloody corpse. The automobile had rolled directly over his chest. By the time he got to the scene Pat was getting to his feet and dusting himself off. The officer was stunned and asked profusely if Pat was all right. Pat assured him that he was fine so the cop wrote him his ticket, got back in his car and drove away. California cops are trained to collect revenue first and deal with lawsuits later. All things considered Pat would have made a fine choice to take the reins, (so to speak) of the horse ranch. I however had to choose someone with a better chance of living long enough to do the job.

One person who was near the top of my short list was a very intelligent guy with all the qualities I was looking for. We were friends and I knew he was smart enough to deal with the chief as well as the many personalities that would challenge his sprit on a daily basis. Shawn had a good sense of humor and most importantly he could be trusted. Trust was a rare commodity but absolutely necessary component to our machine running smoothly. We all had a lot to loose and we were dependent on one another. What happened at the ranch stayed on the ranch. Unfortunately for Shawn there were things going on in his life that were way beyond his control. Shawn was from Los Angeles and his father had been chosen for jury duty. Not a big deal normally but the trial that his father was sitting through involved a strange little mad man named Charles Manson and his misguided followers. The story was unfolding all around us and Shawn's dad was stuck right in the middle. This story isn't about the Manson trial but the Manson trial is part of the story.

Shawn started showing up late for duty or not at all. The ranch didn't operate the same way as the rest of the base and I had no problem covering his ass. The chief would ask "Have you seen the red headed Mic?" and I would respond "Shawn drove out to La Mesa to get a load of Omolene for the herd" Omolene is a Purina product made from oats and molasses and horses can't get enough of the stuff. The horses couldn't live on hay alone and we used the Omolene to supplement their diets. We had plenty stored up but now I would have to hide it someplace until Shawn showed up.

I was worried about Shawn and when he finally came to work the next day he was drunk and hungover. I took him aside and he told me, very slowly, that things were not going well a home. The family was falling apart as the Manson trial dragged on. The jurors eventually would be sequestered for 255 days. The longest trial in history up to that point. Jurors get $15.00 per day in LA today. Whatever they were getting in 1970 wasn't enough and employers are supposed to hold your job open for you but they don't have to pay you in your absence. I've never been chosen for jury duty but when I am I will simply tell them. "I don't believe in law and order" I'm not certain how this will turn out.

Shawn was finally discharged for personal reasons due to family issues caused by a blood thirsty lunatic with a swastika tattoo between his eyes. My search for a replacement continued. When a new guy showed up one day to fill in for Shawn I looked him up and down and said. "Screw it, you will have to do." The stunned and bewildered look on the new guy's face told me that I had left something out of my welcome aboard speech. To late now I thought, I've got work to do and my last days in the worlds most dangerous navy were at hand. I grabbed the new kid and dragged him over to the old stake truck we used for mending fences. I looked him sternly in the eyes and just said. "Get in." He did as he was told. I out ranked him and he was already in tons of trouble or he wouldn't have been assigned to my outfit. I had no Idea why he got sent to the ranch and frankly I didn't give a shit.

I was going to get the fresh meat up to speed or die trying. I fired up the truck, ground it into gear and we sped off just slightly ahead of a giant cloud of dust. The truck was an old deuce and a half (two and a half ton) from one of our past wars. It was like the truck you see in all the war movies with a bunch of soldiers riding in the back. Some had a canvas cover some were open, ours was stripped down to the flat bed with stake fences placed into railing slots on the sides. As we picked up speed the new kid looked a little scared and he yelled over the roar of the engine. "Where are we going?" I yelled back "It doesn't matter. This ride is all about the trip. It's not about the destination." Now he really looked scared. This was his initiation and the sooner we got it over with the better. The truck was running well but still took a while to get up to scary speed. I yelled over to the kid riding shotgun "Hey, what's your name kid?" I'm like twenty-one years old and I'm calling somebody kid. He looked at me fearfully and yelled back "My name's Jesse" I thought that somehow Jesse just might be the perfect name for someone who was going to take over for me at the ranch. You know, like in Jesse James. Billy would have been an awesome name as well. I glanced over at Jesse as he was about to piss in his pants and decided this wasn't the time to ask him if he wanted to change his name.

We were up to speed. I have no idea what that speed was because we had used the speedometer cable to tie the muffler to the frame of the truck on a recent trip to the base. I didn't need my muffler flying loose and taking out a ranking officer when I had pot in the glove compartment. Ranking officers were a dime a bushel but my freedom had no price…at the time.

Jesse was just starting to enjoy the ride down a stretch of dirt road when I saw the hair pin curve up ahead. I had pulled this maneuver with other new guys in the past and it never failed to provide the desired results. Sometimes it got a little smelly depending mostly on what the individual had had for dinner the night before. Instead of slowing down for the curve I sped up. You could see the hard left turn from a half mile away. Straight ahead the earth seemed to disappear. Jesse was screaming at me "stop you crazy bastard we're going to die" That was my cue. I reached up to the top of the steering wheel with both hands and squinted my eyes almost shut and hit the gas as far as it would go. Jesse was screaming so loud you could hear him back in where ever it was he came from. I didn't turn at all and simply drove over the cliff. It wasn't much of a cliff really, just a five foot drop off that wasn't visible from the road. We went airborne for a few seconds that to Jesse seemed like an eternity. We came down hard but more or less unharmed and I was already figuring how I would explain the damage to the truck to Dick finger. The front shocks were toast but the leaf springs were still intact. About then was when I heard the banging on the roof of the truck. What the hell is that?

I suddenly remembered why I was driving the flatbed that day. We were preparing to go out and repair some sections of broken barbed wire fence when Jesse showed up. We had already loaded up a roll of barbed wire, some tools, and a bag of U shaped fence nails. By we, I meant me and the two guys in the back of the truck. I had completely spaced them out. If I had looked in the rear view mirror, even once, I would have noticed their legs directly behind us out the back window. Jack and Danny, a couple of misfits who worked with us sometimes were standing on the flatbed, hanging on by their finger nails.

I slowed down, stopped in the middle of the dirt road and jumped out to survey the damage to the truck and my passengers. Jesse was fine, apart from the mental stress he had just endured. Danny was bleeding from a cut on his chin. His face came down on the roof of the truck when we went over the cliff. Jack did have a number of small puncture wounds suffered when he fell backwards onto the roll of barbed wire and he was going to recover but was badly in need of a new shirt. The truck shocks were bleeding red fluid from the ruptured seals but the six tires were still attached to the axles. All things considered we were looking good. By we, I meant me. Everything and everyone else was going to need a little work. The side rail fences of the truck were out on the range somewhere as were the tools and barbed wire. The flat bed was completely flat...and empty. Looking back I can see how things could have gone badly but Jesse had gotten a well rounded tour of our side of the base and I think he understood we weren't fucking around out there on the ranch.

Now that my replacement was trained to my satisfaction there were still a number of details to deal with as far as the Navy was concerned. I needed to get checked out by the people who payed us to be sure they didn't print any more checks with my name on them. I also would have to get examined by the base medical staff to make sure I wasn't to damaged after serving almost four years of constant wear and tear in the Navy. I planned to get all of this done on my last day. Before that day I needed to talk with my legal council to find out if I was going to be allowed to leave on my own or with an armed escort to a place I really didn't really want to go

I drove over to the base one morning, unannounced. We didn't have a phone at the ranch and no one had a cell phone back then. I know, right?

Rant Alert: What the hell did we do before cell phones. We didn't communicate with one another constantly and we got a whole hell of lot of work done. Today they say the American worker is the most productive worker on the planet. Imagine how productive we were when we weren't sitting in front of a computer all day playing electronic games and checking up on our Facebook and Twitter accounts. At least the people who eat lunch in their trucks and take showers when they get home from work are still getting something done.

I went directly to the legal office and asked to speak to my lawyer. They were expecting me. Wait? What? My case was sitting open on the lawyers desk. Shit like that happened to me all the time during my last two years in the service. No one knows why. Well, somebody knew but it certainly wasn't me. My new lawyer was sitting behind his temporary desk. (Apparently I had six other lawyers since my first) The new guy had a proud grin on his not very smart looking face. He informed me that all charges had been dropped due to lack of evidence. They never had that much to start with. One little burnt up seed wasn't something I wanted to spend the rest of my life in prison over and perhaps keeping a lid on my feelings about the war these last two years was more important to them. This was something I have always believed. Whatever had happened, in a few days, I would be allowed to pack up all my shit and go on my way.

I thanked my new lawyer…for what…I have no idea. I then calmly walked out of his office. There was a strange sense of relief as I felt the warm California sun on my face. I had put the possibility of prison away in a closet in my mind. For two years I made believe that the government wasn't going to drop the hammer on me, but I knew all to well that at any moment the worst could descend on me like sewer rats. Now I could finally let it all go. Somewhere inside I secretly wanted to rip all my clothes off and dance around the parking lot until my feet got sore, but discretion took hold of me, shook me a couple of times and reminded me that if I did my freedom dance I would need a bad, government issue lawyer, all over again. Thanks discretion you have served me well.

CHAPTER 14

Much closer to the end my friend

I haven't mentioned the part where I got married and had a son during my last year in the service. My first wife was a good woman and a great mother. She had nothing at all to do with what was happening to me on base and that was how it had to be. We lived off base in an apartment in a quiet neighbor hood in San Diego. Our small apartment complex looked like a Spanish hacienda. White stucco walls with a vivid red tile roof. There was a long wide stairway up from the street and it was painted dark red in contrast to the bright white stucco. Green vines with red flowers hung from the top of the stairway and there was a court yard at the top. In the courtyard you walked on a red painted concrete sidewalk, past some goofy little banana trees with tiny bananas on them. The courtyard had a coy pond and a small Japanese foot bridge in case you wanted to cut across. There were ten apartments situated around the courtyard and ours was the first one on the right at the top of the stairs. It was a paradise and we loved it there. The best part was that we were only paying around three hundred a month rent including utilities.

We got to know some of our neighbors and one couple in particular made us feel right at home. John and Michele lived in the big apartment directly across the foot bridge from us and they invited us over to their place on a regular basis. John always had a quantity of quality marijuana and He, Michelle and I would get high and talk and laugh until late at night. My wife wasn't a pot smoker but she enjoyed watching us get stoned and listening to the crazy shit John and I came up with together. John wanted to start a magazine that would be a Mexican version of Playboy and he wanted me to do the artwork. I was glad that he didn't want me to write the captions for the cartoons because I never understood the humor in Mexican jokes after they were translated into English.

John and Michelle threw a party at their apartment and even went out and got a real tiger skin rug for their living room floor. It was huge and you had to be careful not to trip over the immense tiger head. The party itself, was off the hook. The second and third things we noticed when we entered the party (first being the tiger rug) were two identical beautiful young women in mini skirts and high heel boots. As it turned out, they were Playboy playmates, the "Collinson" twins. They were the first paired set in Playboy history to that point. We were in awe as we checked out the people who showed up at the party. All the men were dressed in elegant suits. The women were wearing the most expensive clothes we had ever seen. I've never been to a runway fashion show but the clothes worn by some of the women at the party would certainly rival anything found on Rodeo Drive. The women them selves gave me the impression that at least some of the men hadn't brought their wives. At first my wife and I were embarrassed to be in the same room with these people but everyone was very respectful and friendly. I took John aside at one point and asked him who all his friends were. He started to list them off as the San Diego elite. Lawyers, artists, business owners, politicians, and of course, playmates. I think the Mayor showed up for a while. Do not quote me on that last remark. I was told this but I wasn't paying enough attention to local politics at the time to say for sure.

John was involved in some kind of business with several of the men at the party but he was not very specific and I didn't ask. John spent most of the evening entertaining his prominent guests and Michelle spent quite a while talking to my wife and I. I think she was just as intimidated by Johns friends as we were. The party was a little boring compared to what I was used to but the food was amazing and there was an excellent wine selection. Not one of the wines came in a gallon bottle with a finger hole on the neck. Someone was lighting up joints in the kitchen and that made the food taste even better. We didn't stay all night long but the party was still going strong when we said our good-byes. My wife and I took the short walk back to our apartment and both of us had a new found appreciation for our friends across the courtyard.

About a week or two after the party I was returning from work at the ranch. I had parked our Olds convertible in the lot next to our apartment. I didn't lock the car or bother to put the top up. No one was going to steal it and there was zero chance of rain at this time of year in San Diego. I grabbed my lunch box and thermos and started climbing the red steps when our neighbor Michelle came blasting out of her apartment leaving the door wide open. She was carrying a pile of clothes and a woven bag stuffed with personal belongings. She ran past me on the stairs screaming "turn on the NEWS!" She disappeared around the corner on her way to the parking lot. I heard the Jaguar fire up, the screech of burning rubber and then just the sound of the finely tuned car as it sped away. That was the last time we ever saw or heard from our friend Michele.

I hurried up to my front door and rushed in to our living room like a crazy man and turned on our second hand television. There were only three stations and at this time of day any one of them would be broadcasting the national evening news. The used TV slowly lit up to the CBS news with Walter Cronkite. Walter was just announcing breaking news from San Diego, California. At first my wife was mad at me for not taking time to say hello. Now she was glued to the image on the screen, as was I. There had been a big drug bust up the coast and suddenly we were looking at a photo of our friend and neighbor, John. They said his name and address. His address was the same as our address. They showed video of a big Hertz rental van parked by a dock with huge piles of cellophane wrapped kilos of what I had to assume was some high quality Marijuana.

John and some very high profile residents of San Diego had been busted after a long investigation with eight thousand pounds of marijuana. The pot had been shipped up from Mexico on a Yacht. This was the biggest bust in the history of Nixon's drug war at the time. About this time my wife and I turned toward each other and said in unison "HOLY SHIT" before turning back to the TV. Both of us knew by now that some of those people we had met at the party were part of this story and at least one of them owned a yacht. I don't think that the Playboy playmate twins had anything to do with the conspiracy but John sure as hell did. We guessed that John was the idea man and had brought the rest of the group together at the party. Most of the people we had met at the party were investors in the enterprise and expected, but never got, a return on their investment. I'm not sure if insurance covers this sort of thing.

The story really hit home, especially the part about the long investigation. Someone was at the party who didn't belong there, besides my wife and I. That same someone knew we were there also. I was nearly about to be discharged from the Navy. I had finally been cleared from all my legal difficulties and was about to embark on the next chapter of my life. Now, something new and unexpected could put an end to that chapter if I wasn't careful. My wife had no real understanding of what I had been going through up to this point and that I was probably still under some kind of investigation by people in grey suits. I regret to this day that she had to share this strange time with me. She didn't deserve it but she was as cool as she could be during the process.

We were preparing for my discharge and getting all of our ducks and chickens in a row. I had been looking around town for a job in case we decided to stay in California. I tried the airlines first, thinking that being a veteran with jet engine experience would get me a job. They had told me at the recruitment office that jet school was a ticket to a job in civilian life. They lied. You need an A&P (airframe and power plant) license to work on aircraft in the United States. In Russia all you needed was a pair of pliers and a roll of duct tape. I would need to attend classes, and get my certification before I could even apply for a job with the airlines even though I had worked on military aircraft and served as a plane captain in the navy. I couldn't wait that long for work. I needed a job within a week of my discharge from the service. You don't save up much money on military pay, especially when you are married with children.

I had resigned myself to the fact that we were homeward bound. I loved California and I would have sold oranges on street corners if it was just me. Our families were back in New Jersey and they would provide support for us until we got back on our feet. We had a baby son to think about and we didn't want to end up with no money, no job, and no home that far away from our roots. With a few days to go on my enlistment I rented a Hertz rental truck and we started to pack up our stuff and load it into big cardboard boxes. One thing that worried me was the fact that our ex-neighbor, John, had used a truck similar to ours in his attempt to smuggle huge amounts of pot into the country. I thought that my fears were just left over paranoia from the crazy FBI investigation I had just gone through. When I got home from work on my next to last day I pulled into our parking lot and there were two men wearing black cotton warmup jackets poking around the Hertz van. I approached them after parking the convertible in the shade. It was hot and I wondered why these two guys had on jackets. I understood the dark Foster Grant sunglasses. It was very bright late in the afternoon, but I suspected these guys wore theirs all night long. As I walked toward the men they hurried to their "dark grey" sedan and drove off.

Note: when I say their car was dark grey what I mean is the car was regular grey but what was going on inside that car made it dark.

I told my wife what had happened when I entered our apartment and she said she thought she had seen someone wandering around the courtyard that afternoon. "It's not paranoia when they are really out to get you"

CHAPTER 15

The End of Days

I still had some chores to do before leaving the base for good. On my last day I arose early and headed off to the Naval air station at Miramar. I thought this was going to be like the last day in high school, visiting friends signing yearbooks. I was in for a few surprises. On my way through Murphy Canyon I saw smoke up ahead and what appeared to be a car on fire by the side of the road. Normally I would have pulled over and given the stranded motorist a helping hand. As I got closer to the car that had a growing case of flames leaping from beneath the hood I realized the car in question was my old 1956 Buick Roadmaster from days gone by. Not only was I able to recognize my ex-car but also the guy I had sold it to. When I got married I thought it only fair to upgrade our ride. We used $500.00 of our wedding money, or I should say we used our wedding money, to buy the 1960 Oldsmobile convertible.

I needed to get rid of my Buick due to parking issues. There was a first class petty officer from the base who needed a reasonably priced vehicle so I sold him the Buick for $5.00. My wife was really pissed but I calmly explained that I had only paid $65.00 for that giant piece of shit over two years ago. She was still pissed. The buyer was a big man. Not football player big but more like to much time at the lunch counter big. I didn't know his real name but his nick name was "Meat and Potatoes," he went by "Meat."

Meat was all happy when I sold him the car. He thought he was getting over on me and he loved making good deals and ripping people off whenever possible. He went freaking nuts with glee when I quoted him the price. That was then but now he looked like he wanted to kill someone as he frantically threw dirt at the car while the flames grew and grew. I slid down in my seat and sped up a little as I passed the horrible scene that was getting much worse every second. I was looking in the rear view mirror from a ways up the highway when the car blew up. It was a fireball explosion that threw Meat back a few feet but he didn't look badly injured. Meat didn't have a lot going on in the eyebrow department after the explosion but I couldn't feel guilty. After all, he was the one driving around in a five dollar car for the last year.

When I got to the base I headed over to the dispersement office to get my military status changed so that I could pick up my last pay check that included my separation money that was going to pay for the van we'd be driving to New Jersey. I was in and out in no time. These military paper pushers could be extremely efficient when they wanted to be. It was Friday and they needed the office completely devoid of work at the end of the work week so they could enjoy happy hour. Government office workers don't have a great deal to look forward to in life and Friday is as close as most of them would ever get to heaven.....Sorry that was harsh.

I had my check folded safely in my shirt pocket as I strolled down the sidewalk toward my car. While I was enjoying my feelings of freedom I noticed a wave lieutenant headed in my direction. She was very attractive and her uniform was perfect in every respect. The shoes were black patent leather and the creases in her pleated skirt were straight and sharp. She wore a cunt cap tilted just slightly. (I apologize but that's what it was called)

I noticed she was glaring at me as we passed each other. I could hear her spin on her heel as she barked at me to stop where I was. I stopped about ten feet away and turned slowly in her direction and asked if I could help her in some way. She stared at me and exclaimed "You didn't salute me sailor" I considered her statement for a moment and answered "No, I did not" Then she yelled at me "You didn't salute me because I'm a woman" Again I paused and responded "That is not true, I have nothing but respect for women, my mother is a woman, I didn't salute you because you are an officer." She was visibly shaken and her eyes started to blink.

She took a quick step in my direction. I took an even quicker, and longer step backwards. Again she strutted toward me and again I jumped back away from her. I was wearing sneakers, she was wearing high heeled patent leather shoes. She didn't have a snow cone's chance in hell of catching me and she knew it. The lieutenant was way to uptight to start screaming and there weren't any people within range to hear her if she did. I was holding all the cards so I just turned and walked away.

Authority has a place but in my world that place is small and cold and very dark. If you want my respect…earn it. Don't tell me to give you respect or you will have me locked up in chains. That's not respect, that is fear, and people should try very hard not to let fear run their lives. Shit happens, and when it does you have to deal with it, but don't waste your life being scared of things that you can't control.

The last thing on my agenda was a trip to the sick bay for my exam. They need to find out if you are to physically and or mentally screwed up to be released into society. There is also the important need to establish if you are eligible for benefits based upon a service related disability. For instance If a service man entered the military with X number of limbs and only had Y number of limbs when he got discharged he would be eligible to Z amount of dollars for ever or until death which ever came first. Z was a number dependent on the difference between X and Y. The size of the compensation, Z, changes regularly and is adjusted for inflation. In high school they told me I sucked at algebra, obviously "They" were mistaken.

I drove over to the sick bay and walked into the sterile waiting area. The person behind the counter was neatly dressed in his perfectly ironed and starched summer white uniform. It had been a long time since I'd seen that look on a sailor. On the line we always wore our bell bottom Seafarer jeans and denim shirt and a blue ball cap. I personally wore an army, khaki jacket on my night shift. At the ranch the only piece of clothing that resembled anything Navy issue were our bell bottoms. We wore tee shirts and hats. Most of the hats were baseball caps but there were a few white "Dixie cups" (the round folding sailor hat that could be fashioned into any number of interesting shapes) Most guys shaped their sailor hats into a square and then rolled down the top edges.

The seaman at the front counter sent me to the audio department for an ear exam. When you work on the line on an airbase the first thing they want to know is, did you go deaf working around jet engines all day for four years. I went into the sound proof booth and listened for the faint sounds emanating from a pair of head phones. Some of the sounds I was listening for sounded like the constant ringing I had in my head always. Much later I found out that the noise in my head is called "tinnitus" When they asked if I could hear the high pitched sound I said yes. There were other sounds that had completely been erased from my hearing spectrum. Many years later I would apply for, and get, a disability for hearing loss and would receive a compensation check from the VA. What's 40 years times $120.00 a month? That's what I lost by not getting a service connected disability after my ear exam that day.

After the hearing exam I returned to the waiting room and waited to see a doctor for my physical exam. The magazines in the waiting room were "Sports Afield" and "Hot Rod" and that was cool. I loved cars and had a subscription to Hot Rod when I was in high school. There was a wait but it wasn't terrible and I had the time to learn how to replace and adjust a four barrel carburetor. Finally I was called in to see my doctor. I walked into the office and sat in the chair next to the desk. A man in a white coat came into the room but I didn't know if he was a doctor or not. They have people called corpsman that function as doctors but are not what the rest of the world would consider doctors. You didn't need a degree to be a corpsman. I once saw two corpsmen flip a coin to see who would get to give the attractive woman in the waiting room her exam. As it turned out my doctor did have a degree and had the rank of commander as well.

The commander, doctor, took one look at me and told me he wouldn't examine me until I got a proper hair cut. I blinked and smiled because I instantly thought he was just screwing with me. I explained that this was my last day in the Navy and all I wanted was his signature on my paperwork. The doctor re-explained to me that he would not examine me unless I got a haircut. He was a commander, doctor, super gigantic asshole, who saw what was going on around him and that his generation was headed to the scrap heap of history. The politics of everlasting war were being confronted by huge numbers of young people that weren't going to take it anymore. This didn't mean he was going to take it lying down. He made it his mission in life to make sure that those young warriors of change would pay for their misguided attempt to move the country in the direction of peace. Long hair was a symbol of that movement and it had to be crushed or at least shortened to within an inch of it's life.

I came to realize that this day was going to be a long one. I grabbed up my paperwork and headed over to the base barber shop. I had never been inside the barber shop on base. I generally got my haircuts off base by a cute hairdresser in Claremont, the town across the airfield from the base. I had just gotten my hair neatly trimmed the day before my discharge and I thought I was looking good. I realized that my hair was a little long, shit I was going to be a civilian in a matter of hours and I didn't want to enter out into the real world looking like the top of a fucking flagpole.

I asked around for directions to the base hair removal center and found it after a couple of tries. When I entered unattractive concrete block building everyone inside went silent. People were looking at me and my hair like we were Bigfoot and his hair. This was bad and I started to flash back to the barbershop scene in Tennessee where I was surrounded by the cast of Deliverance. I was torn between running out the door or staying for the second worst haircut of my life. Some of you are thinking "So what's the big deal, suck it up and get the damn hair cut."Having hair was a big deal to some of us in the service, or at least it was until buzz cuts came back into style.

(Note: To the guy driving the car in front of me with a head about the size of a sixty watt light bulb. You were ill advised when someone told you that you would look cool with all your hair cut off. Perhaps the, "Just got out of prison" look is cool for someone with a normal size head, but when I pull up behind a car being driven by a doorknob.....it just freaks me out.)

The barbers in the shop hurried through their other customers like they were Lucy and Ethel in the chocolate factory. They all wanted to get a shot at my poor head. The winner hustled his last victim out of the shop and motioned for me to step up. When my turn arrived I slowly walked to the chair and I kept telling myself "It will grow back…someday it will all grow back." My hair was really quite long compared to everyone else and the barber really let me have it. I asked him to just give me a trim but he thought I said. "Make me look like a prisoner of war." So he did just that. When he finished he spun the chair around so I could see myself in the mirror. My hair looked as if it had been attacked by a pack of wolverines on meth. I could also see the smug grin on the barbers face. I was depressed when I walked out of the "little shop of hair horrors." I didn't want to go home on my last day in the Navy looking like I had lost the war. I returned to the doctor's office and after listening to him ream me out for twenty minutes for what I had no idea, he finally signed my form. I put on my ball cap and walked out.

I took my paperwork back to the movie theatre where the commander who was still the superior officer I worked for had his office. When I walked into my commanders office he had a strange look on his face. "Don't I know you from somewhere?" He asked. I answered that yes indeed he did. I had been in special services for two years and he had been my boss for both of those two years. He shook his head and said, "I knew you looked familiar."

I explained that I worked at the horse ranch and that this was my last day in the Navy and that he could do me a huge favor by signing my release papers. He looked puzzled and asked "This horse ranch? Is that mine?" I told him that I was pretty sure the ranch was a part of special services and that he was the commander in charge of that, so yeah. He asked me "Where is this horse ranch?" I told him that I had worked there for well over a year, for him, and that it was probably best that he didn't know where it was. After a moment of deliberation he agreed. People in management are typically experts at covering their own backsides. Being in charge of something and not knowing it could pose a problem to someone in a position of authority, career wise.

My commander realized there was a real possibility that something rather large had slipped between the cracks, and by cracks I mean his ears. The space occupied by his standard size, government, issue, brain had missed something quite large. That something was a horse ranch that he knew not one little thing about. He had signed paychecks, he had signed purchase orders for everything at the ranch, that wasn't stolen. This included the horses and tons of hay, but like a typical administrator he never read any of the stuff in his in-basket. He was much to busy dealing in pool tables and rubber bands to keep track of tiny details, like the ranch, even if this tiny detail was as big as the rest of the airbase. There is a very good chance that my commander never signed any of his own paperwork but rather had one of his subordinates do it for him.

I love management. When you realize that the people in charge of you don't know who you are and yet without all that college educated guidance you manage to do a superior job and build a fully operational horse ranch with only the help of a few convicted felons and several very good looking female ranch hands, it is very gratifying. To be fair I couldn't have done my job without those lovely young cowgirls. They knew how to work around the animals and they loved every minute, and so did I. The women at the ranch taught me a valuable lesson that I've kept close ever since. When you choose a course for your life, don't let the money you'll make be your only guiding light. You need to find a path that makes you happy, something that makes you feel fulfilled and valuable. The paycheck is a bonus but sometimes the less money you have to live on the happier you are. This seems counter intuitive but when you have large amounts of money you have to keep track of it, you have to protect it, you have to account for it, and you have to pay taxes on it. This can be a real pain in the ass. If you wind up with lots of money you will also have a difficult time figuring out who your real friends are.

After some negotiations I managed to get my commander to sign my discharge papers. I had one more stop before making my last drive home. I headed out the front gate and crossed the freeway overpass that lead to the entrance to the horse ranch. I drove slowly down the dirt road toward the bunk house where all of my fellow cowboys and cowgirls were waiting to throw me a going away party. Unlike the commander the ranch hands knew who I was but also were aware that this would be the last time that any of them would ever see me again. My Hertz rental van was packed. I had collected the damage deposit from my landlord. My wife and my baby son and I would be New Jersey bound the next morning.

When I arrived at the bunk house the place was full of friendly faces. A while back I had learned how to get the unfriendly faces transferred simply by stating that they were scaring the horses. Everyone was cool with this and there were plenty of shitty jobs on base that needed low rent workers to do them. I always had a place to send people who would otherwise mess up the well tuned machine that was the ranch. Someone needed to paint and polish all the cannon balls and other military yard sale junk that decorated every open space and all the buildings. Brass cannon shells make lovely ashtrays when polished with a liberal amount of Brasso.

The girls were all dressed in their finest country outfits that made the rest of us look like rag dolls. Our cowgirls were looking extra good and one in particular, I must admit, really caught my eye. Debbie was the same young woman who had caused me to dump that giant load of warm wet horse shit on my dumb head one day. It was my own fault but I blamed her just the same. Debbie seemed to be in charge of the party and handed me a beer when I entered the bunk house. She was extra friendly towards me and we sat together on a bunk while the other ranch hands reminisced and told stories of their experiences with me while I was running the ranch. I was flattered by the attention I received from Debbie that afternoon and I noticed looks of longing from several of the guys at the party. Debbie was the daily fantasy of most of the male workers at the ranch and I think Natasha was acting a little weird also. I wanted to think Natasha was jealous of Debbie but I had a feeling she was jealous of me. Natasha was tall, beautiful, mysterious, and no one was sure just where her sexual desires led her.

Most of the stories told that day revolved around wild drug induced thrill rides in the ranch trucks and everyone was laughing at my expense. I had to remind some of them that they were laughing now but at the time they were crying like babies and shitting in their bell bottom pants. I want to make one thing clear to the friends and relatives of those young men and woman who worked with me at the ranch. Not one of them died or was seriously injured. The cowboy who spent some time in the ER was the only serious casualty but that was his own damn fault and none of us felt the least bit guilty for his misfortune. Near death experiences are good for you. Take it from Kelly Clarkson, what doesn't kill you makes you stronger.

The party went on all afternoon and we drank the beer stored in the horse feeder. The feeder was a long aluminum half can that was once used to transport helicopter rotor blades. Originally our chief thought that the metal boxes used to ship back the soldiers bodies from Viet Nam would make great feeders to replace the wooden ones. The transport caskets were only used once and there were thousands of them to be had for the asking. The problem with the wooden feeders was that the horses chewed them up faster than we could build them. The problem with the caskets was that the horses wouldn't go near them. Horses are weird animals and they have the instincts of a Voo Doo priest. We steam cleaned those metal boxes but the damn horses could still smell death and refused to eat the hay we put in them.

The ranch hands had cleverly covered the ice and beer with hay just in case the chief showed up. Of course when the chief finally did show up he parked his pickup, got out and helped his new girlfriend get down from the passenger seat, and then calmly walked over to the feeder and reached in and pulled four cans of beer out from under the hay. The chief hadn't been born yesterday and like the horses he could smell beer just like they could smell death. He pulled the tabs from two of the cans and dropped them into the cans to prevent the sharp tabs from winding up on the ground where a horse could step on it and tear up the soft underside of its hoof. We watched from the window as the chief handed a beer can to his cute young girlfriend and headed toward the bunkhouse. We all wondered how our old beat to shit supervisor always managed to surround himself with good looking young girls. Personally I guessed that the chief had plenty of cash stashed away from all of his shady business deals and spent some of it freely on gorgeous young women. This is pure speculation on my part, for all I knew he had a dick that would make the horses jealous. For those of you who may never have seen one, aroused horse dicks are as big around as a soda can and nearly a yard long.

The chief entered the crowded room and found me and Debbie still sitting on the bunk chatting and enjoying the party. He was well aware that this was my last day, unlike our commander, Our chiefs only concern was that I had picked a replacement for myself so that he wouldn't have to. I chose this moment to announce that I had indeed found a suitable replacement. Jessy was all trained and ready to go. I also decided to say my good bye's and get home and prepare for the trip back to New Jersey. My young wife would be home, efficiently rounding up all the stuff we would need on our long journey and stashing it all in the cab of the van. Our one year old son would be riding in a 1971 version of a car seat propped up on the insulated plastic cover of the engine compartment. This arrangement would get you jail time these days but back then you could still transport your whole family around in the bed of a pickup truck.

I started making my way around the bunk house while taking time to say something personal to everyone. I was going to miss this place and these people and I wanted them to know it. I gave Natasha a hug and reminded her to never forget her New Jersey cowboy. She gave me a spooky smile and told me never to forget her either. I assured her I couldn't forget her if I tried. "You better not try" she responded. She didn't include "or I'll hunt you down and kill you" but that part was understood. I told the chief not to buy any more horses with missing body parts. He smiled and told me, "Don't get to far off the trail son." This was a cowboy thing and I nodded so he knew I was going to do my level best to stay on or damned near the trail. We both knew that his trail and mine would never intersect. "Not never, not ever, forever, amen."

I walked over to Pat and told him to be careful. He was all healed up and his wife had given birth to a baby boy around the same time that my son was born. He was a proud father and his son was going to need a dad that didn't spend half his life in the emergency room. I wound up my good bye's and headed out to my car where I found Debbie leaning up against the drivers door. As I approached she opened her arms and gave me a big warm hug that lasted way longer than I expected and then she gave me a long wet kiss that caught me by surprise. I was stunned and like most guys in that kind of situation, confused. I had always liked Debbie, even before I got married but never guessed she had any feelings for me. Now it was to late to change anything. I was married with a son and a big truck loaded with all our stuff. For better or not, we were about to head to the East coast. Hey girls it's all about timing and guys are not real smart when it comes to picking up on hints. This rule is multiplied when the girl is young and beautiful. Oh well, this was not the time for double guessing my decisions. It was time to move on and try to grow up and find a way to feed and house my family.

I gave Debbie one last strong hug and turned her around, so that I could get at my car door handle. I tenderly put my left hand to her face and gazed into her beautiful blue eyes. I unlatched the door with my right hand as I gently stroked her cheek and opened the door and slid into the car. I said goodbye softly and closed the door as I started the engine, put it in drive and very slowly drove away. I felt a little sorry for Debbie but I knew she would be over this moment before the sun went down or as soon as I was out of sight and so would I. The big car rolled slowly as I waved goodbye to everyone but accelerated quickly as I pulled away. My brain was awash in memories as I got up to speed.

I gazed across the desert toward the small hills and remembered the time Dave and I had backed up one of those hills in the Ford pickup. We had been careful not to silhouette our selves and parked just below the crest of the hill. The truck was a brownish beige and blended into the hillside perfectly. We were free to light up a joint and gaze over the base as jets came in for landings to the South. We were telling tales, laughing and enjoying our buzz when both of us stopped instantly as the ground shuddered and shook as a terribly loud thunderous sound grew in our ears. I couldn't see anything but as I looked in all directions at once I happened to spot something in my rear view mirror. There was a giant pipe capped with a large flash deflector advancing over the top of the hill directly behind us. I started the truck, popped the clutch, and stomped on the gas almost all at once. Any other truck on base would have stalled out instantly but our mechanic, "Dick Finger," had our little "52" Ford tuned like a fine violin. The M48A3 Battle tank surged over the top of the hill and nosed down right on the spot where we had been parked only seconds before. I sped down the hill side while trying my best not to hit a rut and flip the truck. At the bottom of the hill we turned back to see which way the tank was going so that we could go in the exact opposite direction. The Marines had thrown a tank party but no one had told us and we nearly wound up being transformed into under paid tread grease. Those were indeed the days and I was going to miss them. I may have had a tear in my eye as I came to the end of the dirt road and prepared to get on the highway and start my new life as an unemployed civilian.

Note: Some say that smoking marijuana inhibits your ability to make correct decisions. In my lifetime I have smoked and consumed a fair amount of this banned substance and based on my own experience have no personal proof of this analysis. I can't speak for anyone else.

I was looking back one last time when I noticed Jesse pulling up along side my car. He was smiling and driving the 52 pickup. I rolled down the window, saluted Jesse, and told him, "Make me proud fuck head"

"You know I will chief" he yelled as he gunned the engine and spun the tires. Jesse liked to call me chief and I had told him that was cool as long as there wasn't an actual chief around. Jesse hung a tight smoking "U" turn on the pavement and sped off in the other direction. I continued on my way, down the freeway onramp and drove toward my new life. What I missed as the wind blew in the still rolled down window was Jesse trying way to hard to impress me by speeding down the road that paralleled the free way. As Jesse tried desperately to catch up with me, he on his road, me on mine, he failed to notice the sharp curve in the road ahead. I was cruising south, blasting tunes, with the wind blowing in what was left of my recently abused hair. At that very same moment Jesse was rolling sideways down a hillside through a fence and onto the north bound lanes of the freeway.

    I didn't hear about the accident until the next day when one of the ranch hands, Bandit, who had stopped by to wish us a safe trip home gave us the news. Jesse was a little banged up but alive and recuperating in sick bay. After hearing that Jesse was going to be OK, my first question was, "How is the truck?" Bandit told us that the old Ford pickup was already in the competent, if somewhat disfigured, hands of Dick Finger who loudly swore he wasn't going to let the savages from the ranch get their hands on that truck ever again....ever. I just smiled. I knew my beloved machine was in good, penis inspired hands.

    This was a defining moment and I realized that my ranch saga was officially over. I had taken on the entire military industrial complex and while I may not have won, I didn't lose, and that simple fact was something that I've carried near the front of my mind ever since. Confidence is something you acquire, something you earn, not something you are born with. I certainly wasn't born confident and self assured but the years in the military turned me into someone who could be depended upon to complete a task, exceed expectations and do it in record time. This is something that todays employers often overlook when they review prospective employees where one of the applicants has military experience. The military person was taught to think outside the box and improvise when there is a job to be done. They don't depend on management to lead them every step of the way. They have been taught to manage themselves and lead when they are called upon.

    Many years have passed since my days in the military but those memory's are still bright and clear. My job was to assure that all the planes that I inspected and launched came back in one piece and they all did. I take pride knowing that all of my pilots came back alive, all my drogue chutes opened, and none of our nations horses or ranch hands died on my watch. The few horses that did die did so on someone else's watch. I also feel good in knowing that I stepped up and protested a terrible war that needed to be ended way before it finally was. It was like not knowing when to get up and leave the casino when you are loosing. You think to your self "If I leave now all the money I've lost up to now will be wasted." The truth is the money you lost was wasted the minute you walked in the door. Next time you go to a casino just pull up to the front of the building, get out of your car, walk up to the building and throw your money at the door and walk away. Better yet just drive on by. If you feel a need to throw your money away give it to a well chosen charity. You will feel much better and so will the people you help.

You don't win a war, you survive a war and then you try to learn from the wasted lives and treasure how not to blindly get in to any more wars. When you are the biggest baddest mother fucker in the valley of death, get the hell out of the valley or the Hobbits who control the high ground will figure out a way to mess you up, no matter how big and bad you are. Our military budget is larger than the combined budgets of the ten next most powerful countries and yet 19 bad actors with plane tickets and Home Depot box cutters took out the World Trade Center. This was a lesson, not an excuse to start new wars with people half a world away. We certainly didn't need to attack a country that didn't have anything to do with destroying an iconic target inside your country.

This book was written as one man's window into what life in the military might have in store for young boys and girls who might decide that serving in the armed forces is the doorway to their future. Just know that doors and windows aren't always what they appear to be from the outside. Always look carefully through those windows before walking through the door. Today the internet provides many more ways to obtain information regarding your choices for the future. Also there are people who have been down the road before you. Talk to these people and get a feel from their experience if this is the road for you. You might try doing some volunteer work at a nearby Veterans hospital. Just be careful if you talk to a veteran who lives under a bridge. His opinions may be a little hard to follow. Remember to leave him a tip.

Thank you for reading my book. If you got this far you are a brave and curious person. Feel free to provide me with any feed back through my Email account. My address is chrispeck1@comcast.net.

Note: If you feel an urge to kill me because of my views please be kind enough to let me know ahead of time. I have developed arthritis in both feet from climbing telephone poles and ladders for the last forty plus years and my escape will be slow and painful. A good head start would be greatly appreciated. If however you enjoyed my first attempt at writing I'm planning to start a new book about my adventures as a telephone man in the towns and cities of New Jersey. Oddly there will be more guns and near death experiences in the telephone man story than in this war time book. Not so odd if you have ever been to New Jersey or watched an episode of the "Sopranos."

Acknowledgments

First, thank you to my Mom who was poor as a church mouse when I was born. She chose to have and raise me the best way she knew how. She was alone until I was in the sixth grade and those first years were hard for her. She pointed me in directions that would challenge me for the rest of my life. Thank you Mom.

My stepdad who I've treated rather harshly in this book for his racist views, was a driving force that made me take a closer look at the world around me. He had an Irish wit and he was a story teller. Those two things had a positive influence on me. He also pushed me to succeed in whatever I chose to pursue in life. Thanks Dad.

The writers who've influenced me are to numerous to mention without starting a new book but I'll try to give some of them their due.

Dr. Hunter S. Thompson:

You took on subjects that others wouldn't and you did it with style and your own sense of humor. You were fun to read but at the end of the day your readers had learned something important.

Wanda Sykes (writer comedienne)

Brilliant sense of humor with the black, lesbian, Eskimo, government worker, perspective. I'll get back to you on the Eskimo thing.

Richard Brautigan

Funny, imaginative, you taught me to look outside the box for my ideas.

Check out "Trout fishing in America."

Ian Fleming

You and James Bond taught me to read and enjoy well told stories. Great attention to details.

Henry David Thoreau

Gave me the perspective to view the world around me. Peaceful yet strong and resourceful he showed me how to create a path to follow.

Lenny Bruce

Showed bravery in taking on an unjust and at times a very cruel world. His strength far outweighed his weaknesses. Overlooked, misunderstood, but a very important influence on our culture.

George Orwell

A visionary who saw what we as a society could do to ourselves without soul and humanity to guide us in the right direction. He taught me that socialism didn't have to be a bad thing. "1984" is all around us now. It is subtle but governments run by wealthy benefactors are taking the power away from voters and Mr. Orwell showed us what could happen next.

Upton Sinclair

Formed some of my early political feelings and gave me a sense of right and wrong when it came to the working people who built this country. If you haven't read "The Jungle" read "The Jungle."

Thom Hartman

This guy could help save our world, I've read a couple of his books and they are inspiring and informative, "Screwed" is an example of a book that everyone should read. As well as "Last days of ancient sunlight" You will never feel the same about modern politics or our environment again.

Leon Uris

History and story telling blended perfectly. He was a great model for any writer. I read Battle Cry in the seventh grade followed closely by Mila 18. These books opened my eyes to the side of war that make you think about the personalities and politics of the people who go to war.

Sarah Silverman(writer comedienne)

Ironic social satire, nose bubble funny yet so much truth you want to cry while you are laughing at stuff people shouldn't laugh at……ever. Very easy to fall in love with.

George Carlin (writer, actor, comic, social commentator)

The king of political satire and truth telling. George could put anything into a humorous perspective that would make you laugh, think, and squirm in your seat all at the same time. I miss this man, as we all should. He was trying to tell us how to see the world with all it's good, bad, ugly, and disturbingly funny.

Martin Cruz Smith

I read "Gorky Park" and was fascinated with the detail of the Russian culture and how much we have in common with our cold war rivals. The people not the politicians. I've read most of Mr. Smiths books over the years and his research has taught me a great deal. He is fun to read and his hero always gets his ass kicked real good before solving his case. I think this is a wonderful way to give his main character a human, side.

Joseph Heller

Helped inspire this book. He pointed to the insanity of war and taught me how to convey that fact with humor. His characters are complex and vividly real. "Catch-22" Every high school student should be forced by penalty of violence to read this book, I'm kidding but this book is that important.

www.ingramcontent.com/pod-product-compliance
Lightning Source LLC
Chambersburg PA
CBHW030318080526
44584CB00012B/612